THE COMPLETE WORKS OF
LIUDPRAND OF CREMONA

Liudprand of Cremona

THE COMPLETE
WORKS OF
LIUDPRAND
OF CREMONA

*Translated with an introduction and notes
by Paolo Squatriti*

The Catholic University of America Press
Washington, D.C.

Copyright © 2007
The Catholic University of America Press
All rights reserved

Library of Congress Cataloging-in-Publication Data
Liudprand, Bishop of Cremona, d. ca. 972.
  [Works. English. 2007]
  The Complete works of Liudprand of Cremona / translated by Paolo
Squatriti.
      p. cm.—(Medieval texts in translation)
  Includes bibliographical references and index.
      ISBN 978-0-8132-1506-8 (pbk. : alk. paper)   1. Europe—History—
476–1492.   2. Otto I, Holy Roman Emperor, 912–973.   3. Nicephorus II
Phocas, Emperor of the East, 912–969.   I.Squatriti, Paolo, 1963–
II. Title.   III. Series.
      D117.A2L513 2007
      940.1'44—dc22   2007011013

CONTENTS

PREFACE

A NOTE ON THIS TRANSLATION

This translation of Liudprand's known writings was inspired by Thomas Noble, whom I wish to thank both for his original idea and for his later suggestions. The translation depends on the edition of Liudprand's works by Paolo Chiesa. Chiesa improved on the previous editions in several regards, for example, by including Liudprand's sermon within the Liudprandine canon and by clarifying the process of composition leading to the variant versions of *Retribution* extant today.[1] Chiesa's new edition thus offered an excellent opportunity for producing a new English translation of all the works of one of the most informative, and certainly the most entertaining, writers of the tenth century. In a period when many of Liudprand's themes are of acute interest, from conceptions of European community to ideas of transgressive sexuality, from intercultural encounter to the creation of new legitimacies for imperial power, the works of Liudprand have a lot to offer.

The translations are my own, including those of the well-known Liudprandine texts that have been translated into English before. Unfortunately the older translations are no longer in print, yet it would have been much harder to finish the translation without the reassurance of F. A. Wright's 1930 translation of the then-known *Works of Liudprand of Cremona* and B. Scott's 1993 rendition of the

---

1. P. Chiesa, *Liutprando di Cremona e il codice di Frisinga Clm 6388* (Turnholt: Brepols, 1994).

Constantinopolitan *Embassy*.[2] I am further indebted to Ross Balza-retti for sharing some of his work on Liudprand with me, to Ray Van Dam and Basil Dufallo for help on some difficult passages, and to Carole Burnett, the editor of this volume. The remaining misunderstandings of Liudprand's words are entirely my responsibility, however.

The scriptural quotations with which Liudprand laced his writings are rendered through the Douai Vulgate, somewhat modified to match Liudprand's text (or recollection). As for the notes to the translation, they seek to ease the task of students in unraveling Liudprand's culture; I have tried to restrict references in the notes to Anglophone sources, imagining the main audience for a translation like this will find these most useful.

In this translation the names of various protagonists in the narrative do not retain the idiosyncratic forms Liudprand gave them. His willingness to spell names in different ways, even in different alphabets, is a distinctive sign of his literary style, but creates confusion for modern readers. Though the names are rendered in standard form here, readers should keep in mind the author's volatile onomastics.

My translation is dedicated to Giacomo, whose precocious taste for Liudprand's stories made my work more fun during a difficult conjuncture in our family's life.

A NOTE ON LIUDPRAND'S CALENDAR

In the early Middle Ages writers used the Roman names for months, as we do today. Like most post-Carolingian writers, Liudprand also preferred the Roman system for denoting days of the month, though he was capable of employing Christian feasts, too. The Roman calendar, widely adopted throughout the Medi-

---

2. B. Scott, *Liudprand of Cremona. Relatio de Legatione Constantinopolitana* (London: Bristol Classical Press, 1993); F. Wright, *The Works of Liudprand of Cremona* (London: Dutton, 1930).

terranean basin and favored by Christian chronographers well into the Middle Ages, called the first day of the month the calends. The nones fell on the seventh day of the four months with 31 days (March, May, July, October), and the ides on the fifteenth. Though the length of the other eight months varied, the nones came on their fifth day, and the ides on the thirteenth day. Calends, nones, and ides were the cardinal points of Liudprand's short-term dating system.

ABBREVIATIONS

CCCM	Corpus Christianorum, Continuatio Mediaevalis. Turnholt: Brepols.
CCSL	Corpus Christianorum, Series Latina. Turnholt: Brepols.
CISAM	Centro italiano di studi sull'Alto Medioevo
PL	*Patrologia Latina*, ed. J.-P. Migne. Paris.
SISMEL	Società italiana per lo studio del medioevo latino

.

INTRODUCTION

✽ INTRODUCTION

LIUDPRAND'S LITERARY ALIASES

Liudprand of Cremona was born around 920 and died in 972. In the course of the fifty-odd years he lived, he used several names, though all were ultimately related to that of Liutprand, the most successful king of the Lombards, who died in 741. At different times and in different situations he was known as Liutprandus, Liudprandus, Liuprand, Lioutio, Liucius, Liuzo, and Lioutsios, and if now we may take the name he affixed to an autograph of his most lengthy work, Liudprand, to be the right one, his mutability gives pause.[1] Unsurprisingly, modern scholars have differed on what to call him as much as on how to interpret him. Italian scholars, those who have been most interested in Liudprand for the past century, still stolidly spell his name Liutprand. In English and German there is less unanimity. The change of heart of Philippe Buc, who reluctantly abandoned Liutprand for Liudprand, demonstrates the peculiar uncertainty surrounding the name of a man who was, after all, one of the preeminent writers of the tenth cen-

---

1. Aside from the name in *Retribution, Embassy,* and *Concerning King Otto,* there are the Greek signature on the *Homily* and various names on the charters he witnessed as bishop; see *Salzburger Urkundenbuch* 2, ed. W. Hauthaler (Salzburg: Gesellschaft für Salzburger Landeskunde, 1910), 91; *MGH Diplomatum* 1, ed. T. Sickel (Hannover: Hahnsche Buchhandlung, 1879), 465–66; *Codex Diplomaticus Cremonae,* ed. L. Astegiano (Bologna: A. Forni, 1983), 33–36.

tury, whose opinions still frame, among other things, our ideas about the tenth-century papacy.[2]

Uncertainty about his name reflects basic ambiguities in the chameleon-like bearer of the name. For one of the most striking characteristics of Liudprand's writing, which is almost the only evidence we have about him, is how variable, or versatile, this deceivingly self-revealing author could be. Thus quite different writers emerge between his earliest known text (the book of *Retribution*, finished in 962 but begun in 958, two years after Liudprand met Recemund, to whom he dedicated it); his newly-discovered sermon (delivered before he became bishop in 961, perhaps in Germany); his apology for Otto I's intervention in papal affairs (written in 965); and his account of his second journey to Constantinople (written in 969).

Liudprand's obvious transformations are probably not signs of psychological instability. Rather, the different tones and styles, and the very different, indeed contradictory, points of view in Liudprand's various texts stem from the vicissitudes of his life. Although born into a powerful and well-connected Lombard family, and taken into the household of the king of Italy very young in 931 or so, according to his typically coy mention of this event (*Retribution* 4.1), Liudprand did not enjoy a smooth rise to positions of influence. His family managed somehow to survive the demise of King Hugh and the rise of Berengar II, for Liudprand says that his stepfather had Berengar's ear and cash to spare in 949 (*Retribution* 6.3). Unfortunately for Liudprand, in 950 he lost Berengar's favor, and evidently so did his whole household (*Retribution* 3.1). Perhaps his family's close ties with King Hugh implied a loyalty to his son Lothar that was deeper than Berengar could tolerate, even after Lothar's liquidation. Regardless, a year before Lothar's widow Adalheid became the focus of anti-Berengarian sentiment (and wife of the German king), Liudprand crossed the Alps, seeking protection and fortune in the east Frankish Kingdom that Otto "the Great" had inherited. Evidently Liudprand was successful in his search. He was probably

2. P. Buc, *The Dangers of Ritual* (Princeton: Princeton University Press, 2001), 15.

at Frankfurt, one of Otto's favorite residences, when the emissaries of the Cordoban caliph reached the court there in 956. This would have been the occasion for Liudprand's meeting with Recemund of Elvira, to whom he addressed *Retribution*.

In the late 950s, Liudprand became involved in Otto's efforts to secure the obedience of Berengar II in Italy. For uncertain reasons he was on the island of Paxos, in the Ionian sea, around 960, diligently writing his book of *Retribution*. In 961, when Otto decided to intervene directly in Italian affairs, Liudprand must have known that his career would receive a boost from the intervention. Years at the Ottonian court had taught him how much the Saxon rulers relied on loyal men placed in episcopal sees. Indeed, before January 14, 962, he was named Bishop of Cremona, a major city on the Po River; in this capacity he involved himself in the new emperor's administration, though Bishop Liudprand did not usually enjoy the prominence he had had during the settlement of papal affairs described in *Concerning King Otto*. For this reason he may have thought the mission to Constantinople entrusted to him in 968, the subject of his *Embassy*, an opportunity to gain visibility at court.[3]

Upon his return to Italy, Liudprand immersed himself in the affairs of his important see, serving Otto's cause in various ways while tending to a bishop's concerns. He witnessed deeds involving the diocese's property and attended synods, and seems even to have received the title of Count of Ferrara. At this point, it may have been Liudprand's *un*-local knowledge, specifically his expertise in Byzantine affairs, that became fatal to him: a twelfth-century source claims he died during his third voyage to Constantinople in 971–72, when Otto finally obtained the marital alliance with Byzantium he had desired so long. Liudprand appears to have died on the return leg of the journey that brought the princess Theophanu

---

3. The increasing power of Italian bishoprics in the 900s is discussed by G. Tabacco, *The Struggle for Power in Medieval Italy* (Cambridge: Cambridge University Press, 1989) 161, 169–76; H. Keller, *Adelsherrschaft und städtische Gesellschaft in Oberitalien, 9. bis 11. Jahrhundert* (Tübingen: M. Niemeyer, 1979), 252, 262–69, 333–41.

westward to marry Otto II and begin her long period of influence within the Ottonian dynasty, even beyond her death in 997.

Since his contemporaries did not notice Liudprand's presence among them enough to write about him, the details of his biography, in the end quite few, derive from Liudprand's own writings. These are copious, but do not give a precise sense of their author; in fact, the point of this introduction is to show that they were written for specific purposes at specific times, and none was frankly autobiographical. Yet autobiography, or self-examination, was something of a tenth-century specialty, and several of Liudprand's contemporaries left behind texts in which they discuss themselves with surprising candor. Indeed, some experts in medieval Latin literature consider this capacity to consider one's self, to discuss the intimate recesses of the soul, a characteristic feature of writing during the last century of the first millennium.[4] Perhaps for this reason readers of Liudprand's works have tended to seek Liudprand's real personality in his writings, though these center on *other* people's behavior, and are only incidentally involved in the literary exercise of self-invention. The picture of Liudprand that emerges from this sort of analysis is not flattering, and Liudprand has been characterized as a shallow, venomous, vain creature, a man worthy of the "leaden century" in which he lived.[5]

The personality of anyone who lived more than a thousand years ago tends to appear somewhat foggy to us. This indistinctness is all the more pronounced in the case of Liudprand, who is

4. C. Leonardi, "Il secolo X," in his *Letteratura latina medievale* (Florence: SISMEL-Il Galluzzo, 2002), 160–61.

5. Since the Counter-Reformation the 900s have enjoyed a poor reputation as violent, anarchic, and immoral. Liudprand's writings are a main source for this interpretation, but Cardinal Baronius's *Annales Ecclesiastici* 10 (Rome, 1601) and its memorable labels (e.g., "leaden century") gave it currency. On Liudprand's superficiality and lack of religious conviction, see G. Vinay, *Alto medioevo latino* (Naples: Liguori, 2003), 351–52; his biliousness is chastised by M. Oldoni, "'Phrenesis' di una letteratura solitaria," *Settimane di studio del Centro italiano di studi sull'Alto Medioevo* 38 (Spoleto: CISAM, 1991), 1007–43, and "Liutprando oltre il magazzino delle maschere," in M. Oldoni and P. Ariatta, *Liutprando di Cremona. Italia e Oriente alle soglie dell'anno mille* (Novara: Europia, 1987).

the sole witness to his self. In addition, Liudprand was first and foremost a great wordsmith, a highly skillful user of literary Latin who had read and studied the classics of Latin literature, pagan and Christian. It is prudent therefore to understand Liudprand's insertion of himself into his compositions as a calculated literary strategy, often an evocation of the style of some previous author. Even Liudprand's moments of apparent candor, such as *Retribution* 4.1's claims of youthful vocal excellence, usually turn out to be literary reminiscences, in this case of Cornelius Nepos's *Atticus* 1.[6] A writer who dropped lines of less famous Roman poetry and prose with apparent effortlessness, as well as the more common lines of Virgil, Horace, Cicero, and Augustine, who adopted models and styles from ancient and late antique masters, and who was imbued with a deep biblical culture, was able to represent himself to readers with the persona most attuned to the circumstances. Thus the bilious Liudprand of *Retribution*, who is also a new Job, persecuted by the nefarious duo Berengar and Willa,[7] or the severe and detached one of *Concerning King Otto*, or the impassioned moralist at the end of his sole known homily, and especially the sarcastic Liudprand giving account of his mission in Byzantium, are all creations of the pen of a versatile and well-read author, and are better suited to literary analysis than to psychoanalysis. Liudprand left behind personae, not personality, and his unusual distinction between the "inner" and the "outer" persona (evident in the intriguing passage about his attempt to be true to himself in *Retribution* 6.1) reflects his acute awareness of how written words could become the best means of self-presentation, or even self-invention.[8]

6. E. Colonna, *Le poesie di Liutprando di Cremona* (Bari: Edipuglia, 1996), chap. 1.

7. H. Hofmann, "Profil der lateinischen Historiographie im zehnten Jahrhundert," *Settimane di studio del Centro italiano di studi sull'Alto Medioevo* 38 (Spoleto: CISAM, 1991), 864.

8. H. Fichtenau, *Living in the Tenth Century* (Chicago: University of Chicago Press, 1991), 31, stressed that "iron-century" aristocrats did not distinguish between the external appearance and the inner person. The chasm between appearances and actuality was a theme that Liudprand investigated throughout *Retribution*: see Buc, *The Dangers*, 23.

Of course, not all the fascinating personae that Liudprand fabricated were elegant allusions to the classical mode. Some personal details (such as the messenger's embarrassment at entering the Byzantine Great Palace without appropriate gifts in 949, or the homilist's unease before famished beggars, or the secret satisfaction at exchanging a few words with friends in Constantinople in 968) are more clearly part of a master narrator's effort to convince readers of the reality of what is written and the openness and sincerity of him who writes. But, like the classical reminiscences, they serve as pillars in Liudprand's construction of a literary voice endowed with an astonishing range of modulations.

Today we have four of Liudprand's writings. Until recently, only *Embassy*, *Retribution*, and *Concerning King Otto* were known, and considerable effort went into showing that Liudprand's literary production was unitary, consisting of three sections to a single "historical novel."[9] Now that Liudprand's *Homily* has entered the canon, it is less easy, less necessary, even, to imagine ways in which Liudprand's entire production may appear coherent, one literary project rather than a series of distinct compositions linked to particular circumstances.

LIUDPRAND AS WREAKER OF *Retribution*

Liudprand's book of *Retribution*, or *Antapodosis* as he called it in Greek, stands out among his compositions. It is longer and more sustained than his other writings. It was not written at a successful or particularly hopeful moment in Liudprand's life, but in exile, during his peregrinations. It takes a surprisingly ample view of the affairs that should concern the historically-minded: in *Retribution*, Liudprand ranges over an integrated "Europe" at once Mediterranean and continental, where the things that happen in Denmark are linked to those occurring in Apulia.[10] Perhaps this broad purview

9. Oldoni, "'Phrenesis,'" 1017; and "Liutprando oltre il magazzino," 12.

10. Byzantine, German, and Italian events most concern Liudprand, and other histories are peripheral. Yet contemporary historians were more parochial: see G. Arn-

is related to the circumstance that the author worked and reworked the text, correcting and adding passages, inserting transliterations of the Greek phrases; the three prefaces in *Retribution* (1.1, 3.1, and 6.1) suggest how differently Liudprand conceived of the book as time passed and he continued revising. Liudprand's other writings offer more of a snapshot of his views at a single moment.[11] *Retribution* is also different from the other known texts by Liudprand in that it has more than one clear target or purpose; for if it began as a pan-European contemporary history to satisfy a Spanish friend (1.1), it soon became a way to get even with Liudprand's main Italian antagonists (3.1), and eventually an outlet or consolation for the unhappiness that a decade of exile caused the author (6.1).[12]

Though it did not often circulate whole, *Retribution* was by far Liudprand's most popular book during the Middle Ages.[13] The work in its entirety, including the author's own revisions, exists only in the so-called Freising manuscript, now in the Bavarian State Library in Munich, which belonged to Abraham, the bishop of Freising (†994). This manuscript, recently reinterpreted by the editor of Liudprand's complete works, gives us a glimpse of Liudprand as he toiled on his *Retribution* and proves that the book was conceived as an "open" text. In other words, Liudprand, like many other medieval writers, did not contemplate a finished book

aldi, "Liutprando e la storiografia contemporanea," *Settimane di studio del Centro italiano di studi sull'Alto Medioevo* 17 (Spoleto: CISAM, 1969), 514, 519; Hofmann, "Profil," 843–56; G. Gandino, *Il vocabolario politico e sociale di Liutprando di Cremona* (Rome: Istituto Storico Italiano per il Medioevo, 1995), chap. 8.

11. P. Chiesa, *Liutprando di Cremona e il codice di Frisinga Clm 6388*, 12–13.

12. On *Retribution*'s plural purposes, see P. Buc, "Italian Hussies and German Matrons," *Frühmittelalterliche Studien* 29 (1995): 211–12; K. Leyser, "Ends and Means in Liudprand of Cremona," in his *Communications and Power in Medieval Europe* (London: The Hambledon Press, 1994), 133–35. For a broad view of the historiographical principle of getting even, see G. Trompf, *Early Christian Historiography. Narratives of Retributive Justice* (London: Continuum, 2000), 3–46. It is significant that Liudprand's sense of what history is conformed to none of the categories envisioned in Part I, "Early Medieval Historiography," in D. Mauskopf Deliyannis, ed., *Historiography in the Middle Ages* (Leiden: Brill, 2003).

13. P. Chiesa, *Liudprandi Cremonensis Opera* (Turnholt: Brepols, 1998), xix–xxxix.

in the way that modern writers do, because of printing and the distribution networks that make their writing irrevocable once it leaves their desks and goes to the publisher; instead he kept his book alive, refining its contents and making additions as the circumstances, and his fancy, dictated. What we have, then, are the last retributive thoughts that Liudprand had the time and energy to write down before death overtook him, not necessarily the version he hoped to transmit to posterity. This serial authorship helps to explain the multiple prefaces and some inconsistencies in the narrative.[14]

Despite some structural awkwardness, *Retribution* remains coherent in its focus on everyone getting his or her just deserts. Liudprand's title has multiple meanings, but all are related to this theme. He advertises one meaning in the second introductory chapter (3.1), using his ink to get revenge against those who brought misery to him and his family (despite favorable descriptions of the Ottonians, the promised reward for those who were kind to him is much less explicit in the book). Retribution is also what God will unleash upon humanity at the end of time, and if Liudprand was not an acutely apocalyptic thinker, pointing out in *Embassy* 39 and 43 the self-fulfilling nature of most prophecy among those who believe it, he was aware of the intellectual debates about the imminence of the end, and the final acts of retributive justice were an inspiration to him.[15] But the preeminent significance of retribution in Liudprand's history of the period 888–950 is the divine retribution that fell upon the people of the recent past who erred or

14. Chiesa, *Liudprandi Cremonensis Opera*, lxviii–lxxxii. J. Sutherland, *Liudprand of Cremona* (Spoleto: CISAM, 1988), 79, suggests that Berengar II's demise made finishing the book unnecessary; Oldoni, "Liutprando," 16–17, 27, finds the incompleteness literarily and biographically logical.

15. Colonna, *Le poesie*, 19–20; W. Brandes, "Liudprand von Cremona (*Legatio* 39–41) und ein bisher unbeachteter west-östlicher Korrespondenz über die Bedeutung des Jahres 1000AD," *Byzantinische Zeitschrift* 93 (2000): 463; Hofmann, "Profil," 864; C. Villa, "Lay and Ecclesiastical Culture," in *Italy in the Early Middle Ages*, ed. C. La Rocca (Oxford: Oxford University Press, 2002), 202, sees the Roman grammarian Quintilian's "redditio contraria" in Liudprand's interest in compensation.

sinned or simply forgot the true source of their successes, just as it fell, inexorably if more benignly, on the meritorious (who were Ottonians, for the most part).[16] Only rarely did Liudprand admit he could not make out the divine logic behind some human event: it is a "mysterious" judgment of God that allowed an Islamic colony to flourish in southern France (1.3) or Alberic to flourish in Rome (5.3), and Liudprand wanted to cry over King Lambert's death (caused, ironically, by an unwarranted act of revenge: 1.44), while he was unsure that the "innocent blood" of King Berengar I had flowed as a result of a crime of the victim (2.68–71).[17] The workings of divine justice among humans could, in sum, sometimes prove inscrutable: in *Retribution* 2.46 Liudprand candidly said that he did not know why Jesus chastised southern Italy with piratical raids from North Africa, and he found unsatisfactory the consolation that God's inexplicable retributive urge had stimulated the locals to a successful military reaction.

For the rest, the meticulous uncovering of human wickedness and, to a lesser extent, virtue serves to show how just was the mechanism of God's universe, and how inevitable was the comeuppance for transgressors of God's law or the bliss for those who applied it to their lives. God does not often intervene directly in Liudprand's narrative: good examples of exceptions are King Hugh's loss of Rome by "the decision of the divine dispensation" (3.46) and God's "just" and "fair" judgment against Hugh's knight shortly afterwards (3.47). But to Liudprand the outcomes he chronicled were manifestations of God's supervision over history whether God showed himself overtly or not.[18]

Underneath this overarching theoretical canopy the chronicler inserted a maze of detail, not all of it logical or necessary to the narrative. Because of certain of these divagations, the book of *Retribution*,

16. Sutherland, *Liudprand*, 52–53, 58–59, 63–67; N. Staubach, "Historia oder Satira?" *Mittellateinisches Jahrbuch* 24–25 (1989–90): 469.

17. See Vinay, *Alto medioevo latino*, 357, on Liudprand's awkward providentialism.

18. Arnaldi, "Liutprando e la storiografia," 510–11.

more than Liudprand's other compositions, gave him a reputation as a scurrilous author whose penchant for "the useful laughter of comedies" (1.1) too often led him far from the well-worn path of sober historical exposition.[19] The sometimes malicious, racy stories and an apparently pathological concern with the sexuality of powerful women contributed to Liudprand's notoriety as a misogynist and a sexually-obsessed slanderer. Compared to other tenth-century writers—indeed, compared to most who wrote between antiquity and modern times—the author of *Retribution* (and, to a lesser extent *Concerning King Otto*) inserted much more sexual material into his narrative. Others who thought and wrote about human sexuality, such as the reform-minded who worried about clerical continence, were more abstract.[20] Yet it is wise to recall that sex and sexuality are modern western concepts and what Liudprand's audience saw "below the sphere of [Willa's] buttocks" (4.12) is not necessarily what contemporary western audiences see.[21]

Recent analyses of this fashionable topic have suggested that Liudprand's inclusion of so many sexual foibles of prominent women was not misogynistic, though the Cremonese bishop wrote within a deeply patriarchal tradition that assumed women were less able to resist sexual urges and were hence likely temptresses.[22] For Liudprand extolled the beauty *and* virtue of some women, provided they were associated with the Ottonian family.[23] Thus his cutting descriptions of the sexual activity of the female members

19. R. Levine, "Liudprand of Cremona: History and Debasement in the Tenth Century," *Mittellateinisches Jahrbuch* 26 (1991): 70; R. Balzaretti, "Liudprand of Cremona's Sense of Humor," in *Humour, History and Politics in Late Antiquity and the Early Middle Ages*, ed. G. Halsall (Cambridge: Cambridge University Press, 2002), 117–18; Staubach, "Historia oder Satira?" 468–69, 482–83.

20. For instance, Agnellus of Ravenna depicted wives as a liability: see P. Skinner, *Women in Medieval Italian Society 500–1200* (London: Pearson Educational, 2001), 75.

21. A point well developed by R. Balzaretti, "Men and Sex in Tenth-Century Italy," in *Masculinity in Medieval Europe*, ed. D. Hadley (London: Longman, 1999), 143–45.

22. Buc, "Italian Hussies." An overview is R. Mazo Karras, *Sexuality in Medieval Europe* (London: Routledge, 2005).

23. E. Colonna, "Figure femminili in Liutprando da Cremona," *Quaderni medievali* 14 (1982): 39.

of the families of the Theophylactine counts of Tusculum, such as Marozia (2.48, 3.18, 3.43–45), or of women linked to the royal Italian lineages (2.55–56, 3.7–10, 4.12, 5.32) are carefully calibrated attempts to show the confusion prevailing in, and the illegitimacy of, households that could and did rival the Ottonians in Italy.[24] Older characterizations of Liudprand as being a "committed misogynist" or someone who "plainly hated women" misunderstand his purposes.[25] A clever writer with deep political commitments, he raised genealogical doubts to further his patrons' cause.[26] Liudprand's reiterated illustration of the degenerate sexual freedom of Italy's ruling clans, contrasted with the tidy sexuality and procreative prowess of Ottonian women, demonstrated the better claim to power that Otto I had.[27]

Moreover, Liudprand's eagerness to haul out the dirty laundry from the cupboards of Italy's mighty families by chronicling sexual excesses and infidelities was not restricted to the females in those families. Closer and less prurient inspection of *Retribution* suggests that *male* extramarital sexual activity is what disturbed Liudprand most. The sexual appetite of Ermengard (3.7), transgressive also

24. This is also why Liudprand glossed over Marozia's later days as a nun: see Levine, "Liudprand of Cremona," 80. Though Liudprand wrote from memory, some of his hostility toward the Theophylacts had to do with the sources he had read: see G. Arnaldi, "Mito e realtà del secolo X romano e papale," *Settimane di studio del Centro italiano di studi sull'Alto Medioevo* 38 (Spoleto: CISAM, 1991), 40.

25. Respectively, Sutherland, *Liudprand of Cremona*, 20, and Levine, "Liudprand of Cremona," 78.

26. Skinner, *Women*, 11, 105–8; Buc, "Italian Hussies," 214–24. Balzaretti, "Liudprand of Cremona's Sense," 124–25, disagrees.

27. Sexual transgressions were just one symptom of the unworthiness of Italy's aristocrats: their women also had too much political authority (e.g., 2.36). Though one of Liudprand's patrons, Adelheid (herself of Burgundian and Swabian origin), managed to export "southern" female authority to Saxony, Italian and especially Byzantine women were accustomed to greater public prominence than northern European audiences expected: see Skinner, *Women*, 93; Buc, "Italian Hussies," 217–18; P. Bange, "The Image of Women of the Nobility in the German Chronicles of the Tenth and Eleventh Centuries," in *The Empress Theophanu*, ed. A. Davids (Cambridge: Cambridge University Press, 1995), 150–54; F. Bougard, "Public Power and Authority," in *Italy*, ed. La Rocca, 39–43.

because it was not class-conscious, or of Liudprand's nemesis Willa (5.32), is not as prominent in the narrative as King Hugh's fatal flaw, namely, his insatiable lust (3.19), or Pope John X's inability to observe canonical continence (2.48).[28] Though Liudprand accepted sexuality as human, in keeping with the Augustinian tradition, he used his writing to suggest that it should be channeled into monogamous, legitimate unions and thus be controlled, so as to ensure harmonious, God-pleasing social relations on earth that would bring peace and prosperity exactly because they pleased God. Given the centrality of blood relationships in his period's dynastic politics, Liudprand's position was sensible.[29] To him, then, it was not sex, or unchaste behavior, that mattered. Rather, it was their untidy consequences, of which he thought he had witnessed far too many.

Liudprand's *Retribution* may have been targeted at those powerful German magnates, many with contacts and histories of involvement in Lombard Italy, who had vouchsafed Otto I's 952 settlement in Italy (whereby Berengar II and his son in effect became Otto's plenipotentiaries south of the Alps).[30] For these men Otto's changed stance after 956, his growing dissatisfaction with his too-independent agents in Italy, and his decision to intervene there, required their approval and support.[31] It was German magnates who would fill the ranks of Otto's avenging army, after all. Moreover, according to the political traditions of the time, the consent of a ruler's faithful men was a precondition for the harmonious relations that guaranteed the ruler's policies a successful outcome.

28. The issue of male sexual transgression is addressed by Balzaretti, "Men and Sex," 145–58. Accusations of sexual depravity against tenth-century popes were a political tool for other antagonists of the papacy: see *The Correspondence of Leo Metropolitan of Synada*, ed. M. Pollard Vinson (Washington: Dumbarton Oaks Research Library, 1985), 15–23.

29. Levine, "Liudprand of Cremona," 78.

30. The book circulated mostly in southern and western German lands.

31. Buc, *The Dangers*, 17–19, 21, 25, 27. It is worth noting, though, that also men not directly involved in Italy's "feudal" politics could tire of them: see S. Wemple, *Atto of Vercelli* (Rome: Edizioni di Storia e Letteratura, 1979), 82–83, 85–99.

Retribution proved that Italian aristocratic politics were different, that is, un-consensual and corrupt, and had been since 888.[32] Liudprand meticulously chronicled the failure of consensus in Lombardy, the arrogance of the powerful there, the reiterated regicide, the manifest disdain for the rules of aristocratic political dialogue, and the unpardonable softness toward unbelievers, because these were arguments in favor of Otto I's novel political directions in the late 950s. A polity like the Italian one evoked by Liudprand needed to be invaded. Men like Berengar II and Adalbert, behind whom pullulated a treacherous and litigious world of Flamberts and Walperts,[33] could rightly be liquidated without their liquidators losing face or honor, no matter what oaths had been undertaken in 952.[34]

Beyond the inclusion of so much detail on the sexual activity of the powerful, another potentially disorienting characteristic of Liudprand's book of *Retribution* is the poetry it contains. Toward the end of his *Embassy* Liudprand had also included some verse, the ditty he supposedly carved into the furniture in Constantinople (*Embassy* 57). But as a poet he is otherwise only known through his fourteen compositions in *Retribution*. These gave Liudprand a chance to display his considerable classical erudition in literal or formal citations of famous Roman poetry. However unusual the introduction of poems like these into historical prose may seem today, it was much less strange at the time when Liudprand wrote. To the extent that he mixed these genres together in his writings, the highly regarded eighth-century historian of the Lombards Paul the Deacon also saw no contradiction between the inventions of poetry and those of history.[35] Prosymetry, in fact, was revered clas-

---

32. Gandino, *Il vocabolario*, chap. 1. Through a negotiated settlement, in 952 Otto I allowed Berengar to retain authority in Italy.

33. See *Retribution* 2.69–71 and 3.39–40.

34. G. Tabacco, *The Struggle*, chap. 4, provides a fine introduction to "iron-century" Italian politics. Further overviews are in L. Provero, *L'Italia dei poteri locali* (Rome: Carocci, 1998) and S. Gasparri, "The Aristocracy," in *Italy*, ed. La Rocca, 75–84. Buc, "Italian Hussies," 213, points out that Saxons had little patience for accommodation with non-Christians, which instead was an early medieval Italian tradition.

35. Colonna, *Le poesie*, chap. 1.

sical tradition, and one of Liudprand's literary models, the fifth-century thinker Boethius, had excelled at it.[36] Since Boethius had also shown Liudprand that writing could be an antidote to the despair of life's vicissitudes, and that exile and peregrination were among the most inspiring muses to the stoical writer, his formal lessons could not be taken lightly either. Thus Liudprand's poems are not an interruption to the listing of history's sober facts, but are a continuation of history by other means, ones that his audience understood and appreciated because they did not separate forms of knowledge as modern audiences expect to do.[37]

Another potentially disconcerting characteristic of *Retribution* is the fairly frequent resort to Greek. Like most English-speakers today, most tenth-century European readers knew no Greek. Instead, Liudprand's knowledge of this language was fair, especially if one considers that, unlike some southern Italians, he was not a native speaker. In 968, when Liudprand used the services of an interpreter in Byzantium some twenty years after his first journey, the reason may not have been his linguistic limitations, but rather a matter of protocol; moreover, Liudprand may have been exercising prudence, in that a translator gave him more time to formulate responses and provided a useful filter against Byzantine courtly subterfuges. Liudprand could understand what contemporary Greek-speakers said when he wanted to; he also wrote Greek, in both miniscule and capitals, and presumably read it, too.

According to Liudprand's own account (6.3), he had learned Greek in Constantinople in 949–50, when he was in his twenties, and he displayed mastery of it in all his writing except *Concerning King Otto*. Since such knowledge of this prestigious, scriptural language was rare in Latin Christendom, it gave Liudprand satisfaction to display it, as well as offering some practical advantages in his peregrinations: learned northern Europeans admired the exotic language with classical *and* biblical connotations. People who knew

36. Hofmann, "Profil," 208; M. Gibson, "Boethius in the Tenth Century," *Mittel-lateinisches Jahrbuch* 24–25 (1989–90): 124.

37. Colonna, *Le poesie*, chap. 3; V. Sivo, "Studi recenti su Liutprando di Cremona," *Quaderni medievali* 44 (1997): 217–18.

it awed them, too. Hence, in *Retribution* Liudprand was ostentatious with his Greek. Greek phrases and technical terms distinguished the learned Italian cleric and also conferred believability upon his texts, giving his considerations on Byzantine affairs an air of authenticity, which would explain why the bulk of the Greek phrases occur in passages where Liudprand considers Byzantine affairs. And Liudprand's use of Greek changed over time. Early on, Liudprand had relied on the wonder his readers would feel when, plowing through his elegant Latin, they found his Greek. Later, when writing the Freising manuscript, the author took the unusual step of transliterating and translating the Greek for his audience, a kind gesture that won readers' appreciation without sacrificing the respect that his knowledge of Greek should elicit.[38]

Related to the question of Liudprand's comprehension of Greek is the one of his evaluation of his world's Greek-speakers, the Byzantines. Scholars have long noted the author of *Retribution*'s respect, even enthusiasm, for Byzantium, in contrast to Liudprand's negative approach in the *Embassy*. While Liudprand wrote *Retribution*'s main redaction, he had not yet wholeheartedly converted to the Ottonian view of the world. The highest, most legitimate human authority remained that of the Constantinopolitan emperor of the Romans.[39] Liudprand had strong opinions about which individuals God invested with emperorship—this was in fact one reason why he depicted Nicephorus Phocas as he did in the *Embassy*, where he did not accord the emperor his proper titles.[40] But *Retribution* betrays few doubts that the new Rome of the east harbored Christendom's supreme authority, which might explain why Liudprand

38. W. Berschin, *Medioevo greco-latino* (Naples, 1989), 26–35, 39, 224–32; F. Dolbeau, "Le rôle des interprètes dans les traductions hagiographiques d'Italie du Sud," in *Traduction et traducteurs au moyen âge*, ed. G. Contamine (Paris: Editions du CNRS, 1989), 146–47, 154–55; J. Koder and T. Weber, *Liudprand von Cremona in Konstantinopel* (Vienna: Verlag der Österreichischen Akademie der Wissenschaften, 1980), 58–60.

39. Sutherland, *Liudprand of Cremona*, 26–28; M. Rentschler, *Liudprand von Cremona* (Frankfurt: Klostermann, 1981), 15–18; M. Lintzel, *Studien über Liudprand von Cremona* (Berlin: Verlag Dr Emil Ebering, 1933), 75–76.

40. S. Kolditz, "Leon von Synada und Liudprand von Cremona," *Byzantinische Zeitschrift* 95 (2002): 560.

did not develop a written rationale for the imperial hegemony Otto I exercised after 962, despite his opportunity to do so in writing *Concerning King Otto*. In *Retribution* the Ottonians are kings, powerful and divinely sanctioned, but not transcendent authorities like the Byzantine emperors in book 1 or book 6. Liudprand resisted the temptation to project backwards in time the realities of the years (roughly 958–62) when he worked on his *Retribution*.

Interestingly, respect for and even awe before the Byzantine "emperors of the Romans" did not mean that Liudprand felt special reverence for the city of Rome and its inhabitants. Rome and especially the Romans are depicted throughout *Retribution* in embarrassing and inglorious circumstances. Tenth-century Rome was indeed not an impressive place. The Eternal City's population occupied a fraction of the ancient urban armature, and although this was western Christendom's largest community, it was shabby and desolate. In addition, learned men like Liudprand knew that since Republican times the appropriate tone to take in speaking of the citizens of Rome had been scornful. From Cato's day on, at least, the literary tradition assumed the city and its inconstant, treacherous, cowardly people to be unworthy of their ancestors. In the end, it seems, Liudprand detected no contradiction between considering Rome an ideal of transnational government, a unifying symbol for Christian Europe, and depicting the real Romans abandoning the defense of their walls because of a hare (1.27). For the Lombard writer knew both conceptions had illustrious literary pedigrees, and he understood the chasm separating transcendent ideal from human actuation of it.[41]

LIUDPRAND AS HOMILIST

Liudprand's single known surviving sermon was discovered about fifty years ago and first published in 1984. To date it is the least stud-

---

41. H. Fichtenau, "Vom Ansehen des Papsttums im zehnten Jahrhundert," in *Aus Kirche und Reich*, ed. H. Mordek (Sigmaringen: Jan Thorbecke Verlag, 1983), 121–23; Kolditz, "Leon von Synada," 554–55; Arnaldi, "Liutprando e la storiografia," 504.

ied of Liudprandine texts. Nevertheless, as the only obviously complete work we have from Liudprand, the *Homily* reveals a lot about the author and his context. Certainly the *Homily* renders it more difficult to dismiss Liudprand as a shallow or opportunistic Christian, for in it the "Italian deacon" displays a tenacious commitment to the tenets of his faith, as well as the usual strong erudition, this time less classical and more scriptural, and steeped in Augustinian theology. Even for readers prepared to regard Liudprand's claims of having experienced miracles (*Embassy* 24, 60–61) as false, or his solemn theological expositions (*Retribution* 4.26) as trite, he emerges from the *Homily* as a courageous believer willing to reproach his ecclesiastical superiors for their lack of Christian charity and pained by clerical indifference to social and economic inequalities.[42]

The *Homily* survived on six sheets of parchment in a single codex. Bound together with it are texts of varied provenance, written by different hands. The book seems to have been assembled in Freising for Bishop Abraham, who was a collector of Liudprand's writings. Abraham needed the volume, some of whose texts are in Old Slavonic, for his missionary activity in Carinthia during the 970s and 980s. This purpose would explain why so much homiletic literature ended up in the volume. Probably Liudprand had his *Homily* transcribed in central Germany, under his direct supervision, and he corrected it himself before folding it and sending it to Abraham (who parsimoniously filled the blank space on its last page with the beginning of the ninth-century sermon that follows upon Liudprand's in the volume). Perhaps Liudprand thought that a sermon addressing the problem of unbelief would suit Bishop Abraham's purposes in a thinly Christianized part of Austria at a time when bishops were duty-bound to teach the faith through sermons.[43] Sermons, as well as writings that adopted the dialogue form as this one did, were

42. B. Bischoff, "Ein Osterpredigt Liudprands von Cremona (um 960)," in his *Anecdota novissima* (Stuttgart: A. Hiersemann, 1984), 20–34, first published the sermon he had discovered decades earlier. He was baffled by Liudprand's temerity in attacking bishops for their stinginess (20). Leyser, "Ends and Means," 130, saw the sermon as evidence of Liudprand's religious commitment.

43. Fichtenau, *Living*, 210.

part of the arsenal that early medieval missionaries deployed when attempting to convince others that the faith was trustworthy.[44] Yet Liudprand did not hesitate to include a reminder that episcopal charity was as important as zealous proselytism.[45]

To modern western readers, one of the most striking aspects of Liudprand's homily is the device of addressing a Jew directly in it. In doing this Liudprand was mixing two traditional genres, namely, the anti-Jewish sermon and the dialogue-based treatise, both much employed by Latin Christians who pondered the relations between Judaism and Christianity. Liudprand, who was well aware that Christianity was only one of many belief systems, neglected Judaism in his other writings. Yet the preacher's imagined interlocutor is a learned, intelligent, and dedicated gentleman who engages Liudprand in a logical debate, drawing heavily on scriptural evidence. This section of the sermon includes several tropes from the literary tradition of the fictional debate between religious opponents. It reeks sufficiently of the classroom so that one might suspect the text originated in a disputation exercise of the kind common in the high Middle Ages, but we know too little about tenth-century schooling and Liudprand's own educational experience to be certain.[46] After 1000 there would develop a richer tradition of similar dialogue texts, with the celebrated school teacher Peter Abelard penning the best-known one, the *Dialogue of a Philosopher with a Jew and a Christian*.[47] But already in the tenth century, clergymen and even Venetian doges worried about Jews who argued successfully against Christian the-

44. B. Blumenkranz, *Juifs et Chrétiens dans le monde occidental 430–1096* (Paris: Mouton, 1960), 75–81; A. Lukyn Williams, *Adversus Judaeos. A Bird's Eye View of Christian Apologiae Until the Renaissance* (London: Cambridge University Press, 1935), 298–305.

45. For the history of Liudprand's manuscript, see Chiesa, *Liudprandi Cremonensis Opera* lxxxiii–lxxxvii. On the importance of the codicological context for understanding sermons, see C. Muessing, "Sermon, Preacher, and Society in the Middle Ages," *Journal of Medieval History* 28 (2002): 75–76.

46. Arnaldi, "Liutprando e la storiografia," 506; L. Ricci, *Problemi sintattici nelle opere di Liutprando di Cremona* (Spoleto: CISAM, 1996), 195–96. Leonardi, "Il secolo X," 160–61, takes up the tradition according to which tenth-century scholars did not learn in schools, but on their own.

47. D. Berger, *The Jewish-Christian Debate in the High Middle Ages* (Philadelphia: Jewish Publication Society of America, 1979).

ology, about Christians who mingled with Jews, whether to gain
exegetical knowledge or for other reasons, and about the attraction
Judaism exercised for Christians. Such worry generated a series of
references to Judaism, treatises on Jewish and Christian belief, and
records of debates among learned men of the two faiths.[48] Liudprand's dialectical exchange with an unbeliever, while participating
in a late antique tradition of literary dialogues between Christians
and Jews, is quite original for the Ottonian period, and betrays the
Christian clerical elite's continuing preoccupation with learned Judaism and with the need to prove the tenets of its faith through
logic and reference to shared authorities.

Tenth-century Judaism was a small presence in Liudprand's
world. Within the Italian peninsula, early medieval Judaism had
flourished in the Byzantine south, and the *Chronicle of Ahimaaz* is
one testament to the vitality of the Apulian communities after the
ninth-century "hebraization" of Jewish culture there.[49] Yet in the
early 900s Byzantium's rulers had begun to coerce Jews to convert
to Christianity, and the *Chronicle of Ahimaaz* refers to the hardships
that Jewish communities endured even in such a remote periphery
of the empire as southern Italy.

In the kingdom of Italy further north, the place where Liud-

48. See B. Blumenkranz, *Les auteurs chrétiens latins du moyen âge sur les juifs et le judaïsme*
(Paris: Mouton, 1963); N. Golb, *Jewish Proselytism—A Phenomenon in the Religious History of
the Early Middle Ages* (Cincinnati: University of Cincinnati Press, 1988), 2–6, 32; Lukyn
Williams, *Adversus Judaeos*, 3–90, 117–223, 348–65. For the long view of Jewish-Christian
polemics, see I. Yuval, *Two Nations in Your Womb* (Berkeley: University of California Press,
2006), chap. 1–3.

49. See *The Chronicle of Ahimaaz*, trans. M. Salzmann (New York: Columbia University Press, 1924). The debate (pp.78–79) between the "archbishop" and rabbi Hana-
neel is an example of the intellectual sparring that early medieval audiences appreciated. During the Carolingian period, Hebrew increasingly replaced Greek and Latin
in liturgical and other contexts: see C. Roth, *History of the Jews of Italy* (Philadelphia:
Jewish Publication Society of America, 1946), 38–65; V. Colorni, "Gli ebrei nei territori italiani a nord di Roma dal 568 all'inizio del secolo XII," *Settimane di studio del
Centro italiano di studi sull'Alto Medioevo* 26 (Spoleto: CISAM, 1980): 286–93; B. Kreutz,
Before the Normans (Philadelphia: University of Pennsylvania Press, 1991), 85–87;
C. Colafemmina, "Hebrew Inscriptions of the early Medieval Period in Southern
Italy," in *The Jews of Italy*, ed. B. Cooperman and B. Garvin (Bethesda: University Press
of Maryland, 2000).

prand grew up, Byzantine intransigence was not embraced, and, anyhow, kings lacked the administrative capacity to be as intrusive as Byzantine emperors could be. Still, some late Carolingian legislation obliging Jews to convert had been promulgated, and King Louis II (†877) had offered Lombardy's Jews a choice between conversion and expulsion. If these policies had an impact, it was transitory, for Jewish traders and landowners are present in Italian documents throughout the tenth century.[50] Around 900, Rabbi Moses of Pavia, an émigré from the Byzantine south, became famous enough to be regarded, later, as the first Talmudist.[51] Liudprand, who grew up in Pavia in the 920s, may have known the Pavian Jewish community.

The Saxon rulers who welcomed the "Italian deacon" in the 950s, and under whose protection the *Homily* probably was composed, perpetuated Charlemagne's and Louis the Pious's liberal policies for Jewish communities.[52] At the Council of Erfurt in 932, for instance, Christian clerics had talked about a disputation between a Christian and a Jew they thought had caused mass conversions of Jews in Palestine, but Henry the Fowler, the first Saxon king of Germany (or East Francia), ignored the attendant clerical pleas for forced conversion to Christianity in the region.[53] Otto I also fostered Carolingian-style policies toward Judaism, even when, in 938–39, the pope failed to uphold with the traditional clarity the canonical position that forced baptism was not desirable.[54] His stance was significant since the presence of Jewish colonies in the

50. Colorni, "Gli ebrei," 247–48, 277.

51. Roth, *History*, 63. At Pavia the young Alcuin saw Peter of Pisa debate with a Jew (*Letter* 172).

52. B. Bachrach, *Early Medieval Jewish Policy in Western Europe* (Minneapolis: University of Minnesota Press, 1977), 66–132; M. Toch, *Die Juden im mittelalterlichen Reich* (Munich: R. Oldenbourg Verlag, 2003), 46, 103–4.

53. Such conversions were contrary to canon law, but may have gained popularity in the West through the example of Romanos Lakapenos in the East, for the Christian clergy constantly worried about "judaizing," or the attraction for Christians of Judaism. Forced conversion to Christianity eliminated this danger.

54. D. Malkiel, "Jewish-Christian Relations in Europe, 840–1096," *Journal of Medieval History* 29 (2003): 64–65.

eastern Frankish kingdom was recent, and perhaps for that reason was disturbing to people who did not benefit directly from their presence in the main cities, as rulers did instead.[55]

In this political climate of toleration, or benign neglect, the exiled deacon was wise to represent his disagreements with a learned Jew as an intellectual exchange, and one that ended in a stalemate. The anti-Semitic extremism of Bishop Rather of Verona, a contemporary whom Liudprand admired, had no place in a homily designed for Ottonian German eyes and ears. Already an established senior cleric when he was in Pavia and its environs in the 930s, at the time Liudprand was entering the service of King Hugh, Rather had a profound impact on Liudprand's writing.[56] Rather was himself a homilist who liked to conjure up imaginary audiences with whom to carry on dialogues in his sermons, though he never took the step Liudprand did of addressing a fictitious Jew in a place (a church) and time (Easter mass) where no Jews are likely to have been.[57] In a Ratherian Easter sermon of 963, the preacher turns abruptly from a theological discussion with St. Paul to exhort his audience of Veronese clergy, before him in church, to share their abundant food with the poor.[58] In a similar sudden change of reg-

55. Toch, *Die Juden*, 5–6. Toch notes (111) that in the Ottonian period Jewish-Christian relations were tranquil, and the few interruptions to the tranquility came from Christian clerical debates about the church's missionary role (and the *Homily* was sent to a missionary bishop). See also M. Toch, "The Formation of a Diaspora," *Ashkenas* 7 (1997): 11–34.

56. Staubach, "Historia oder Satira?" 470–84.

57. Carolingian canon law restricted Eucharistic celebrations to Christians, though in practice Jews continued to witness Christian rituals, especially outdoor ones: Blumenkranz, *Juifs*, 52–54. Easter was the period when Christian hostility against Judaism was likeliest to surface, as the late winter feast of Purim might become the occasion for Jews to express antipathy for Christianity, which might take the form of crucifixion-mockery: see Malkiel, "Jewish-Christian Relations," 65–67; E. Horowitz, "'And It Was Reversed': Jews and Their Enemies in the Festivities of Purim," *Zion* 59 (1994): x.

58. *The Complete Works of Rather of Verona*, ed. P. Reid (Binghamton, NY: Medieval and Renaissance Texts and Studies, 1991), 338–42. Liudprand cited Rather's second Easter sermon in *Retribution* 1.12 and *Concerning King Otto* 10. Early medieval homilists, lacking late medieval how-to manuals, learned their craft from other sermons: see T. Hall, "The Early Medieval Sermon," in *The Sermon*, ed. B. Kienzle (Turnholt: Brepols, 2000), 203.

ister, Liudprand's *Homily* abandons its initial, Jewish interlocutor in section 21 and aims a final set of arguments about being generous to the needy at the homilist's "dearest brothers," fellow clergymen.

But if Rather's writings are a valuable key to the form of Liudprand's *Homily*, the two homilists parted ways on content. The *Homily* does not echo with the vehemence Rather imparted to his claims that he had spent his episcopal career "uninterruptedly reviling" Judaism, to the point of reproaching any who greeted a Jew in Verona, and of condoning a cleric who struck a Jew there in the course of a debate.[59] The Veronese bishop was embattled, and Rather's 966 treatise is a self-defense, implying that most people in Verona disapproved of his activities, including the anti-Jewish ones. But he shared with the exiled deacon, and perhaps with the Lombard clergy more generally, an anxiety over the challenges posed by Jews to Christian theological positions. Liudprand's opposition to any doubts about the Incarnation and Crucifixion was more Olympian and intellectual, while Rather depicted his own hostility as a legitimate defensive reaction against people who aggressively denied the truths of Christianity, among them the basic idea that God had become human in Jesus. Even if Rather's exculpatory treatise and Liudprand's *Homily* were divorced from the more easy-going realities of everyday social relations between Jews and Christians, they give insight into the culture of educated clerics with backgrounds in Lombardy around the middle of the tenth century.

LIUDPRAND AS IMPERIAL APOLOGIST

Like the *Homily* and the *Embassy*, Liudprand's *Concerning King Otto* was an occasional piece, composed in specific circumstances for a particular purpose. Unlike the *Homily* and the *Embassy*, this text seems to have enjoyed a fairly wide readership, for it survives in a reasonable number of manuscripts of medieval date (nine, usually attached to parts or the whole of *Retribution*, mostly from southern German

---

59. *The Complete Works of Rather*, ed. Reid, 435–36, 505–7.

lands).[60] If we do not have an autograph, we nonetheless have a contemporary version whose copying Liudprand must have overseen. This is the original text, then, even if incomplete, written around 965 and describing events that took place between 961 and 964. These events were pivotal for Liudprand's career and life, as they transformed him from a foreigner and exile hanging on at Otto I's court into a powerful lord in his native land, Lombardy. Though *Concerning King Otto* is about the Saxon ruler's occupation of Italy and dealings with the papacy, its subtext is about the triumphant return of a down-and-out deacon as the valued collaborator of the new government, and as bishop of a vital see on the river Po.

If they had this important personal dimension for Liudprand, the events outlined in *Concerning King Otto* mattered even more to northern and Mediterranean Europe's grand politics. The title assigned royal status only to Otto, and Liudprand barely mentioned Otto's imperial coronation, perhaps to minimize a ceremony that demonstrated papal superiority. Otto's imperial status, however, was a precondition for everything else in the treatise: once the western empire had a militarily credible hegemon again, Germany, Italy, and Byzantium confronted a new situation.

It is with the repercussions of Otto's decisions to embrace a Carolingian conception of the Roman Empire that this treatise grapples. Tenth-century writers knew that empires need not be Roman, and the Saxon chronicler Widukind, for one, consistently ignored the legitimating force of Roman-ness in Otto's empire, preferring the legitimization that Otto's trans-ethnic power and his victories against paganism conferred.[61] Yet an emperor who had been elevated in St. Peter's in Rome and called himself emperor of the Romans (among other epithets) understood that deeper involvement in Italian and Roman affairs would be his lot after February 962.[62]

60. Chiesa, *Liudprandi Cremonensis Opera*, xix–xxxix.

61. C. Erdmann, *Forschungen zur politischen Ideenwelt des Frühmittelalters* (Berlin: Akademie Verlag, 1951), 44–47.

62. C. Erdmann, *Ottonische Studien* (Darmstadt: Wissenschaftliche Buchgesellschaft, 1961), 174–77; G. Sergi, "The Kingdom of Italy," in *New Cambridge Medieval History*,

Italian affairs occupied Liudprand less, in this treatise, than the specifically Roman ones. He mentioned Otto's "mopping up" operations against Berengar II and Adalbert (whom the narrative robs of any initiative in the unsuccessful Roman uprising of 963, in order to increase John XII's culpability). He also notes that by late 962 the leading potentate in southern Italy, Pandulf of Capua, had aligned himself with Otto and would block papal messengers sent to Constantinople. In spite of these minor departures, Liudprand's text centers on the Eternal City and what transpired there in the first years of Otto's imperial reign.

Pope John XII, alarmed by incursions into Roman territory that originated in the duchy of Spoleto, held by Adalbert, had begged for Otto's protection. He had then rewarded his savior by crowning him emperor, but his conception of proper relations between Rome, its bishop, and its emperor, did not match Otto's. Their disagreement was inevitable. The generation of Roman aristocrats who witnessed Otto's coronation was not accustomed to a papacy that acted as more than a local agency. For fifty years the Theophylacts had had a stranglehold on the main offices through which legitimate authority flowed in Rome, and the relative tranquility this one clan imposed depended on this control as much as on their landholdings around Tusculum (today's Frascati). To maintain this situation, the Roman bishop was expected to concern himself primarily with Roman matters, even to the detriment of his other vocation as universal pontiff, responsible for the spiritual health of all Christians.[63]

Such an introverted papacy did not fit Otto's requirements after 961. Now the senior Theophylact, John XII, should return the papacy to an international dimension, as a prominent bishopric in a new, Saxon-led Roman empire. Along with members of the Ottonian family, bishops were a vital cog in the mechanism of Ottonian governance, and leading bishops, especially the one who conferred imperial authority, could not continue to occupy themselves exclu-

---

ed. T. Reuter (Cambridge: Cambridge University Press, 1999), 3:357–60; E. Muller-Martens, "The Ottonian Kings and Emperors," ibid., 248–54.

63. P. Llewellyn, *Rome in the Dark Ages* (London: Constable, 1993), 296–313.

sively with local, petty issues, independent from the emperor and his strategies.[64]

The decision to depose Pope John XII was both unprecedented and momentous. It was also hotly contested within the western church. Despite the elisions that later people made in the record, there survive several signs of the doubts Otto's action evoked among Germany's clergy, a category of men essential to Otto's political success.[65] Clerics trained in the Carolingian tradition cannot have approved of this way of redefining relations between secular and ecclesiastical leadership. One of Liudprand's contemporaries in Italy, the bishop of Vercelli called Atto, knew that from usurpation of authority, or the illegitimate assumption of prerogatives, all manner of disorder ensued, including disasters for any unlucky enough to live under the unsanctioned authority's sway.[66]

For Liudprand, to whom Otto seemed an excellent, just, and legitimate ruler, the imperative was therefore the propagation of a "correct" understanding of what Otto had done, much of which he had witnessed, though he did not make recourse to the stereotype of the eyewitness account in this case. *Concerning King Otto* is a lucid defense of the rather high-handed way in which Otto had behaved toward a pope who had failed to conform to his needs. In order to convince readers of the justice and legitimacy of Otto's policy, Liudprand adopted an unusually staid, august, impassive style in his Latin, quite unlike the style employed in, for example, the book of *Retribution*. Yet this style matched the supernaturally detached, patient, paternal behavior of the text's protagonist, Otto. The dispassionate exposition, the inclusion of documents, the careful listing of participants at events, are all part of Liudprand's narrative strategy, and win him a credible position from which to shed light on what *really* happened.

64. On bishops and governance, G. Tabacco, "Regno, impero e aristocrazie nell'Italia postcarolingia," *Settimane di studio del Centro italiano di studi sull'Alto Medioevo* 38 (Spoleto: CISAM, 1991), 255, 265.

65. See Adalbert's *Continuatio Reginonis*, for example, well explicated by Lintzel, *Studien*, 20–34.

66. Fichtenau, *Living*, 384; Wemple, *Atto of Vercelli*, 63, 85–99. Liudprand's ideas on the papacy are weighed in Sutherland, *Liudprand*, 37–40.

The author's desire to prove the righteousness of the papal demotion also surfaces in the brutal character assassination of John XII. Such denigration was part of the standard repertory of classical rhetoric, but Liudprand wielded it with fresh efficacy. In order to make his portrait more convincingly hideous, the emperor's bishop overlooked any "virtuous" deeds of John and the Theophylacts, such as fostering monastic reform in Rome.[67] Instead, Liudprand harped on John's unbridled sexuality, even more than his horrifying indifference to proper liturgical procedure and his murderous bent, because the aristocrats who would read his text knew that curbing sexual passions was essential to family dynamics and political order. In this way Liudprand proved that John was an unworthy leader, an unfit member of the elite. His sexual liaisons, moreover, were scandalous to any clerics involved in contemporary efforts to increase the clergy's dedication to celibacy, an obsession of tenth-century reformers. Quite aside from the shocking places where the canonically illicit unions took place, and from the fact that they involved women toward whose male relatives the pope was honor-bound to show respect, John's affairs, luridly described, were the sort of thing that could change tenth-century opinions.[68] In deliberate contrast to John's behavior, Liudprand evoked Otto's. The king-emperor, decently married to Adelheid, thus emerged as an indulgent father to the young pope, as the long-suffering but understanding senior male in the new Roman family, who disapproved but knew that boys would be boys and was even willing to wait until John's youthful ardor had simmered down.

Liudprand also insisted that Otto had not acted alone, for tenth-century politics was supposed to involve aristocratic support, and tyranny, or failure to build up aristocratic consensus around decisions, was the hallmark of bad rulers like Berengar II and Adalbert, whom Otto had ousted from Italy.[69] Liudprand showed that Otto

---

67. Llewellyn, *Rome*, 308–10, using the fine research of B. Hamilton.

68. Balzaretti, "Men and Sex," 143–59; Gandini, *Il vocabolario*, chap. 6.

69. Gandini, *Il vocabolario*, chap. 1; J. Nelson, "Rulers and Government," *New Cambridge Medieval History* 3, ed. Reuter, 102, 119; Buc, *The Dangers*, 21–23; F. Brunhölzl, *Geschichte der lateinischen Literatur des Mittelalters* (Munich: W. Fink, 1975), 2: 372–74.

had moved south in response to various magnates' appeals, had enjoyed the support of the Roman aristocracy,[70] and had humbly listened to the opinions of the senior clerics who alone had reached the decision that John XII was unfit to rule. When Otto had resorted to violence, as he did in early 964 on a scale remarkable enough that a Byzantine emperor was still talking about it four years later (*Embassy* 4), it was a last resort and a response by a heroic and outnumbered band to unacceptable Roman treachery and oath-breaking.[71]

Otto emerges from Liudprand's apology as perfect in his virtues. He had handled a prickly situation with wisdom and fairness, according to the best political traditions of the tenth-century aristocracy. His forbearance was superhuman. His kindness was infinite. He was, in sum, a saint, an executor on earth of the divine plan, more, even, than he had been in the book of *Retribution*. Liudprand's new Otto in this respect differed from the Otto of other Saxon chroniclers, and the saintly emperor in this treatise may be the highest point of Liudprand's attempt to show that Otto's actions were justified because he enjoyed divine favor. Tenth-century readers could tell who was right from his success, popularity, and God-given privilege of seeing things turn out favorably. The holy glow surrounding Otto in Liudprand's short text was another useful confirmation that he had done the right thing in his dealings with the first popes of his imperial years.[72]

LIUDPRAND AS EMISSARY

The Liudprand best known in the twenty-first century is not the same one who enjoyed some modest notoriety in the 900s. This is because Liudprand's currently most celebrated text, the *Embassy*, was, to judge from its manuscript dissemination, not engaging to

70. Though even Liudprand could not overlook the three rebellions against Otto's arrangements that took place in 962–64.

71. On the Romans' bad reputation, see Fichtenau, *Vom Ansehen*, 121–23; on Liudprand's use of violence, Gandini, *Il vocabolario*, chap. 5.

72. On Otto's sanctity, Gandini, *Il vocabolario*, chap. 1.

medieval readers. Indeed, no medieval manuscripts survive today of this amusing account of Liudprand's diplomatic journey to Constantinople in 968, and his adventuresome return in the winter of 968–69. The sole known copy has been lost since being used for the first edition of 1600. Thus only an early modern edition (though a reliable edition, from what can be divined) preserved the text that gives Liudprand any fame he enjoys today.

The reasons for the disinterest of medieval readers in the *Embassy* are uncertain. It is possible that the author himself did not imagine his text would circulate beyond the dedicatees, namely, Otto I, Adelheid, and their son Otto II, together with their intimates. For Liudprand had a lot to lose if his *Embassy* were to have gained wide audiences. Sailing to Byzantium was a family tradition, and Liudprand, who had become the Ottonians' Byzantine specialist, must have expected to return to Constantinople after 968. In fact it seems he did, with a high-ranking delegation, in 971, in what became his last voyage.[73] A well-known piece of vitriolic anti-Byzantine satire would have been an embarrassment even after the regime change of December 969 (whereby the more amenable John Tsimiskes replaced the emperor Nicephoros Phocas); it might have needlessly shut some diplomatic doors on Liudprand, whose stature in the Ottonian world depended on his ability to navigate these passages. Certainly the text lost one of its more obvious practical purposes after the palace coup that elevated Tsimiskes, and in the détente of 970–71 it would have been wise to lock it into a cupboard.

Other practical functions for this *Embassy* are equally difficult to decipher.[74] It was presumably written during 969.[75] In the preced-

73. Liudprand's father in 927 and subsequently his stepfather in 941 represented King Hugh in Byzantium, before Liudprand's own 949 trip for Berengar II and his mysterious trip to Paxos of about 960. That Liudprand died returning from Constantinople in 972 is now more widely believed than it used to be: see Leyser, "Ends and Means," 126; Sutherland, *Liudprand*, 99–100.

74. Lintzel, *Studien*, 49.

75. Brandes, "Liudprand von Cremona," 446, suggests that the *Embassy* was written some time after December 969, when Nicephoros Phocas died, because Liudprand seems already to know the accuracy of his grim prophecies for this emperor.

ing two years Otto I had sought to apply pressure on the Byzantines, seemingly in order to obtain a satisfactory definition of Ottonian and Byzantine spheres of influence, as well as a prestigious princess for Otto II to marry, thereby contributing to the family's imperial stature. Otto I's campaign in southern Italy foundered, and in 969 Otto's most precious ally there, Pandulf of Capua, fell into Byzantine hands and was shipped off to captivity in Constantinople, where he may have helped the negotiators of 971–72 obtain Theophanu, Otto II's future wife. If Liudprand's *Embassy* was supposed to provide Otto with fresh intelligence for his war (chap. 29), or well-informed, usable advice on how to move forward in dealings with the eastern emperors (52), by the time Otto might have read it, the text was obsolete.

If instead the *Embassy*'s real targets were southern Italy's various rulers, to prove in what high regard the Ottonians held them and how little respect the Byzantines accorded them, though they were Constantinople's traditional allies, the text came at an extraordinarily awkward time, that is, after a half-century of Byzantine successes in the region.[76] Pandulf had been captured in the spring of 969 at Bovino, where the German army was routed. Gisulf, the ruler of Salerno, welcomed the Byzantine victors of Bovino during the summer of 969, entertaining them lavishly and perpetuating the Lombards' traditional equidistance between Byzantine and western emperors. Later triumphs for the German reinforcements and Otto's arrival in early 970 were preludes to the pacification of summer 970.[77] The latter months of 969 and the early ones of 970 were an inauspicious moment at which to circulate a treatise mocking Byzantine ways.

Regardless of whether or not Liudprand wrote for the southern Lombards, he repeatedly addressed his Ottonian patrons in the *Embassy*, not any southern princes, and one obvious purpose of the

---

76. For the Byzantine revival in Italy, see Tabacco, *The Struggle*, 136–43, 176–78.

77. J. Gay, *L'Italie méridionale et l'empire byzantin* (Paris: A. Fontemoing, 1904), 312–18; H. Mayr-Harting, "Liudprand of Cremona's Account of his Legation to Constantinople and Ottonian Imperial Strategy," *English Historical Review* 116 (2001): 541–44.

text was to explain why his mission had failed to produce favorable results for the people who had sent him on it. There is no sign that Liudprand suffered any Ottonian ill will after returning empty-handed from Constantinople in early 969. He continued to act as a responsible bishop in a strategic see, attending councils and witnessing documents.[78] Yet the petulance Liudprand chose to display in his account sounds like a justification for deeds that had been criticized. Likewise, the unprecedented, persistent, and explicit anti-Byzantinism in the text may be an attempt to explain why the legate had failed to reach an accord with Nicephoros: how could anyone come to terms with a vain garlic-eater?[79] Still more, the reiterated pinpointing of dates and times suggests that Liudprand hoped to allay any suspicion that he had dallied in the east, an area he had liked in 949[80] and whose rulers he had once considered more legitimate than any in the Italian peninsula. Thus the most immediately visible prompt behind a text that flashily exhibits loyalty to Ottonian causes, distaste for things Byzantine, and an envoy's conscientious use of every daylight hour, is the need to prove that Liudprand had not been fraternizing with the enemy while Otto I waited testily "to achieve that Apulia be reintegrated into our Italian kingdom, having been taken away from the Greeks."[81]

In his account of his exchanges with Nicephoros Phocas and his administration, Liudprand went out of his way to show that quite the opposite of fraternization had taken place. In fact, Liudprand's *Embassy*, perhaps more than his other writings though they, too, are concerned with the establishment of difference, reflects the participation by men and women of letters in the slow crystallization of

78. Leyser, "Ends and Means," 128; Sutherland, *Liudprand*, 97–99; B. Scott, *Liudprand of Cremona. Relatio de Legatione Constantinopolitana* (London, 1993), xv.

79. The novelty of Liudprand's depiction of Byzantium is treated by Rentschler, *Liudprand von Cremona*, 17–18.

80. See *Retribution* 6.

81. According to a diploma of Otto from November 2, 969, while Liudprand was laboriously finding his way home: see *MGH, Diplomatum* 1, 504. K. Leyser, "Theophanu Divina Gratia Imperatrix Augusta," in *The Empress Theophanu*, ed. A. Davids, 14–16, stresses the import the Ottonians ascribed to the marital alliance.

cultural boundaries during the European tenth century.[82] The gifted nun Hrotswita of Gandersheim, a contemporary of Liudprand's who lived in an exclusive, powerful, royally sponsored convent in Saxony, signaled the same mounting intransigence when she included in her limited selection of hagiography some modern martyrs, Christians who had actively sought confrontation and death in Islamic Spain a couple of generations earlier.[83] Of course, the new bristling, more antagonistic attitude toward people whose religious and cultural background made them seem "other" was not a universal phenomenon in the "iron century." Southern Italians, who had a long and sometimes painful familiarity with Arab raiders, read historians who did not always cast "the Saracens" as animalesque, laughable, immoral monsters. In fact, in this historiography some Saracens proved their humanity, and even their righteousness, on the battlefield or on the gallows.[84]

Liudprand's description of Byzantine customs in the *Embassy* exceeds other early medieval ethnographic description both in its level of detail and in the sharpness of its scorn. There were other Italian historians of the tenth century who disliked Byzantium, but even they never matched Liudprand's venom. John the Deacon, a Venetian with solid patriotic grounds for his negative descriptions of Byzantine governance, was bland by comparison.[85] Liudprand, who is the narrative's protagonist, was better informed than most other pre-modern ethnographers; his stay in Constantinople in 968 was long, even if not unusually so, for a period when movements were difficult and the cadence of diplomacy slow.[86] Liudprand had been there before and had a store of family lore about the city and its

82. Leyser, "Ends and Means," observed Liudprand's interest in firming up Latin Europe's cultural identity.

83. Leyser, "Ends and Means," 141–42; K. Baxter Wolf, "Christian Views of Islam in Early Medieval Spain," in *Medieval Perceptions of Islam*, ed. J. Tolan (New York: Garland, 1996), 85–108, reviews the ups and downs of religious identity in Iberia.

84. L. Berto, "I mussulmani nelle cronache altomedievali dell'Italia meridionale," in *Mediterraneo meridionale*, ed. M. Meschini (Milan: Vita e Pensiero, 2001), 6–7, 11, 19–20.

85. L. Berto, "La storia degli altri," *Archivio veneto* 155 (2000): 5–20.

86. Leyser, "Ends and Means," 135.

people on which to rely in giving his adventures literary form. He had some native informants and could speak the local language. Greater exposure to and knowledge of the alien culture thus partly explain his decision to satirize cultural minutiae.

In addition to this better data on Byzantium, the negative discourse also depended on literary calculations. Liudprand's characterizations of the Byzantine *nomenklatura* were made from a position of superior information about *two* cultures (Latin and Byzantine) that allowed the bishop to manipulate his readers and stimulate the reactions he desired in them, for he understood precisely what would surprise and scandalize his western audience even if to him such things were no longer strange.[87] A good example of this is the haughty and distant figure of the emperor, sure to alarm western magnates accustomed to more accessible lords.

On the other hand, the years spent around the Ottonian court may have taught the exiled deacon the need for the rejection of strange ways (the same ways that had seemed attractive in 949, as reported in *Retribution* 6) and the construction of a proud new cultural polity, the fused Lombards-Saxons-Franks-Lotharingians-Bavarians-Swabians-Burgundians, whom Liudprand lists as a single entity in *Embassy* 12, which corresponded to the christianized portions of the Ottonians' realm. As in other ethnic discourses, the rejection of a set of "alien" ways in the *Embassy* was intimately related to the propagation of another set of authentic, good, homespun ones. Thus when Liudprand drew deep lines of division between the proper culture of "us" and the absurd one of "them," his ethnic sensitivity was both constructive (of the Ottonian polity) and destructive (of the allegedly ridiculous and wrong-headed Byzantine world).

During the 950s and 960s, then, Liudprand had deepened his appreciation for the importance of cultural difference and developed a new opinion of Byzantium. He was not quite agile or disengaged enough to rectify this opinion in the 970s, when the political winds changed, or at least there is no sign that he altered his *Embassy* in

87. Scott, *Liudprand of Cremona*, xx–xxi.

light of the new friendship between Saxons and Byzantines. But the period when the Byzantine Empire had allied itself with the Fatimid rulers of Islamic North Africa while mounting a campaign against the rulers of Christian South Italy was a bewildering one.[88] Liudprand duly referred to the sins of the Christians to explain this odd, "fratricidal" turn of events, though he knew that southern Italians had engaged in a century of opportunistic ententes with Islamic powers, and understood the advantages that interfaith agreements could bring to their practitioners (like that Recemund of Elvira, to whom he dedicated his most voluminous work). Unlike the book of *Retribution*, which invoked a pan-Christian solidarity against the threats of "outside" infidels of various kinds, the *Embassy* broadened the ranks of the enemy against whom the Ottonian West should guard, inserting the Christian Byzantine Empire on the black list. Such a position might resonate in the circles in which Liudprand's Constantinopolitan friends probably moved, which might be Macedonian-legitimist and thus nostalgic for the regime of Nicephoros Phocas, but more importantly it might convince that Saxon elite, accustomed to fighting against unbelief on the eastern frontier, that the Ottonians' new Byzantine antagonists in Italy were just as worthy targets as the pagan Liutizi, described by the Saxon historian Thietmar of Merseburg in his great *Chronicon*.[89]

Texts like Liudprand's that addressed the encounter with cultural difference were something of a specialty of the long tenth century. Notker of St. Gall, who included in his *Deeds of Charlemagne* many observations about travel to Byzantium that Liudprand echoed, was a forerunner. Adalbert, a contemporary of the bishop of Cremona, wrote a biography of St. John of Gorze with extensive sections about John's tribulations as the Ottonian ambassador to the Umayyads in Cordoba. Also in the Islamic world, in the generation preceding Liudprand, the bearers of diplomatic

---

88. Indeed, Nicephoros Phocas's Fatimid alliance had other goals, namely, rendering Byzantine campaigns in Syria easier by creating trouble on the Ikshidids' western frontier in Palestine.

89. 6.22–25.

messages could turn their experiences into polished literary ethnologies. And about a generation after Liudprand's visit to Constantinople a Byzantine bishop of Synada, Leo, penned an account of his own experience of alterity in Rome, where he had been sent on the emperor's (and patriarch's) business. Neither Harun ibn-Yahya nor Leo of Synada reached Liudprand's strident pitch of indignation in their evaluations of the strangeness of a foreign place. Their descriptions are much closer to that Liudprand wrote in *Retribution* 6 a decade before 968, about his visit to the imperial city in 949, a text that can be taken as a sample of how Liudprand could polish his travel notes into "proper" history, or as a trial run for the *Embassy*.[90] But, like Liudprand, all these authors used the occasion of their travels to reflect on the value of customs with which they were familiar.[91]

But if written rather than oral reports to sovereigns of the results of a messenger's mission were increasingly common in the 900s, the form of Liudprand's *Embassy* remains unique in the early medieval Latin canon. It is unusual enough that some are convinced that the extant format represents travel notes to himself, which the author used to compose a (lost) official report upon his long-awaited re-entry into Italy.[92] This seems improbable, for, though the work is incomplete, there is no mistaking the high level of literary accomplishment in the *Embassy*. Writing the *Embassy* offered an excellent *literary* opportunity because it was an account of exile, of longing for a return home, of sufferings, almost of a Passion endured in a steadfast, morally courageous way.[93] This autho-

90. Oldoni, "Liudprando," 33.

91. Leyser, "Ends and Means," 139–40; D. Queller, *The Office of the Ambassador in the Middle Ages* (Princeton: Princeton University Press, 1967), 14, 110; A. Vasiliev, "Harun ibn-Yahya and his description of Constantinople," *Seminarium Kondakovianum* 5 (Prague, 1932): 149–63; Nelson, "Rulers and Government," 126; and R. Fletcher, ed., *Moorish Spain* (London: Weidenfeld and Nicolson, 1992), 67–68.

92. Leyser, "Ends and Means," 129. Vinay, *Alto medioevo latino*, 377, suggested instead that the *Embassy* is a "public" transcription of an original document reserved for Otto's eyes only.

93. H. Vinckier, "Liudprandi Passio," *Medieval Perspectives* 1.1 (1986): 54–64; see also Vinay, *Alto medioevo latino*, 378.

rial stance was in the best tradition of Rather of Verona, whom we have met before as one of Liudprand's literary models. Though he, too, had wandered a good deal, compelled to leave his diocese and seek Otto I's favor and protection, Liudprand's great teacher never generated such adventuresome material from which to construct himself as a virtuous hero, able to endure hardships with ascetical toughness. Yet exile and its trials were the foundation of Rather's personal narratives. Together with the Roman poets Juvenal, Martial, and that Terence who often inspired Liudprand's tone, Rather suggested to Liudprand the voyage of the exile as a form that the diplomatic report was a pretext to deploy.[94] More than an official diplomatic paper, full of the hard details of negotiation, layered with vital information on the political situation of the antagonist, and more than a pragmatic text designed to get a tardy emissary off the hook with his employer, the *Embassy* is a lovingly crafted piece of writing, an occasion to flaunt the virtuosity of the writer's Latin (and Greek), a chance to show off his deep learning in copious citations of the classics or the Bible, while also paying homage to a contemporary author he admired. It is impressive literature, a kind of signature for a bishop whose selection early in 968 for the delicate, indeed "impossible," mission of winning Byzantine favor for Otto while he campaigned in Byzantine Italy had represented a major advancement toward the inner circles of Ottonian power.[95]

94. Vinay, *Alto medioevo latino*, 378; Staubach, "Historia oder Satira?" 47–84.

95. Sutherland, *Liudprand*, 96–97; on Liudprand's Latin, see Ricci, *Problemi*, 193–96. Lintzel, *Studien*, 53, is right to stress that the *Embassy* rests on literary tropes and does not resemble formal reports.

THE COMPLETE WORKS OF
LIUDPRAND OF CREMONA

 RETRIBUTION

Book One

CHAPTER HEADINGS

IN THE NAME OF THE FATHER AND SON AND HOLY SPIRIT, HERE BE-
GINS THE ΑΝΤΑΠΟΔΟΣΕΩΣ[1] BOOK OF THE KINGS AND PRINCES OF THE
EUROPEAN AREA, COMPOSED BY LIUDPRAND, DEACON OF THE PAVIAN
CHURCH, ÈΝ ΤΉ ΕΧΜΑΛΟΣΊΑ ΑΥΤΟΎ,[2] FOR RECEMUND, BISHOP OF THE
SPANISH PROVINCE OF ELVIRA.

1. Preface.[3]
2. About the castle of Fraxinetum and its location.
3. How the Saracens first took Fraxinetum.
4. How through the Provençals' [mutual] envy the Saracens devastated
Provence, with the locals fostering it.
5. Which emperor then ruled the Greeks, which kings ruled the Bulgarians, Bavarians, Franks, Saxons, Swabians, and Italians, and what pope
reigned in Rome.

1. "Retributive" (Greek). See *Retribution* 3.1 for Liudprand's own clarification of his
title. In the interest of fidelity to Liudprand's text, the Greek in this volume retains
Liudprand's forms, including his use of diacritical marks.
2. "During his wanderings."
3. Liudprand added these chapter headings in the second redaction of the text,
between 959 and early 962.

41

29. Why there was enmity between Formosus and the Romans.

30. About Pope Sergius, who ordered Formosus to be exhumed from his tomb and to be deposed while dead.

31. About the body of Formosus, cast into the river by Sergius and found by fishers and hailed by images of the saints.

32. How Arnulf besieged a castle called Fermo and took a deadly potion from Wido's wife.

33. About the evil deeds that Arnulf's men did.

34. About Arnulf's retreat and Wido's pursuit.

35. That the Italian people did not care about Arnulf, and about Margrave Anscar, who was hiding at Ivrea.

36. About the sordid death of King Arnulf.

37. About King Wido's death and the election of his son Lambert, who was made king.

38. About the expulsion of Lambert and the recall of Berengar.

39. About Count Maginfred, who was beheaded by Lambert for rebelling.

40. About Margrave Adalbert and Count Hildeprand, who came to fight against Lambert.

41. About when King Lambert rushed on Adalbert and Hildeprand at night, and killed their soldiers and took them alive.

42. How Lambert was killed in Marengo by Hugh, son of Maginfred, as vengeance for his father's death.

43. That Berengar properly obtained the kingship after the death of Lambert.

44. A eulogy for King Lambert.

HERE BEGINS THE FIRST BOOK

1. Greetings to the reverend lord Recemund, full of every grace, bishop of the Elviran church, from Liudprand, deacon of the Pavian church, but not by his own merit.[4]

For two years, dearest father, because of the smallness of my talent, I have neglected that request by which you urged that I put

---

4. Rabi bin Zaid, known as Recemund in Latin Europe and called "bishop" as a courtesy, was a Christian cleric who served the caliphs of Cordoba and became am-

down in writing the deeds of the emperors and kings of all Europe, not as one who, reliant on hearsay, can be doubted, but as one who is reliable, like an eyewitness. The following things deflected my resolve to begin my task: the abundance of things to discuss, about which I am scarcely an expert; the envy of detractors who, swollen with snobbery, sluggish in reading, and, according to the phrase of the learned Boethius,[5] wearing a scrap of the cloak of philosophy while thinking they have on the whole garment, will address these insulting words to me: "Our predecessors wrote so much that readers are now much rarer than things to read"; then they will babble that comical saying, "There is nothing to say that was not said before."[6] I answer their howls this way: those who love knowledge are like people afflicted with dropsy who, the more they drink the more they burn with thirst; that is, the more frequently they read the more avidly they seek new things to learn. So, if they tire of the complicated readings of witty Cicero, at least they will be reanimated by such stories as the ones here; for unless I am mistaken, just as our vision, without the interposition of some substance, is blunted when struck by the sun's rays, lest it see them pure, likewise it is clear the mind is weakened by constant meditation on the doctrines of the academicians, the peripatetics, and the stoics, if it is not refreshed either by the useful laughter of comedies or the delightful history of the heroes. For the execrable rite of the ancient pagans, which is, I say, not just unhelpful but even not a little harmful to hear about, is recorded in books;[7] so why should there be silence about wars of generals as worthy of praise as those of Julius, Pompey, Hannibal and his brother Hasdrubal, and Scipio Africanus, and of famous emperors—since, especially in their case, the goodness of our Lord Jesus Christ must be evoked inasmuch as they lived virtuously and,

---

bassador to Otto I in 955, an occasion when he must have met Liudprand. Elvira was an ancient south Iberian bishopric on the site of today's Granada.

5. Boethius was a sixth-century statesman and thinker, whose *Consolation of Philosophy* 1.3 is echoed here.

6. Terence, *Eunuchus*, prologue, 41.

7. The utility of classical (hence pagan) books was a topic that preoccupied other Ottonian writers, like Hrotswita of Gandersheim.

inasmuch as they did evil, his healthful correction is to be recalled through them? Nor should it bother anyone if I insert into this booklet deeds of weak kings and effeminate princes. For the just virtue of almighty God, the Father that is, and Son and Holy Spirit, is one thing which rightly crushes such people for their crimes and which honors others for their merits. This, I say, is the true promise of our Lord Jesus Christ to the saints: "Take notice and hear my voice, and I will be an enemy to your enemies and will afflict those who afflict you. And my angel shall go before you."[8] Through Solomon, Wisdom, which is Christ, also calls out, "The whole world shall fight for him against the unwise."[9] Even someone who has been snoozing realizes what is happening every day. To demonstrate this, take one example from the countless available, and, with my voice falling silent, let the village called Fraxinetum speak, which is known to lie on the border of the Italians and the Provençals.[10]

2. As it is plainly exposed to all, one fact I reckon scarcely escapes you, indeed one you know better than I—since you can learn about it from the residents, who are tributaries of your king, that is, Abd ar-Rahman[11]—is that the village's site is shielded on one side by the sea, and is defended on the other sides by a very thick grove of thorny plants.[12] If anyone were to enter it, the arching of the prickly plants would so grab him, their very sharp rigidity would so puncture him, that he would not have the possibility of advancing or retreating, unless with great toil.

3. But by a mysterious and—since it could not be otherwise—just judgment of God, a mere twenty Saracens, having left Spain with a small ship, were transported there against their will by the

8. Ex 23.21–23.

9. Wis 5.21.

10. The doings of the Islamic brigands in southern France had been the subject of Recemund's embassy. Today's La Garde-Freinet is on the site of Fraxinetum (in Arabic Farachsa), in the tellingly named Massif des Maures, close to the modern resort of St. Tropez.

11. The Umayyad caliph Abd ar-Rahman III (912–61).

12. *Fraxinus* is the Latin name for "ash tree," and Fraxinetum means "ash wood," but the ash is not thorny.

wind.[13] These pirates, having disembarked by night and secretly entered the town, slaughtered the Christians—O horror!—and claimed the place as their own; and they prepared Moor's Mountain, right next to the village, as a refuge against neighboring peoples, making the thorny wood bigger and thicker for their protection by this agreement: that if anyone should cut even a branch from it, he would depart mankind by a sword's blow.[14] And thus it turned out that every access except one very narrow road was forfeited. Therefore, trusting in the harshness of the site for protection, they secretly began to inspect the neighboring populations all around; they sent many messengers to Spain who extolled the place and promised that they considered the neighboring populations to be nothing. In the end they only brought back with them scarcely a hundred Saracens who would accept the truth of their claims.

4. Meanwhile the Provençals, the nation that was closest to them, began to squabble among themselves through envy, to throttle one another, snatch property, and to do whatever evil they could think up. But since one faction could not quite do for itself what envy and pain demanded, it called to its aid the aforementioned Saracens, who were no less clever than perfidious, and with them crushed a faction of neighbors. Nor was it enough to murder neighbors, but truly they reduced to desolation the fruitful earth. But let us see what just envy procured for itself according to a certain author who described it, saying:

> More just than envy there is nothing, which continually
> Corrodes its author and tortures the soul.[15]

Which, while it seeks to deceive, itself is deceived; while it strives to extinguish, is itself extinguished. What happened, then? The

13. For a sense of what Islamic shipping was like in the tenth century, see J. Joncheray, "The Four Saracen Shipwrecks of Provence," in *Barbarian Seas*, ed. S. Kingsley (London: Periplus, 2004), 102–7.

14. Apparently an early example of a special interest group fostering environmental legislation.

15. *Anthologia Latina*, n. 485b. The *Anthologia Latina* is a late antique collection of verse, much of it classical, that enjoyed wide dissemination in the 9th–12th centuries.

Saracens, since they could do little with their own men, defeating one faction with the help of another, ceaselessly increasing their troops from Spain, began to hunt down by all means those they at first seemed to defend. Therefore they ravaged, they exterminated, they made it so that no one was left. Now the other neighboring nations began to tremble since, according to the prophet, "One of them pursued a thousand, and two chased ten thousand."[16] And why? "Because their God had sold them and the Lord had shut them up."[17]

5. In that same period, Leo Porphyrogenitus, son of the emperor Basil, father of that Constantine who up until now happily lives and reigns, ruled the empire of the Constantinopolitan city.[18] The strong warrior Symeon governed the Bulgarians, a Christian but deeply hostile towards his Greek neighbors.[19] The Hungarian people, whose savagery almost all nations have experienced, and who, with God showing mercy, terrified by the power of the most holy and unconquered king OTTO, now does not dare even to whisper, as we will relate at greater length, at that time was unknown to all of us. For they were separated from us by certain very troublesome barriers, which the common people call "closures,"[20] so that they did not have the possibility of leaving for either the southern or the western regions. At the same time, once Charles surnamed "the Bald" had died,[21] Arnulf, a very powerful king, ruled the Bavarians, Swabians, Teutonic Franks, Lotharingians, and brave Saxons;[22] against him Sviatopolk, duke of the Moravians, fought back in a manly way.[23] The commanders Berengar and Wido were

16. Dt 32.30.
17. Ibid.
18. Leo VI (†912) and Constantine VII (†959).
19. Simeon the Great (†927).
20. See 5.18, n. 33, below, on these Alpine fortifications.
21. In October 877.
22. Arnulf of Carinthia (†899), who skillfully exploited Carolingian weakness in East Francia after 887. See E. Goldberg, *The Struggle for Empire* (Ithaca, NY: Cornell University Press, 2006), 335–46, for some context.
23. Sviatopolk (or Svatopluk) was duke of this Slavic group in the northwestern Balkans, 870–94.

in conflict over the Italian kingdom. Formosus, the bishop of the city of Porto,[24] was the head of the Roman see and universal pope. But now we shall explain as briefly as we can what happened under each one of these rulers.

6. Leo, then, most pious emperor of the Greeks, of whom we made mention above, that is, the father of Constantine Porphyrogenitus, having obtained peace on all fronts, ruled the empire of the Greeks in a holy and just way. I call a *porphyrogenitus* one who is not born into purple cloth, but in the mansion that is called Porphyra. And since this thing has come up here, we shall record what we heard about the birth of this Porphyrogenitus.

7. The august emperor Constantine, from whose name emerged the name of the city Constantinople, ordered τὸν οἶκον τοῦτον[25] to be built, on which he imposed the name Porphyra; and he desired the lineage of his noble progeny to see the light there, in such a way that any who were born from his stock would be called by the magnificent name of Porphyrogenitus. Whence several people claim that also this Constantine, son of the emperor Leo, traces his origin from his blood. But the truth of the matter is as follows.

8. The august emperor Basil, his forefather, was born into a humble family in Macedonia and went down to Constantinople under the yoke of τῆς πτοχείας—which is poverty—so as to serve a certain abbot. Therefore, the emperor Michael who ruled at that time,[26] when he went to pray at that monastery where Basil served, saw him endowed with shapeliness that stood out from all others and quickly called τον ηγούμενον[27] so that he would give him that boy; taking him into the palace, he gave him the office of chamberlain. And then, after a little while he was given so much power that he was called "the other emperor" by everyone.

9. Truly, as almighty God visits upon his servants whatever just censure he wants, he did not allow the emperor Michael to be of sound mind to the end of his life; God acts thus so that the one

---

24. At the estuary of the Tiber, an important see within the Roman province.
25. "This very house."   26. Michael III (†867).
27. "The abbot."

he more heavily tested in this lowly world he may more mercifully recompense in the heavens. For, as is related, at the time of his fits Michael ordered even his intimates to be condemned to death; but, returning to his senses, he wanted them restored, so that unless those he had ordered killed were returned, those who had done it would be condemned with a matching sentence. Through this fear, those he ordered condemned were spared. But when he did this often and repeatedly to Basil, the latter accepted the following advice—how horrible!—from his servants: "Lest by chance the insane order of the king be carried out one day by the zeal of those who dislike you or harbor hatred, instead kill him and take the imperial scepter." This he carried out without delay, partly impelled by fear, partly deceived by lust for power. And so once he was killed, Basil was made emperor.[28]

10. Then, once a little time had passed, our Lord Jesus Christ appeared to him in a vision, holding the right hand of the lord emperor whose murderer he was, and addressing him thus: "Ἵνα τι ἐσφαξες τὸν δεσποτην σου βασιλεα?"[29] Awakened, he realized he was guilty of a great crime, and, quickly returning to his senses, he pondered what he should do about this. And then comforted by the healthful and truly acceptable promise of our Lord through the prophet, that on whatever day the sinner repents he shall be saved, with tears and moans he confessed to being a sinner, a criminal, a spiller of innocent blood. Having accepted good advice, he made friends for himself by the mammon of iniquity so that he might be freed from the eternal fire of hell by the prayers of those whom he had consoled in this world with material subsidies. He built close to the east side of the palace, with precious and marvelous workmanship, a church which they call Nean—meaning "new"—in honor of Michael, the highest archangel and prince of the heavenly militia, who is called archistrategos in Greek.

11. But now it will not disturb this booklet to insert two things, worthy of memory and laughter, which the son of this Basil, the

28. Basil I (†886), who founded the Macedonian dynasty.
29. "Why did you kill your lord the emperor?"

aforementioned august emperor Leo, did. The Constantinopolitan city, which formerly was called Byzantium and now New Rome, is located amidst very savage nations. Indeed it has to its north the Hungarians, the Pizaceni, the Khazars, the Russians, whom we call Normans by another name, and the Bulgarians, all very close by; to the east lies Baghdad; between the east and the south the inhabitants of Egypt and Babylonia; to the south there is Africa and that island called Crete, very close to and dangerous for Constantinople. Other nations that are in the same region,[30] that is, the Armenians, Persians, Chaldeans, and Avasgi, serve Constantinople. The inhabitants of this city surpass all these people in wealth as they do also in wisdom. Indeed, it is their custom to place every night at two-way, three-way, and four-way intersections throughout the city armed soldiers who guard it for the purpose of protecting the city, lest they be overcome by the neighboring nations. And it is done so that if the guards run into anyone walking anywhere after sunset, once he has been seized and immediately beaten with rods, he is kept in prison under vigilant custody, with bound feet, until he is to be presented at a public trial on the next day. And by this arrangement the city is kept unharmed not only by enemies but even by robbers. So Leo the august emperor, wanting to test the trustworthiness and tenacity of the guards, descending alone from the palace after sunset, reached the first guard outpost. When the guards saw him fleeing and retreating from them as if in fear, after seizing him they interrogated him about who he was and where he was going. He said he was one of many and sought a brothel. To him they quickly retorted: "Once you are ferociously beaten we will keep you with bound feet in custody until tomorrow." To this he answered: "Μη αδελφοὶ μη!"[31] Take what I carry, let me go where I will!" And hav-

---

30. Liudprand used the term *climata*, from the Greek for "region," here. Ancient and then medieval geographical theory usually divided the world into seven zones. See N. Lozovsky, *The Earth is Our Book* (Ann Arbor: University of Michigan Press, 2000), 10–22, for background, and J. Block Friedman, *The Monstrous Races in Medieval Art and Thought* (Cambridge, MA: Harvard University Press, 1981), chapter 3, for treatment of the influence that these zones were thought to have on their inhabitants.

31. "Wait, brothers, wait!"

ing taken twelve gold coins, they straightaway sent him away. Leaving there, he came to the second guard post, where, seized just as in the first one and having given 20 gold coins, he was let go. When he came to the third, he was seized, but he was not released, having given gold coins, as in the first and second posts; instead, with everything confiscated, with his feet tightly bound, beaten for a long time with punches and whips, he was kept in custody until the next day, to be handed over for trial. Once these soldiers had left, the emperor called the prison guard to himself, saying: "φιλε μου,[32] do you recognize the emperor Leo?" "How can I recognize him," he answered, "when I cannot remember seeing him? On the rare occasion when I looked on from afar (since I was unable to get close) while he processed through the public, he seemed to me something marvelous and not a man. It would be better for you to pay attention to how you will get out of here unharmed than to ask such a thing. Fortune does not sustain the two of you equally, σε εις την φυλακην και αυτον εις τὸ χρυσοτρικλινον.[33] These ones are too small; heavier chains shall now be added to ensure that you do not lack an interlude in which to think about the emperor!" At that, "Wait!" he said, "wait! For I myself am the august emperor Leo who strode out from the honor of the palace under a bad star." The prison guard, however, hoping that what he said was not true, spoke: "Am I," he said, "to believe the emperor is a dirty man who squanders his wealth on prostitutes? Since you neglected it yourself, for your own good I will open your eyes on astrology . . .[34] Mars is now in triangle, Saturn faces Venus, Jupiter is squared, Mercury is angry with you, the sun is round, the moon is in a leap year, so bad luck closes in on you." But the emperor said: "So that you may prove what I say is true, when they will have given the morning signal (for we do not dare to try it earlier), come with me to the palace when I go down there under a better star. Kill me if you do not see me received there as the emperor: it will have been no less a crime for me

32. "My dear."
33. "You are in prison and he is on the golden throne."
34. There is a gap in the text here.

to have claimed to be the emperor, if I am not he, than to kill someone. If, however, you fear that you may suffer some harm on account of this, may God repay it to me and add to it, if you do not
receive a reward rather than a punishment for this." Thus, the prison
guard having turned credulous, once the morning signal had been
given, as the emperor said, he accompanied him up to the palace.
And when the emperor came there, marvelously received as if by
people who knew him, his companion was stunned with great wonder. Reasonably enough, as the guard contemplated all the officials
rushing to him, offering up praises, adoring him, removing his san-
dals, and doing ever more things for him, he thought of death there
and then, and that he had lived enough. The emperor said to him:
"Now think about your astrology, and if you shall accurately state
under what star you came here, you shall prove that you have knowledge of augury. But beforehand, I ask that you state what the disease may be that turned you so pale." To this the guard answered:
"The highest of the goddesses of fate, CLOTHO, now ceases her
spinning; truly, her companion LACHESIS wants not to work any
longer at winding [threads]; ATROPOS, the most fierce of them all,
awaits only your imperial sentence so that she may snap the cords
of my life, yanking my joints into pain. The cause of the pallor of
my face is that my spirit sank from my head and led the blood along
with it into the lower part of my body."[35] Then, chuckling, the emperor said: "Recover your spirit, recover it, and with it take four
pounds of gold coins; and answer no one's questions about me, except to say that I ran away." Once these things had been done thus,
the emperor ordered that the guards who let him off once he was
arrested, and who freed him from custody after he had been beaten,
come to him; and he said to them: "Did you catch any thieves and
adulterers while you were on duty and overseeing the safety of the
city?" Those who had let him go after taking a bribe answered that
they had seen nothing, while those who had taken him into custody

35. The personification of fate as three daughters of Zeus and Themis was elabo-
rated early in Greek theology: already Hesiod (*Theogony* 904–6) knew Clotho, Lachesis, and Atropos. In this episode Liudprand displayed his classical erudition through
the unlikely spokesman, the dutiful guard.

after he had been beaten answered this way: "Δεσποτία σοῦ η αγια[36] ordered that if guards were to seize anyone walking about after sunset, having seized him and beaten him with rods, they should hand him over into custody. As we followed your orders, most holy master, last night we seized some fellow heading for the brothels, beat him, and, having put him in prison, we detained him to be turned over to your holy rule." The emperor said to them: "The might of my rule right now commands that he be quickly brought forth here." Without delay they ran back to lead the chained man forth; when they heard he had escaped they returned to the palace half-dead [from fear]. When they announced the escape to the emperor, all of a sudden the emperor, having disrobed himself to show his body, heavily beaten by them, said: "Δεῦτε, μη διλησεται![37] I myself am the one whom you whipped and whom you now believe to have escaped from prison. For I know and truly believe that you thought you were beating not the emperor, but the emperor's enemy. My authority not only desires but even orders that those who let me off not as an emperor, but as a common thief and a threat to my life, be deprived of all their property and, beaten and half-dead, be expelled from the city. To you on the other hand I grant not just my riches, but also all those of that perverse crew." And how judiciously he managed that situation your paternity will be able to understand from this fact:[38] that from then on the other guards watched over the city most diligently, tending to things as if he were present even with him absent. And in this way it turned out that the emperor never again went out of the palace by night, and the guards faithfully guarded his realm.

12. I judge it absurd to cover in silence the other prank that he performed.[39] For the sake of the emperor's welfare the Constantinopolitan palace is guarded by outposts of many soldiers; quite

36. "Your holy majesty."
37. "Come, fear not!"
38. Recemund is called "father" because of his quasi-episcopal status.
39. Displays of cleverness, often involving trickery, were valued by tenth-century élites: see H. Fichtenau, *Living in the Tenth Century* (Chicago: University of Chicago Press, 1991), 404–9. They are a prominent feature of Liudprand's historical style.

a lot of rations and daily pay are issued to the guards. After their repast, during the hot period of that day, it was the turn of 12 of these guards to rest together in a house. It was the custom of the emperor to sneak through the whole palace when all were resting. On a certain day, when he came to the place where the aforesaid 12 had given themselves over to heavy sleep, having thrown off the door latch with a small bit of wood, like someone quite skilled at it, he provided himself access for entry. While eleven really slept, as guile tricked guile, the twelfth was awake and, having crossed his arms over his face, he began to snore as if he were asleep, and most carefully considered everything the emperor did. Thus, once the emperor had entered, when he determined all were sleeping, he placed a pound of gold coins on the chest of each of them; and quickly he retreated in silence and shut the door as it had been before. For he did this so that, perplexed, they might also celebrate over this windfall, and might marvel in no small way about how this happened. But then, once the emperor left, the only one who had lain awake rose and took for himself the gold coins from the sleepers, and went back to bed; after that he made himself sleep. Therefore the emperor, curious about his prank, ordered those twelve whom we mentioned to come to him after the ninth hour,[40] and addressed them in this way: "If by chance any vision frightened or brought delight to the sleep of any of you, my authority orders that he state it here; and no less my authority orders that anyone who, upon awakening, saw something novel, must inform me of it." The men, since they saw nothing, answered that they had seen nothing; and, greatly marveling over the episode, "in silence they held their mouths still."[41] The emperor, therefore, imagining that they were quiet not because the thing was unknown, but out of some craftiness, grew very angry and began to threaten the reticent guards with several awful things. When the one who was aware of every-

---

40. Since ancient times, the hours of the day were twelve, equal in length, and calculated to fit between sunrise and sundown. The ninth hour came in late afternoon, three hours before sunset.

41. Virgil, *Aeneid* 2.1.

thing heard this, he addressed the emperor with a most humble and pleading voice as follows: "φιλανθρωπε βασιλευ,[42] I do not know what these men saw; I saw a delightful dream, and would that it return to me often. While eleven of my companions present here were really, but unluckily for them, sleeping today, I saw that I was awake, not asleep. Suddenly there appeared your imperial majesty, shutting the door almost stealthily, having entered secretly, and it placed a pound of gold on each of our breasts. And when your emperorship seemed to walk away again and in my vision I saw my companions sleeping, I, rising swift and gleeful, took the pounds of gold coins of the eleven sleepers and put them in my pouch, where there already was one pound, for, in order not to exceed the Ten Commandments, they should not be 11, and indeed on account of the memory of the apostles, they were added to mine and became 12. This vision, O august emperor—and may good things befall you—did not at all terrify me but made me happy. O let no other dream-interpretation please your emperorship! For it is clear that I am μαντην και ονιροπολον."[43] Once he heard these words, the emperor swelled with great laughter, and, truly admiring the prudence and cleverness of this man, he promptly said: "Before now I heard that σε ουτε μαντην ουτε ονιροπολον;[44] now, however, you have declared this so openly that you make no use of circumlocution. But since you could not have the capacity of lying awake or the knowledge of prophecy unless a divine gift had been given to you, whether it is true (as we hope, indeed believe) or false—καθως ο Λουκιανος[45] it tells of a certain fellow who discovered many things while he was sleeping and found nothing when he was awakened by the cock's crow—either way, let whatever you saw, felt, and even found be yours." After hearing these words, by assuming their different points of view anyone can imagine how full of consternation the others were, and how full of joy this man was.

---

42. "Kindly emperor."
43. "A prophet and dream-interpreter."
44. "You were neither a prophet nor a dream-interpreter."
45. "In Lucian." Lucian was a poet and philosopher of the second century A.D.

13. Meanwhile Arnulf, the strongest king of the nations living below the star Arcturus,[46] could not overcome Sviatopolk, duke of the Moravians, whom we mentioned above,[47] with the latter fighting back in a manly way; and—alas!—having dismantled those very well fortified barriers which we said earlier are called "closures" by the populace, Arnulf summoned to his aid the nation of the Hungarians, greedy, rash, ignorant of almighty God but well versed in every crime, avid only for murder and plunder; if indeed it can be called "aid," since a little later, with him dying, it proved to be grave peril, and even the occasion of ruin, for his people alongside the other nations living in the south and west.[48] What happened? Sviatopolk was conquered, subjugated, made tributary; but that was not all. O blind lust of King Arnulf for power! O unhappy and bitter day! The fall of one small man became the castigation of all Europe! How much widowhood for women, childlessness for fathers, corruption of virgins, enslavement of priest and peoples of God, how much devastation of churches, desolation of rural districts does blind ambition bring! Read, I beg it, these words of truth himself, who says, "For what does it profit a man, if he gain the whole world and suffer the loss of his own soul? Or what exchange shall a man give for his own soul?"[49] Arnulf, if the severity of this true Judge did not terrify you, at least the thought of the community of all mankind should have tempered your rage; for you were a man among men, however exalted in rank, still not dissimilar in nature. A weak and poor condition, the human one: the species of animals, snakes, or birds, which intolerable ferocity or deadly poison renders separate from mankind (since there are basilisks, vipers, or rhinos and griffins, which even in their very appearance seem dangerous to all), nevertheless carry on placidly and harmlessly among themselves on account of their common origin

46. A star in the Boötes constellation, which circles the "Bears" (Big and Little Dipper) around the North Pole. Liudprand means, "people of the northern areas."
47. See 1.5, above.
48. The alliance between the east Frankish king and Hungarians took place in 892.
49. Mt 16.26.

and affinity. On the other hand man, formed in the image and likeness of God, aware of the law of God, capable of reason, not only tries not to love his neighbor, but also strives mightily to hate him. Let us see then what John said about such matters, and not any old John, but the famous virgin, aware of the heavenly secrets, to whom, as a virgin, Christ from the cross commended his virgin mother: "Whoever hates his brother is a murderer; and you know that no murderer has eternal life abiding in himself."[50] But let us get back to the issue. After having conquered Sviatopolk, duke of the Moravians, once he obtained peace, Arnulf oversaw his realm; meanwhile the Hungarians, having observed the outcome and contemplated the region, spun evil schemes in their hearts, as became apparent when events unfolded.

14. While these things were happening, the king of Gaul, Charles, surnamed "the Bald," exchanged this life for the next by dying.[51] While he was alive, two overmighty noble princes from Italy served him, of whom one was called Wido, the other Berengar. These two became so close by alliance of friendship that they promised each other the following, by swearing oaths: if they were to outlive King Charles, the one would support the other's coronation, namely, so that Wido would receive what they call Roman France, and Berengar Italy.[52]

But as there are several kinds of uncertain and unstable friendships which in different ways connect the human species by the sociability of love—for in some cases a preceding recommendation later causes friendship, and in other cases it is a similarity of business interests, or military service, or art or studies—so still, just as such friendships arise from different relationships, whether

50. 1 Jn 3.15.
51. The emperor Charles the Bald died in 877. Liudprand presumably meant Charles the Fat (†888), the last Carolingian to rule Italy (879–87) and to have a chance of ruling the entire Carolingian world.
52. Wido II (†894), the Widonid from Tuscany, and Berengar I (†924), the Unruoching from Friuli, were the leaders of two of the most powerful clans of Frankish origin that the Carolingians had established in Italy after 774.

for profit or pleasure or necessity, they are dissolved by the agency of any reason for separation; such is the model of friendship, such, I say, because it has in many cases and very often been proved that by no means can those who enter an alliance of friendships under the principle of conspiracy preserve concord unbroken. Clearly that most crafty enemy of the human race works to shatter friendship so that he may turn men into oath-breakers more quickly and shrewdly. For if we were asked about real friendship by those who know less, we would answer that concord and true friendship cannot exist except between men of purified morals and sharing equal virtue and objectives.[53]

15. It happened therefore that both of them, that is, Wido and Berengar, missed Charles's funeral. As soon as Wido heard of his death, however, he set out for Rome and received the anointing for the entire Frankish empire without the advice of the Franks. But the Franks appointed Odo king since Wido was absent. Berengar, following Wido's advice as he had promised, swearing an oath, took over rulership in the Italian kingdom, and Wido quickly set out for France.

16. And as he wanted to enter that part of France they call Roman, crossing the kingdom of the Burgundians, there met him messengers of the Franks telling him to go back because, worn out by the long wait, as they could not be without a king for a long time, they had elected Odo with all assenting. It is said, however, that the Franks actually did not take Wido as their king on account of this. For when he was coming to the city of Metz, which shines most powerful in the kingdom of Lothar, Wido sent ahead his servant who was to prepare food for him in the royal style. And the bishop of Metz received an answer like this from the servant, when he served him much food according to the custom of the Franks:

53. "Friendship" was a special kind of social bond among aristocrats, essential to the political dealings of tenth-century élites: see G. Althof, *Family, Friends, and Followers* (Cambridge: Cambridge University Press, 2004), 67–90. Here Liudprand attacks the basis of aristocratic politics, and perhaps indirectly endorses Otto I's more autocratic style of rule: see P. Buc, *The Dangers of Ritual* (Princeton: Princeton University Press, 2001), 25–27.

"If you give me at least a horse, I will arrange things in such a way that King Wido will be satisfied with a third of all this after he has feasted." When the bishop heard this, "it is not proper," he said, "for such a king to rule over us, who prepares himself a cheap ten-coin meal." And so it happened that they abandoned Wido and instead elected Odo.[54]

17. Wido, not a little disturbed by the messages of the Franks, began to waver between many thoughts, both about the Italian kingdom, which he had promised to Berengar by swearing an oath, and about that of the Franks, which he now realized he could not obtain. Caught between both possibilities, since he could not become king of the Franks, he decided to break the oath he made to Berengar; and having gathered an army as best he could—he obviously drew on some line of affinity among the Franks—and having hastily entered Italy, he approached the inhabitants of Camerino and Spoleto with confidence, as relatives of his;[55] with the help of money he won over even the supporters of Berengar, as they were disloyal. And thus he prepared war against Berengar.

18. At last, once troops had been gathered on both sides, they prepared civil war near the river Trebbia, which flows five miles from Piacenza. In the battle, though many fell on both sides, Berengar took flight, and Wido obtained victory.

19. Without delay, with just a few days intervening, having gathered a horde, Berengar prepared war against Wido at Brescia's wide fields. There, after an enormous slaughter, Berengar broke free by escaping.

20. Now in truth Berengar, unable to resist Wido because of the small size of his army, called to his aid that most powerful King Arnulf whom we mentioned before,[56] promising that he and his descendants would serve his power if with the assistance of his

54. Count Odo of Paris had the strong aristocratic connections in West Francia that Wido lacked. Reluctantly, Charles the Fat had acknowledged his sovereignty in 887, in preference to his own (illegitimate) son, still too young. Wido also managed consecration (at Langres), but without local support had to retreat.

55. The Widonids' power base was in this part of central Italy.

56. 1.5, 1.13, above.

strength he would overcome Wido and restore him to the Italian kingdom. King Arnulf, obviously impressed by the generosity of such a promise, sent his son Zwentibald, whom he had generated with a concubine, along with a strong army, to Berengar's aid, and they arrived in all haste at Pavia.[57] Wido had so fortified the stream called Vernavola that soaks Pavia on one side, as much with palisades as with an army, that neither side could fight the other, given the stream flowing between them.

21. Already twenty-one days had passed while, as we said, neither side could harm the other, and every day one Bavarian, reproaching the lines of the Italians, shouted that they were weaklings and poor riders. To the increase of this insult he jumped amidst them and knocked the spear from one man's hand and thus returned elated to his side's fortification. Therefore Hubald, the father of that Boniface who later, in our times, was margrave of the Camerinans and Spoletans, desiring to avenge so great an insult against his people, having taken up his shield, soon went out to meet the aforementioned Bavarian. Not only remembering his earlier triumph but also emboldened by it, certain of victory, that fellow advanced elated against him; and he began at times to spur on his agile horse with vigorous charges, and at other times to pull him back with tightened reins. The aforementioned Hubald began to advance straight on. When they reached the point that they struck each other with blows, in his usual way the Bavarian began to gallop in swirls with the horse taking various complicated turns, so that with these maneuvers he could trick Hubald. Instead, when, according to these tactics, he turned his back so that, suddenly turning around, he could strike Hubald from behind, the horse upon which Hubald rode was vigorously urged on with spurs, and the Bavarian was pierced between his shoulders through to his heart with a spear before he could wheel around. Then Hubald, taking the horse of the Bavarian by the bridle, abandoned the stripped corpse in the middle of the stream's bed, and thus he returned all the happier to his men,

57. After ruling Lotharingia for five years, Zwentibald died in 900.

triumphant, the avenger of their insult. Once this had been done, no small fear gripped the Bavarians, and no small boldness the Italians. Hence, having taken counsel with the Bavarians, and having received several loads of silver from Wido, Zwentibald went back to his own country.

22. Therefore, when he saw that favorable prospects had become unfavorable, along with Zwentibald Berengar turned to the might of King Arnulf, pleading and promising that if he helped him he would place himself and all of Italy under his authority, as he had promised earlier. Aroused by the allure of so great a promise, as we said before, and, having collected no mean army, Arnulf went to Italy. And there Berengar carried Arnulf's shield so as to give the faith of his promise a guarantee of plausibility.

23. Welcomed by the Veronese, Arnulf set out for Bergamo. There, as the locals, trusting in the most solid impregnability of the site, indeed deceived by it, did not want to rush to his feet, he took the city by storm after having camped there, and killed and butchered; even the count of the city, named Ambrose, he had hanged before the door of the city gateway with his sword, belt, bracelets, and other very costly clothes on. Once he had done this, no small terror gripped the princes of all the other cities; whoever heard of it felt both his ears prick up.

24. Both the Milanese and the Pavians, terrified by this reputation, could not bear to wait for his arrival; instead, having sent an embassy ahead, they promised they would obey his commands. Arnulf therefore sent Otto, most mighty duke of the Saxons[58]—forefather of the most glorious and unconquered King Otto who now lives and happily reigns—for the purpose of defending Milan: he himself headed straight for Pavia.

25. Finally Wido, unable to withstand this thrust, began to flee toward Camerino and Spoleto. Without delay the king chased him eagerly, conquering by force cities and castles and all that resisted him. There was no castle, even one fortified by nature itself, pre-

---

58. Otto the Great's grandfather, who died in 912.

pared to resist his strength for long.[59] And this is no surprise, as the very queen of all cities, that is, great Rome, could not sustain his thrust.[60] Indeed, when permission for him to enter the city was denied by the Romans, having called his soldiers to himself, he spoke thus:

26.

"Great-souled warriors and bright, by the aid of Mars,
Through whose zeal weapons glint with gilded metal
While the Rome-dwellers are used only to constructing empty texts;
Gather up your courage, let rage provide weapons for you,
Pompey is not here, nor that blessed Julius
Who tamed our fierce ancestors by the sword.
For the best in nature that fellow led off to the Greeks
Whom the holy British mother first showed the light.[61]
For the current residents the main occupation is handling a curved
        fishing rod
Not handling shining shields."[62]

27. When he had uttered these verses, their spirits uplifted, the heroes disdained all life in their lust for praise. At last they hastened to attack the walls in bands, covered with shields and cane pallets; they also prepared many war machines, and while they were doing this a small hare, alarmed by the crowd and terrified by its clamoring, began to flee toward the city.[63] When the army, as is usual [on such occasions], chased it with brisk bounds, the Romans threw themselves from the wall, thinking the army was attacking them. Seeing this, having dumped against the wall their baggage and the saddles on which they sat on horseback, the people scaled the wall

59. The ease with which Berengar is represented as capturing castles, aristocrats' warehouses, and means of territorial control, is meant to impress readers.

60. In 896.

61. Constantine the Great's departure for Constantinople in the early 300s was associated with an exodus of Roman aristocrats. Constantine was born in Britannia to Helena, later canonized.

62. This composition echoes Virgil, Martial, Persius, and Juvenal.

63. Since Herodotus (*Histories* 4.134) the fleeing hare that became militarily significant was a *topos* in accounts of battles.

on this pile. In fact, a certain portion of the people, having taken up a tree trunk close to fifty feet long, shattered the gate; and they took by force that Rome which they call Leonine,[64] in which lies the blessed body of Peter, prince of the apostles. The other Romans, who were across the Tiber, driven by fear of this, bowed their necks to Arnulf's domination.

28. At that time the most observant Pope Formosus was being vigorously tormented by the Romans, and upon his insistence King Arnulf came to Rome. At his entrance he ordered many Roman nobles who were hastening to confront him to be beheaded to avenge the harm done to the pope.

29. The cause of the animosity between Pope Formosus and the Romans was this.[65] When Formosus's predecessor died, it was a certain Deacon Sergius of the Roman church whom a certain part of the Romans had elected as its pope; another part, and not a tiny one, wanted a bishop of the city of Porto called Formosus, to be made pope for his true faith and knowledge of heavenly doctrines. And when the time came for Sergius to be ordained vicar of the apostles, that part which supported the faction of Formosus drove Sergius from the altar, with a tumult and great insult, and made Formosus pope.

30. And Sergius went down into Tuscany since the aid of the most powerful margrave Adalbert would help him; and so it was done. For once Formosus had died and Arnulf had vanished back into his own country, the one who was made pope after Formosus's death was expelled and Sergius was appointed pope by Adalbert.[66]

64. Walls were built around the Petrine basilica and nearby structures by Pope Leo IV, in the mid-ninth century, after an Arab raid had revealed the inadequacy of the late antique circuit.

65. The pontificate (891–96) of Formosus was exceptionally divisive for Roman aristocratic politics. Beyond foreign policy (pro-Byzantine or pro-western stances), the legitimacy and consequences of bishops' changing sees was at issue. See B. Schimmelpfennig, *The Papacy* (New York: Columbia University Press, 1992), chapter 4.

66. Stephen VI was actually the successor of Formosus who presided over the famous "Cadaver Council" of mid-897. Boniface VI, elected in the same month of Formosus's death, died within fifteen days (April–May 896). See J. Sutherland, *Liutprand of Cremona* (Spoleto: CISAM, 1988), 38–40.

Once appointed, as if impious and ignorant of holy doctrines, Sergius ordered Formosus to be extracted from his tomb and placed on the seat of the Roman pontiffs, dressed in his priestly attire. To him he said: "When you were bishop of Porto, why did you usurp the universal Roman see in a spirit of ambition?"[67] Once these things were done, he ordered the corpse, stripped of its holy vestments and with three fingers cut off, to be tossed into the Tiber, and, after degrading them to their former stations, he again ordained all those whom Formosus had ordained. And how badly he acted in this, most holy father Recemund, you may realize in this detail: since even those who before the betrayal received greeting or apostolic blessing from Judas, the betrayer of our Lord Jesus Christ, were not at all deprived of these after the betrayal and suicide by hanging, except those whom wicked crimes perhaps had defiled. Indeed, blessings which are imparted by Christ's ministers are infused not by the priest who is visible, but by the unseen one. "Therefore neither he that waters is anything, nor he that plants, but God that gives the increase."[68]

31. Of what great authority and observance Pope Formosus was we may deduce from this: that when his body was later found by fishers and taken to the church of blessed Peter, prince of the apostles, certain images of saints greeted him reverently when he was placed in the tomb. For this fact I heard repeated very often by very observant men of the city of Rome. But now, forgetting these things, let us return to the order of the narrative.

32. King Arnulf, having become master of what he desired, did not desist from chasing Wido, and, having set out for Camerino, he besieged the castle called Fermo, and firm by nature, where Wido's wife was; Wido meanwhile lurked in uncertain places. Thus this aforementioned castle called Fermo, and firm by its nature, was circled with a ditch, and every war machine by which it could be seized was prepared. And when Wido's wife was being pressed on

---

67. Previously no bishop had become pope; canon law forbade episcopal translations (changes of see), as Liudprand knew (see 2.48, below).

68. 1 Cor 3.7.

all sides by great hardships, and any hope of escape was completely denied her, with her viper-like cunning she began to investigate ways to cause the death of King Arnulf.

And having called to her side someone most intimate with King Arnulf, with great gifts she asked that he help her. When he asserted that he could not do anything, unless she hand over the city into his lord's power, nevertheless that woman, not only promising but actually doling out a measure of gold then and there, prayed again and again that his lord the king should drink of a certain cup from her, once the fellow had delivered it, since it posed no danger of death but only placated the ferocity of the mind. And one of her servants, so as to prove the trustworthiness of her words, drank of it in his presence, stood in his sight, healthy, for an hour, and left. In truth let us proffer that true sentence of Virgil's here: "Holy hunger for gold, to what ends do you not drive men's hearts?"[69] Having taken the lethal cup he hastened back to the king. Once Arnulf had drunk it, such an overwhelming drowsiness suddenly filled him that for three days the clamor of the whole army could not awaken him. It is said that when his retinue disturbed his slumber first by making noise, then by touching him, even with his eyes open he could feel and utter nothing properly; for, having lost his wits, he seemed to low, not to articulate words. In fact this turn of events compelled all to retreat, not to fight.[70]

33. I believe that King Arnulf incurred this malady by the just censure of the severe Judge. When propitious things everywhere were forming the empire of this great man, he attributed everything to his own strength and did not pay the honor due to almighty God. The conquered people's priests of God were being dragged off, holy virgins were being oppressed by force, married women were being raped, and not even churches could serve as refuges for those who fled. For within them people used to hold dinners, make lewd gestures, sing bawdy songs, have parties; and—most hideous!—women actually prostituted themselves there.

69. *Aeneid* 3.56–57.
70. After his coronation as king of Italy Arnulf fell ill and retreated to Bavaria.

34. At length, as King Arnulf retreated very laboriously, King Wido slowly came after him. And when Arnulf was descending Mount Bardone,[71] he determined with the counsel of his men that he should blind Berengar and thus securely take over Italy. But one brother-in-law of Berengar, who enjoyed no small intimacy with King Arnulf, as he came to know of this plan promptly revealed it to Berengar. As soon as Berengar understood the plan, having given the lamp he held before the presence of King Arnulf to someone else, he fled and came swiftly to Verona.

35. From then on all the Italians disdained Arnulf as worth nothing. Whence, when he came to Pavia, no small uproar broke out in the city, and so great a massacre of his army ensued, that the underground passages of the city, also called "sewers" by another name, were choked with their bodies. When Arnulf saw this, since he could not pass through Verona, he retreated by Hannibal's route, which they call Bardone and Mount Jupiter.[72] When he reached Ivrea, Margrave Anscar was there, by whose incitement the city was rebelling. Truly Arnulf promised by swearing an oath he would never leave that place until they delivered Anscar to his presence. But that man, as he was very timid, most similar to the one about whom Virgil says, "lavish in wealth, and valiant of tongue, though his hand was cold for battle," left the castle and hid in the stone caves near the wall of the city. He did this, however, because that way the inhabitants could legitimately claim to King Arnulf that Anscar was not in town. Thus the king accepted their oath and left on the trip he had undertaken.

36. And having reached his country Arnulf died of a horrible disease; he gave up the ghost, ardently tormented by those tiny worms they call lice. Indeed it is said that these worms proliferated in such a way that they could be diminished by no therapy of the doctors. Whether, according to the prophet, he should be stricken

71. Presumably the Apennine peak near Parma, on a route linking Ligurian sea and Po basin. Though this would represent a roundabout route from Fermo to Pavia, Wido is said in 1.37 to have died on the nearby river Taro.

72. The Great St. Bernard.

with a double punishment for such an enormous crime, that is, the unleashing of the Hungarians, or whether he attained a future forgiveness through torments in the present world, we leave it to the knowledge of the One about whom the apostle says, "Therefore, judge not before the time, until the Lord come, who both will bring light to the hidden things of darkness and will make manifest the counsels of the hearts: and then every man shall have praise from God."[73]

37. Righteous God prepared the anguish of widowhood for the wife of Wido, who had arranged for Arnulf's death. For, as we said before, while King Wido followed the retreating Arnulf from behind, the former died near the river Taro.[74] When Berengar heard of his death, he quickly came to Pavia and powerfully took over the kingship. The vassals and supporters of Wido, lest Berengar should take revenge for the injustice brought on by them, and since the Italians always want to have use of a pair of kings since they can manipulate the one through his fear of the other, appointed as king the son of the dead king Wido, named Lambert, an elegant youth, and, though still an adolescent, quite warlike.[75] So the people began to come to him and to abandon Berengar. And as Berengar, on account of the scarcity of troops, could not block Lambert, who was advancing on Pavia with a large army, he sought out Verona, and there, secure, he passed the time. But after not much time King Lambert came to be seen as burdensome by the nobles, since he was a strict man; so they sent messengers to Verona and asked that King Berengar come to them, to expel Lambert.[76]

38. In addition, the very wealthy count of the city of Milan, Maginfred, rose up, a rebel against Lambert for five years, and he not only defended the city where he had rebelled, that is, Milan,

73. 1 Cor 4.5. In this chapter Arnulf is equated with king Antiochus (Acts 12.23; 2 Mc 9.9), and his death is the right one for whoever brought hardship onto the faithful.

74. A tributary of the Po flowing northwest of Parma. Wido died in 894.

75. Lambert of Spoleto (†898). Lambert had been co-ruler with his father since 892.

76. Lambert's strongest north Italian support lay in Emilia. The Adda River separated what were in effect two kingdoms of Italy.

but also greatly depopulated neighboring places thereabouts that served Lambert. The king could not stand to let the deed go unavenged, often pondering the psalmist's verse: "When I shall take a time, I shall judge justices";[77] and after a little while he ordered the rebel condemned with a death sentence. This act brought no small fear to all the Italians.

39. And finally, at the same time Adalbert, the noble margrave of the Tuscans,[78] and Hildeprand, most powerful count, tried to rebel against him. Indeed, so great was the power of Adalbert that he alone among all the magnates of Italy was surnamed "the Rich." It was by the inspiration of his wife, called Bertha, later in our own time mother of King Hugh, that he began such nefarious schemes. For, having gathered an army, he hastened resolutely with Count Hildeprand to reach Pavia.

40. Meanwhile in Marengo, about forty miles from Pavia, oblivious of these things, King Lambert was occupied with hunts. And when the previously mentioned margrave and count crossed Mount Bardone with their immense but weak army of Tuscans, the state of affairs was announced as it stood to King Lambert, hunting in the middle of a swamp. Actually he, as he was steadfast in spirit and mighty in strength, would not bear to have his soldiers prepared, but having gathered those hundred soldiers whom he had with him, he hastened to confront them at a gallop.

41. As soon as he reached Piacenza, it was announced that they were encamped near the river Stirione, close to the suburb in which the most holy and precious body of the martyr Domninus is venerated. Ignoring what the impending night had in store for them, stinking of drink after many frivolous songs, the rebels abandoned themselves to sleep, to snoring; and to some their intemperance in consumption brought nausea.

Therefore, the king, as fierce in spirit as he was crafty in mind, attacked them in the dead of that same night, and killed the sleep-

---

77. Ps 74.3. Liudprand's citations from the Psalms are designated by means of the Vulgate numbering.

78. Margrave Adalbert II of Tuscany (†915).

ers, and slaughtered the yawners. At length he came to those two who were the leaders of that army. And as it was the king himself who broke the news of the glorious raid to them, and not someone from their horde, terror itself stole their ability not just to fight but even, I say, to flee. In truth, Hildeprand, having escaped by flight, abandoned Adalbert hiding in the stable among the beasts. When he was discovered and led into the presence of the king, the latter spoke to him thus: "We believe your wife Bertha to have prophesied with sibylline spirit when, through her insight, she promised you would become either a king or a donkey. Truly, since she did not want to make you a king or, more likely, could not make you one, lest she be caught lying, she turned you into a donkey, since she drove you into the stable with the Arcadian farm animals." Beyond this they captured several men along with this one, and overcame them, and led them into Pavia, and kept them in prison.

42. Once these things had been done in this way, King Lambert was occupied again with hunting in the same place, Marengo, until what should be done with the prisoners could be determined by the decision of all the princes. But would that this hunt had targeted wild animals and not kings! For they relate that while this Lambert was chasing boars, mounted with loosened reins, as the custom is, he fell and broke his neck. Actually, I would say it is absurd to lend credence to this claim. For there is another account of the death of that man which seems to me more likely, and is told by all sorts of people.[79]

Maginfred, count of the Milanese city, of whom we made mention just above, when he was condemned to death for crimes against the state and king, left his only son Hugh as heir to his possessions. When King Lambert saw that along with having a remarkable physique he surpassed many in bravery, he tried to alleviate the boy's great pain from the death of his father by conferring upon him as many favors as possible; whence he gave him the privilege of intimacy beyond that accorded to all others. So it happened that while

79. Liudprand omitted this sentence and the rest of chapter 43 when he wrote his first draft, probably in 958–59.

King Lambert hunted in the place called Marengo—for there lies a glen of wondrous extent and pleasantness and in addition suited to hunting—with all of them rushing here and there, as the custom is, the king stayed behind in the glen with one man, namely, Hugh. And as the king awaited the passage of a boar and, staying in one place for a long time, wearied of the long wait, he granted himself a little rest, committing to that untrustworthy companion the watch over his respite, as if he were trustworthy.

Thus, with everyone gone, the mind of the guard Hugh, betrayer and murderer, forgetful of the many favors conferred upon him, began to mull over within himself the death of his father. He did not consider that his parent had incurred a just death; he did not fear to violate the oath he took to the king; he did not blush to be called vicar of Judas, betrayer of our Lord Jesus Christ; and, what is more serious, he did not fear he would undergo an eternal punishment; rather, he broke the sleeping man's neck with a good-sized stick using all his might. Indeed, he hesitated to strike with the sword lest the thing prove clearly he was the author of the sin. The perverted mind arranged the whole thing so that it could give an attestation to those who found the corpse that Lambert had fallen from his horse and departed humanity by breaking his neck, not by the wound of a sword, but by the manifest collision with wood; and the truth of this matter lay hidden for a great many years.

But when in the course of time King Berengar obtained the kingdom in a manly way, with none resisting him, the treacherous Hugh himself made the crime emerge as his own, as he was its author, and it was fulfilled as the king and prophet says, since "the sinner is praised in the desires of his soul, and the unjust man is blessed."[80] But he could hardly have done otherwise, on account of those words of truth, who says, "For nothing is covered that shall not be revealed, nor hidden that shall not be known."[81]

43. Once these things had happened in this way, King Berengar was honored with an amplified form of his original royal dignity; Margrave Adalbert and the others headed home.

80. Ps 10.3.
81. Mt 10.26.

44. It is right, dearest father Recemund, to write crying and to cry writing about the death of so great a king. For in him resided the probity of honest morals, holy and awe-inspiring severity, and a man whom youth adorned with a magnificent body, a holy old-timers' wisdom also beautified; clearly he brought more honor to the state than the state brought to him. If sudden death had not taken him, he would have been the one who, in the era after the power of the Romans, would have subjugated to himself the whole world in a manly way.

HERE ENDS THE FIRST BOOK

Book Two

HERE BEGIN THE CHAPTER HEADINGS
OF THE SECOND BOOK

12. About the skirmishes of the battle, in which the Hungarians won and afterwards fled.

13. About the fact that the pagans awaited the Christians across the river Brenta, on account of the exhaustion of their horses, and asked them for peace, which the Christians did not grant.

14. What decision the Hungarians reached on account of their desperation, and what they said.

15. How the Hungarians, having laid ambushes, rushed on the Christians and won.

16. How they enjoyed victory not on account of their strength, but on account of the sin of the Christians.

17. How at that time Louis, king of the Franks, died and Conrad was ordained in his place.

18. Who the princes were under him, among whom there was also Henry, duke of the Saxons.

19. About the fact that Henry and other princes rebelled against King Conrad and were defeated by him, and why Arnulf fled into Hungary.

20. King Conrad, dying, exhorts all the princes to peace and to elect Henry king; to whom he also sends the royal symbols.

21. With King Conrad dead, Arnulf returns from Hungary and prepares war on King Henry.

22. With a most prudent speech Henry assuages Arnulf's wrath.

23. At the insistence of his soldiers Arnulf becomes a vassal of King Henry.

24. The Hungarians, having heard of the death of Conrad, enter Saxony.

25. Though ailing, King Henry rushes against them.

26. How he exhorted his troops to fight.

27. About the good vow of King Henry.

28. About the messenger who announced the Hungarians were in Merseburg.

29. The Hungarians send out scouts, having questioned their prisoners about the war.

30. About the battle with the Hungarians.

31. About the good advice of King Henry, and his victory; and where this victory is depicted.

32. About a certain Louis, whom the Italians invite to rule over them.

33. That Margrave Adalbert, who was the son-in-law of King Berengar, did this.

34. About this same Adalbert, who first was good and afterwards turned bad.

35. That King Louis took an oath and returned home, for fear of Berengar.

36. That Adalbert, mighty margrave of the Tuscan province, by the inspiration of his wife Bertha deserted Berengar and sent for Louis, so that he might come.

37. Louis is welcomed by the Italians, and Berengar flees to Verona, whence he is also expelled by Louis.

38. Louis sets out for Lucca and is honorably received by Adalbert.

39. Because of Adalbert's power Louis is affected by envy, on account of which Adalbert abandons his fidelity to him.

40. A description of the Veronese city and the river Adige and the bridge over it.

41. How, while Louis stayed in Verona, once the city's guards had been bribed by Berengar, he is captured and deprived of his sight.

42. About the Hungarians, who used to ravage Italy at that time.

43. About the Saracens of Fraxinetum, who devastated part of Italy as far as Acqui.

44. About the African Saracens who occupied Apulia, Calabria, and Benevento, and held Mount Garigliano as their redoubt.

45. For what reason the Saracens left Africa.

46. That this was done by the will of God and for our chastisement.

47. Why John of Ravenna was pope at that time.

48. How the pope was elected by the prostitute Theodora.

49. About a certain African who came to the pope and gave him advice about the tactics by which he could fight the Africans.

50. That this same African by laying ambushes killed the others.

51. About the advice of Landulf, prince of Benevento.

52. About the fact that the pope, having sent messengers to Constantinople, received aid from the emperor and fought the Phoenicians.

53. That the Greeks, as soon as they arrived, built a castle close against the mountain.

54. That all the Phoenicians were killed and captured, and why the glorious apostles Peter and Paul were seen in the battle.

55. Adalbert, margrave of the Tuscan province, dies, whose son Wido is stationed in his place, but his mother is captured by Berengar.

56. How many children people suspected Bertha bore to Adalbert.

57. About the fact that many princes rebelled against Berengar, along with the Milanese archbishop Lambert, and why they did this.

58. About the palace count who was captured and unwisely entrusted to Lambert.

59. That Berengar requested the prisoner, and why he could not have him.

60. About Rudolf, king of the Burgundians, who took the daughter of Duke Burchard as wife and was invited by the Italians to come to them and be their king.

61. How the Hungarians, friends of King Berengar, killed Odelric, and took Adalbert, the king's son-in-law, and Count Gislebert, alive.

62. By what cunning Margrave Adalbert tricked the Hungarians and escaped from them, redeemed at a low price.

63. About Gislebert, captured, whipped, and led before the king, and mercifully dismissed and honored by him.

64. About this same fellow, who left on account of King Rudolf and brought him back.

65. About the civil war that arose between Berengar and Rudolf.

66. That Rudolf obtained victory through his relative Boniface.

67. Rudolf returns to Burgundy with the consent of the Italians.

68. Concerning the Veronese, who decided to kill Berengar.

69. A prudent speech of King Berengar to Flambert.

70. About a gold cup given by the king to Flambert.

71. That King Berengar was killed on the advice of Flambert.

72. About the king's blood staining a stone up to this day.

73. About the soldier Milo, who avenged King Berengar and hanged his killers after three days.

HERE END THE CHAPTER HEADINGS

HERE BEGINS THE SECOND BOOK

1. After the life-blood of King Arnulf, deserting his limbs, left his body lifeless, his son Louis was ordained king by all the people.[1] But the death of so great a man could not escape the notice of the Hungarians, just as it could not escape anyone in the whole world; and so the day of his death was to them merrier than all holidays, more pleasing than all treasures. But why?

2. In the first year after his death and his offspring's ordination, having assembled a very big army, the Hungarians claimed for themselves the nation of the Moravians,[2] which King Arnulf had subdued with the aid of their might; they even occupied territories of the Bavarians, destroyed castles, burned churches, massacred communities, and drank the blood of their victims so that they would be feared more and more.

3. Therefore King Louis, perceiving their cruelty and the decimation of his people, so aroused the spirits of all his men with fear that, if anyone considered being absent from the war which he was about to launch against the Hungarians, he would without doubt end his life in a noose. That numberless horde of the worst of peoples hastened to encounter his greatest of armies. Nor would you see a soul thirsting for a cold draught more avidly than that cruel nation longs for the day of battle; for nothing pleases them except to fight. Indeed, as I learned from the book written about their origin, their mothers cut their boys' faces with very sharp blades as soon as they come into the world so that, before they may receive the nourishment of milk, they may learn to endure wounds. The wounds that are inflicted on the bodies of the living in place of grief for dead relatives lend some credence to this story; truly they cry with blood, instead of tears, as would ἄθεοι καὶ ἀσεβοῖς ἀντὶ τῶν δακρείων.[3] Having gathered an army, hardly had King Louis

---

1. Louis IV, "The Child" (†911) was crowned aged barely 7, in 900.

2. See 1.13, above.

3. In Greek, "the godless and the impious in place of tears." Liudprand's ethnography draws on Jordanes, *Getica* 24.

come to Augsburg, which is a city on the border between the Swabians, Bavarians, and eastern Franks, when an unexpected and, even
more, an unfortunate approach of this people was announced. On
the following day both lines of battle assembled on the meadows
along the river Lech, places suited to martial deeds by virtue of
their ample space.[4]

4. Before Aurora left the saffron couch of Tithon,[5] the nation
of the Hungarians, thirsting for slaughter, avid for war, attacked
those yawning, that is, the Christians; for arrows, rather than noises,
awoke several, and others, pierced in their cots, neither the clamor
nor their wounds aroused, as life departed from them more quickly
than sleep. Then there broke out heavy fighting all around, and the
Turks, turning their backs as if in flight, laid many low with their
arrow shots.

> When almighty, awe-inspiring Eloim begins to bury in dark clouds
> The light of golden-haired Phoebus
> And when the North Star resounds with clamor from its loftiest
>   height,
> Frequent fiery lightning bolts fly, sent from the thundering throne;
> Then those men suddenly quake, who turn black into white,
> And they fear to review their crimes in an informed spirit,
> Equally to fall into the fire of heaven.
> Not quite straight fly the arrows shot from empty bows
> And stout breastplates are split from behind.
> As noisily as hail strikes the crop, plummeting upon it
> And at the same time echoes on and rattles the mighty roofs,
> So now resound the tight helmets, struck by clasped swords,
> And so fall the bodies, pierced by the exchange of arrows.[6]

When Phoebus, descending, occupied the seventh hour, and
blithe Mars favored Louis's side, then the Turks, since they were
crafty, feigned flight, having laid ambushes. And when the people
of the king, unaware of the deceit, chased them with a mighty

4. Louis faced the Hungarians on the Lech in 910.
5. Virgil, *Aeneid* 4.85; *Georgics* 1.447.
6. There are many reminiscences of Virgil and Juvenal in this poem.

thrust, the ambushers, falsely vanquished, fell on them from all sides and annihilated the supposed victors. The king himself marveled that after being the victor he was now vanquished, and it was all the more burdensome for him because unexpected. There you could see the meadow and the fields completely littered with corpses, and rivers and banks turned red by the blood that mixed in; then the neighing of horses and the clamor of trumpets terrified those fleeing more and more, and emboldened their pursuers more and more.

5. Moreover, the Hungarians, having carried out their scheme, unable to satisfy their evil cravings with so great a massacre of Christians, instead ravaged and totally burned the kingdoms of the Bavarians, Franks, Swabians, and Saxons so as to satiate their lust for perfidy. Nor was there anyone who could withstand their advance except with great strain or in places strongly fortified by nature; and the people were made tributary to them for several years.

6. During this time a certain Adalbert—not any person but the great hero himself—nurtured no small hatred for the state, in the castle called Bamberg.[7] For often King Louis, having gathered everyone, led raids against him; the aforementioned hero prepared for battle with him not near the castle, as most people are accustomed to do, but removed from the fortification. The soldiers of the king, before they learned by experience to marvel at his audacity, preceding the king, were considering how to entice Adalbert from his castle with a preliminary encounter and kill him. Adalbert, however, not only aware of this preemptive move but even thrilled by it, advanced against them so far from the castle that the king's soldiers did not recognize he was one of the enemy until his sword, impatient to kill, rampaged on their necks. Therefore, when the hero Adalbert had resolutely carried out his rebellion in this way for seven years, Louis, knowing he would never conquer the strength of that man's audacity except through some deception, consulted

---

7. Liudprand inserted this episode after the original composition of the text in 958–59. Adalbert's Babenberger lineage competed for supremacy in Franconia with the Conradines, close allies of King Louis.

Hatto, archbishop of the see of Mainz, about what he should do regarding this business.[8] And he, who was powerful in exercising duplicity, said: "Stop; I will free you of these worries. I will arrange it so he comes to you; you take care lest he ever go back again." Then Hatto, animated by confidence since he had turned many things from unfavorable into propitious, went to Bamberg as if to join Adalbert. And he said to him: "Even if you think there is no other life than the present one, you would still be acting unwisely since you rise up, a rebel against your lord, especially since you do what you do for nothing; and because you succumb to the ferocity of your spirit, you do not understand how much you are loved by everyone, and particularly by the king. Therefore, take my advice and accord me your trust; accept an oath by which you may without any hesitation leave the castle and return. If you do not believe the promises of my priesthood, at least do not distrust my oath, since I will arrange it so I will lead you back here just as I will lead you safe and sound from this castle." Thus Adalbert, lubricated by the sweet honey of praise, indeed deceived by it, accepted the oath from Hatto and invited him to dine together with him immediately after. But Hatto, mindful of the trick that he wanted to play a little later, forbade him by all means to dine. Without delay Hatto departed from the castle with Adalbert following close upon him, holding his right hand. When Hatto saw him outside the castle: "It pains me," he said, "O outstanding hero, that I did not refresh my body with some food according to your advice, especially as a long journey lies ahead." Then Adalbert, unaware of how much discomfort and how great a misfortune his phrases would bring, said: "My lord, let us turn back and, lest the body dissolve itself by the mortification of fasting, let it be refreshed by a little food." Assenting to this invitation, Hatto returned by the same road by which he had led Adalbert out, still holding his right hand while re-entering the castle. Without delay food was consumed, and on

8. Hatto (†913), a member of a powerful Swabian clan and one of Louis's godparents and closest advisers, was the bulwark of the throne after 907. He had been important also at the court of Arnulf, Louis's father.

the same day they traveled to the king. An uproar rose through the nearby castles; no small tumult broke out when it was announced that that very Adalbert was coming to the king. The king, not a little excited by his arrival, ordered the magnates to come to him and to sit in judgment. And he said to them: "We have learned from the facts rather than from mere rumor what great massacres Adalbert caused over almost seven years, how many of our companies he destroyed, how many catastrophes of pillage and arson he brought us. For this reason we await your sentence as to what retribution he may now receive for this so egregious evil." By the decree of all, according to the statutes of the early kings, Adalbert, judged guilty of treason, was sentenced to beheading. And as he was being dragged in chains to his death, noticing Hatto he said: "You will be guilty of perjury if you allow me to suffer death." To which Hatto replied: "I promised you would be led out from your castle just as hale and hearty as you would be led back; and I perceived I had done that when I led you back into the castle safe and sound right after having led you out." Then Adalbert, lamenting that this had happened to him and sighing over having understood Hatto's trick too late, followed his executioner as unwillingly as he would willingly have lived, if allowed to.[9]

After a few years had elapsed, since there was no one in the eastern or southern lands who could resist the Hungarians (for they had made the nations of the Bulgarians and the Greeks tributary), lest there might be anything still unknown to them, they assailed the nations who are seen to live under the southern and western skies.[10] Having gathered an immense, numberless army, they sought out wretched Italy.[11] And then they planted their tiny tents, indeed their rag heaps, along the banks of the river Brenta. Having

9. Adalbert's execution took place in September 906.

10. Here Liudprand again uses the term *climata*, on which see n. 30 in 1.11.

11. The excavation of a "Hungarian" tomb in the western Alps, whose young occupant wore a necklace of Italian coins, including one of Berengar I's, suggests the impact Hungarian raids had on Italy: M. Schulz-Dorlamm, "Die Ungarneinfälle des 10. Jahrhundert im Spiegel archäologischer Funde," in *Europa im 10. Jahrhundert*, ed. J. Henning (Mainz: P. von Zabern, 2002), 111, 116–17.

sent out scouts for three days so that they might evaluate the lay of the land and the density or sparseness of settlement, they received responses like this from the returning messengers:

7. "This plain, full of many farmers, is surrounded on one side, as you can see, by very rugged but fertile mountains, and on the other by the Adriatic Sea. It is endowed with several towns, and highly fortified ones; though its population's weakness or strength is unknown, still its vast numbers are obvious; so we do not advise attacking it with so few troops.

8. "In truth, while there may be several things that drive us to fight—our taste for triumphs, our strength of spirit, our skill at fighting, and especially the presence here of those things we long for, of which there are so many that we have never before seen quite as many in the whole world, and never imagined we could— nevertheless our advice is that we return home (for the road home is neither long nor difficult, since it can be covered in ten days or less), and return here after we have gathered all the strongest of our people; and let then our numbers, like our valor, become the terror of the locals." Without delay, once they had heard this they returned to their own lands and passed the whole bitter period of winter making weapons, sharpening swords, teaching war maneuvers to the young.

9. When the sun, abandoning the sign of Pisces, occupied Aries,[12] they sought out Italy, having gathered a vast, numberless army. They bypassed the heavily fortified cities of Aquileia and Verona, and with no one resisting they came to Ticinum, which is now called by a new, better name, Pavia. There King Berengar could not marvel enough at such an egregious and new evil—for before then he had not even heard of the Hungarians' name. Therefore, he ordered to come together as one all the Italians, the Tuscans, the Volscians,[13]

12. Around March 20, 899.

13. This Italic population of south Latium and north Campania was assimilated by Rome after the fifth century B.C. By using an archaic name little known to post-classical authors (Orosius and Frechulf are exceptions) Liudprand displayed erudition. Berengar's authority never extended into former Volscian country.

the Camerinans, the Spoletans, some in writing, some through messengers, and an army three times bigger than the Hungarians' was formed.

10. And when King Berengar saw so many troops around him, puffed up by the spirit of pride and attributing the [coming] triumph over his enemies more to his numbers than to God, he gave vent to license, staying alone with some companions in a certain small town. What happened? As soon as the Hungarians noted so great an army, they, subdued in spirit, could not decide what to do: they were afraid to engage in battle, but above all they could not bring themselves to flee. Truly, between these two possibilities escape prevailed over fighting; they crossed the Adda River by swimming, with the Christians chasing them in such a way that many drowned because of the great rush.

11. Finally the Hungarians, having taken no foolish advice, by means of an intermediary asked the Christians that they be permitted to go home safe, once they had returned all their booty with all their gains. This request the Christians decisively denied, and they insulted the Hungarians—what a pity!—and they searched about for chains with which to bind their enemies rather than weapons with which to kill them. When the pagans failed to soften the spirits of the Christians with their offer, having decided the original plan was best, they tried to free themselves by taking flight, and, fleeing thus, they came to the very wide fields of Verona.

12. The vanguard of the Christians pursued the rearguard of the Hungarians; and an early skirmish broke out in which the pagans obtained victory. But with the stronger army approaching, and remembering their flight, they followed the road they had taken.

13. And the Christians caught up with the idolaters alongside the river Brenta; for their exhausted horses denied the Hungarian force the possibility of fleeing. Thereupon, both the battle lines assembled simultaneously, separated only by the bed of the aforementioned river. Then the Hungarians, pressed by great terror, promised to surrender every furnishing, the prisoners, all their weapons, having kept back only one horse apiece on which they

could return home; and beyond that they added to their offer the condition that if only the Christians should allow them to go back alive, they would promise never to enter Italy again, after giving up their children as guarantees. Alas! The Christians, deceived by their swollen pride, chased the pagans with threats as if they were already defeated and continuously shot back this kind of απολογειαν[14] at them: "If we accepted the gift surrendered to us, especially since it comes from dead dogs who have virtually surrendered, and entered into any kind of treaty, insane Orestes himself would swear that we were unsound of mind!"[15]

14. Therefore, the Hungarians, rendered hopeless by that message, having gathered their strongest fighters into a unit, consoled each other by exchanging the following speech: "There is nothing worse that can befall men than this which we see right here; since there is no space for pleading, and all hope of escape has been removed, to bow our necks is to die; why should we be afraid to rush onto their weapons and inflict death with our own death? Our fall must not be imputed either to fortune or to feebleness, must it? For to succumb while fighting in a manly way is not to die, but to live. Let us leave to our descendants the same great fame, the κλιρονομειαν[16] that we received from our forefathers. We must believe in ourselves, at least in our experience. Often we have defeated many with small numbers: a large assembly of unwarlike plebeians is only exposed to slaughter. Very frequently Mars kills the one who flees and zealously protects the one who stands and fights. And these people, who would not take pity on us as we pleaded, do not know and do not understand the fact that to win is good, but overkill is most odious."

15. Thus, uplifted in spirit by this exhortation, they laid three ambushes on the flanks, and rushed into the middle of their enemies, fording the river straight across. For many of the Christians, worn out by the long wait caused by the negotiations, had gone

14. "Response."
15. Persius, *Satires* 3.118. In Greek mythology, Orestes killed his mother Clytemnestra.
16. "Heritage."

down through the fortifications so they might be refreshed with food. The Hungarians struck down these men so quickly that they pierced the food in their throats, while they denied others, whose horses they took, the possibility of escape, and because of this they pressed more lightly on them, since they saw they were trapped without horses. Finally, to increase their predicament, there was no small dissension among the Christians. Several men clearly not only did not inflict violence on the Hungarians, but hoped the enemy would kill their own companions; and these perverse people acted so perversely in order that they might rule more freely alone once their neighbors were slain. These men caused their *own* deaths, too, when they neglected to come to the aid of their companions and rejoiced in their deaths. Thus the Christians run away while the pagans rampage, and those who earlier could not obtain mercy even with gifts, later would not spare those who were begging for mercy afterward.[17]

16. At length, with the Christians killed and scattered, the Hungarians traversed all the places of the kingdom, ravaging them; nor . . .[18] was there anyone who resisted their presence except by chance in heavily fortified places. Clearly their strength prevailed, since a certain part of them depopulated Bavaria, Swabia, Francia, and Saxony, while another part did the same to Italy. But actually it was not their strength that earned this success, but God's true words, more lasting than the earth and heaven, could not be changed, as when through the prophet Jeremiah every nation, personified by the house of Israel, was threatened, saying: "Behold, I will bring upon you a people from afar, a strong people, an ancient people, a people whose language you shall not know, nor understand what they say. Their quiver is like an open sepulcher; they are all valiant; and they shall eat up your grain and your bread, they shall devour your sons and your daughters, they shall eat up your flocks and your herds, they shall eat your vineyards and your figs; and with swords they shall destroy your strong cities, wherein you trust.

17. This battle occurred on September 24, 899.
18. There is a lacuna here in the text.

Nevertheless in those days, says the Lord God, I will not bring you to utter destruction."[19]

17. Then in the same period King Louis died. Conrad, a man of the stock of the Franks, vigorous and knowledgeable in the ways of war, was ordained king by the whole people.[20]

18. Under him were the very mighty princes Arnulf of Bavaria,[21] Burchard of Swabia, Everard the very mighty count in Francia, and Gislebert duke of Lotharingia. Among them Henry, most mighty duke of the Saxons and Thuringians, stood out.

19. In the second year of his holding the kingship, the aforementioned princes, especially Henry, rose against him in rebellion. But King Conrad outclassed them as much by the force of his wisdom as by the vigor of his strength, and he led them back to his allegiance. Arnulf, however, impelled by great fear of him, fled with his wife and children to the Hungarians and stayed there as long as the glow of life sustained King Conrad.[22]

20. Then, in the seventh year of his reign, he recognized that the time of his summons to God had come. And when he had the aforesaid princes come to him, with Henry alone absent, he spoke thus: "As you can see, the time of my calling from corruption to incorruptibility, from mortality to immortality, is close. Wherefore I fervently ask that you always pursue peace and concord; when I leave mankind, let not any lust for ruling and no ambition to command inflame you. Elect Henry, most prudent duke of the Saxons and Thuringians, as king, and make him your lord; for he is both mighty in knowledge and abundantly endowed with the severity it takes for fair judgment." Once these things were said, he ordered that his crown (which was not made out of gold, a metal with which almost any kind of prince shines, but which, I say, was not

19. Jer 5.15–18.
20. Conrad, duke of Franconia, ruled the East Frankish kingdom, 911–18. His rise was facilitated by the fall of Adalbert's house (2.6, above).
21. Liudprand often called Arnulf (†937) Arnald.
22. Virgil, *Aeneid* 1.387, 4.336.

just decorated but *burdened* with most precious gems), and also all his royal vestments and scepter, be brought there and, to the extent he could, he uttered words like these: "I ordain Henry heir and vicar to the royal dignity with these regal ornaments; and I not only advise, but I implore you to obey him." His demise followed this command, and soon after that everyone's obedience. For with Conrad going to his death, the aforementioned princes brought Duke Henry the crown and all the royal vestments; and they recounted in its proper order everything that King Conrad had said. At first he humbly refused the apex of the royal dignity, and after a little while took it on without ambition.[23] Truly, had pallid death, which thumps its foot equally in the taverns of the poor and the towers of kings,[24] not snatched King Conrad away so quickly, it would be he whose reputation ruled over many nations of the world.

21. At that same time Arnulf, returning with his wife and children from Hungary, was honorably received by the Bavarians and eastern Franks; nor was he just received, but he was vigorously encouraged by them to become king. When King Henry perceived that everyone else complied with his orders and only Arnulf resisted him, he set out for Bavaria, having gathered a very sturdy army. When Arnulf heard of this, he could not stand to wait for the king's arrival in Bavaria, and, having assembled what troops he could, he set out to meet him: clearly he, too, desired to become king. And when they reached the point where both had to commit to battle, King Henry, like a wise and God-fearing man, considering that irreparable damage could befall either side, summoned Arnulf to speak with him alone. Accordingly, Arnulf, thinking that he was going to a duel, arrived at the agreed-upon place alone and at the established time.

22. King Henry, setting out to confront him, addressed Arnulf thus:

---

23. The duke of Saxony Henry the Fowler ruled the East Franks, 918–36. Seeking to avoid office was standard behavior in early medieval narratives about good people.
24. Horace, *Odes* 1.4.13–14.

"Why do you resist God's order with unsound mind?
Note that the people want me to be king
By Christ's command, which sustains the mechanism of the world.
Even Tartarus fears him, Flegeton respects him;[25]
He pulverizes splendid kings, willing them to be terrified for a while
And exalted for a while; he raises up the poor, if he wants,
For which may they give the proper praises to God for centuries.
Do you really, O haughty one, criminal, perfidious one, hard, fierce,
Touched by the prick of envy and wild longing,
Desire to waste Christians' lives?
If the people wanted to elevate you as king,
Certainly I would be the one who desired it most."[26]

With this fourfold type of speech—that is, abundant and brief, dry yet florid—King Henry, who was prudent in soul, softened Arnulf's resolve and returned to his followers.

23. When Arnulf recounted all these things to his followers, he heard an αποκρισην[27] like this from them: "Who can doubt the pronouncement of the wise man, indeed of true wisdom, that says: 'By me kings reign, princes rule, and the wise decree justice,'[28] and that of the apostle, saying: 'Every ordinance is from God; and he that resists the power resists the ordinance of God.'[29] For certainly in that election all the people could not be of one mind if he were not chosen before the creation of the world by the highest Trinity that is the one God. If he will be good, he shall be worthy of love, and God shall be praised in him; if instead he shall be bad, he shall be tolerated placidly: for the faults of many subjects demand that they be burdened, not ruled, by their governors. It seems fair and just to us that you elect this man king so as not to dissent from the other electors; but he should bless such a fortunate and wealthy man as you with terms like these, and so assuage the anger of your

---

25. Tartarus and Flegeton were custodians of the ancient pagan underworld.
26. The composition echoes lines from Virgil, Boethius, and perhaps Lucretius.
27. "Response."
28. Prv 8.15–16. Liudprand's text replaced "the powerful" with "the wise" (*prudentes*).
29. Rom 13.1–2.

spirit that what your ancestors did not have should be granted to you, namely, that all the bishops of Bavaria should submit to your authority, and it should be within your power when one dies to ordain another one." Arnulf, agreeing with this excellent and good advice from his followers, became a soldier of King Henry, and from him, as was just said, it was conceded that Arnulf be honored by the bishops of all Bavaria.

24. At this same time, when the Hungarians heard of the demise of King Conrad and Henry's succession to the kingship, they addressed each other with this kind of talk: "Perhaps a new king wants to use new methods. Let us go up there, having assembled no small force, and let us investigate whether King Henry wants to pay the right tribute; and if he deviates from the other kings' way—while we do not believe it possible—let his kingdom be depopulated by slaughter and by vast fires. First let us invade the borders not of the Bavarians but of the Saxons, where the king lives; in that way if by chance—which we do not hope for—he wants to gather an army, it will not be able to reach him in time either from Lotharingia or from Francia, Swabia, or Bavaria. Also, the lands of both the Saxons and the Thuringians will easily be decimated since it is neither protected by mountains nor supported by highly fortified towns."

25. A very serious illness was holding King Henry back when the imminent arrival of the Hungarians was announced to him. Hardly had he finished hearing the messengers' words when, having sent messengers throughout Saxony, he ordered all who could to come to him within five days or risk execution. Therefore, having assembled a very strong army in four days—for this custom of the Saxons according to which no one is allowed to avoid military service after his thirteenth year is praiseworthy and should be imitated[30]—with a body lacking in strength but invigorated by his fortitude of mind, he mounted his horse as best he could. Then, having gathered together his troops, he stirred up their lust for battle with words like these:

---

30. This aside suggests Liudprand envisioned non-Saxon readers for his text.

26.

"The Saxon nation was once famous,
A lion gnashing its teeth through numberless wars;
It resisted Charlemagne with bloody sword
Who subdued the whole world to himself.
He who had conquered everywhere was chased off, conquered.
And if he subdued us all upon his return
That was arranged by God's piety because
He wanted us to partake of eternal life.
Now an evil nation of Turks, ignorant of Christ and hostile to God,
Delights in putting to the sword all the people of the church;
Alas, my heroes! Listen up since now
They want to bend our necks to paying tribute!
Lift up your spirits in a manly way!
I ask you to cut off their limbs, to slash hard at them!
Let there be a burning rage, a holy lust, against them!
Let them carry our gifts back to the waves of the Styx,
Let them count hot coins by the fire of hell!"[31]

27. The king saw the spirits of his men aroused for battle by such exhortations; having enjoined silence on everyone, he added this, touched again by the spark of a divine gift: "The deeds of the early kings, the writings of the holy Fathers, reveal to us what we ought to do. For it is not difficult for God to cast down many with a few, but only if the faith of those who hope to carry off such an exploit merits it; the faith, I say, not just of recitations but of good deeds, and not just of the lips, but also of the heart. Therefore let us swear and give promises as the psalmist says to; indeed, I shall go first since I seem to be the foremost among us by office and rank.

"Let the simoniacal heresy, hateful to God and condemned by the most blessed prince of the apostles, Peter, which until now was rashly preserved by our predecessors, be removed from our

31. The last two lines contain sarcastic references to the afterlife beliefs of the ancient pagans. This lyric employs a meter unusual in the tenth century, displaying thus the author's versatility.

kingdom by every means.[32] Instead, let the charity of unity bind together any whom the devil's guile divided."

28. The king aspired to say many more things like this when a messenger announced that the sly Hungarians were in Merseburg, a castle set at the border of the Saxons, Thuringians, and Slavs. The messenger also added that they had taken captive no small number of children and women, and had made an immense massacre of men; and they had said that they would leave no one surviving older than the age of ten, since in this way they could create no small terror among the Saxons. Yet the king, as he was steady in spirit, was not frightened by such news, but increasingly exhorted his men, saying that they must fight for their fatherland and die nobly.

29. Meanwhile, the Hungarians were inquiring of the prisoners whether they would have to fight. And when it was asserted by the prisoners that it could not be otherwise, having sent out scouts, they investigated whether this might be true. The scouts sighted King Henry with a huge army close by the aforementioned castle of Merseburg. Finally, as soon as they could return to their companions, they announced the arrival of the army: nor was the one who bore them this message of war any other messenger than the king himself.

30. With hardly any delay battle began, and frequently there was heard the holy and plaintive cry "κυριε ελεισον"[33] from the Christians' side, and from their side the devilish and dirty "Húi, húi."

31. Before the beginning of the encounter King Henry had given his men wise and healthy advice like this: "When you will begin to head out into the game of Mars, let no one try to advance beyond his comrades, though he has a faster horse; instead, take the first strike of their arrows on your shields, having covered each side with them; then rush on them with the fastest charge and with the most vehement attack, in such a way that they cannot fire a

32. Simony, whereby ecclesiastical offices and functions are purchased, was especially abhorrent in reforming clerical circles in the tenth century.
33. The Greek invocation "Lord, have mercy" was part of the Latin mass.

second volley of arrows on you before they feel the cuts of your
weapons upon them." Therefore, the Saxons, mindful of this most
salutary warning, charged with an orderly, even line, and there was
no one who outran the slower with a faster horse; and they took
on their shields the harmless strikes of the Hungarians' arrows,
having covered each side with their shields just as the king had
said; only then, as that most prudent man had directed, did they
surmount the enemy with a vigorous charge, in such a way that
life escaped from the Hungarians with a moan[34] before they fired
the second bolt of arrows. And it happened by the piety of divine
grace that it proved better for the Hungarians to flee than to fight.
Then their swift horses seemed slack; beyond that, the ornament
of their breastplates and the repute of their weapons were not protection but burdens for the Hungarians. Having thrown down their
bows, cast off their swords, and removed their breastplates, too, so
that their horses could run faster, they applied themselves only to
flight; in fact, almighty God, who gave them their audacity in fighting, wholly denied them the means of escaping. Therefore, once
the Hungarians had been killed or chased off, the immense horde
of their prisoners was set free, and their moans changed into a
song of joy. This triumph, worthy of praise and memory, the king
ordered depicted in the upper chamber of the palace at Merseburg
by ζογραφεῖαν,[35] in such a way that you may see the actual event
itself rather than an imitation.[36]

32. While these things took place, almost all the Italians, having
sent him messengers, invited a certain Louis, born of Burgundian
blood, so that he might come to them and take for himself the
kingdom from Berengar.[37]

34. Virgil, *Aeneid* 11.831.

35. "By a picture."

36. Until the time of Henry, this had been a vital fortress on the eastern frontier
of Saxony (see 2.28); his military successes changed the significance and nature of the
outpost.

37. Louis III of Provence arrived in the wake of Berengar's defeat by the Hungarians (2.6–16); he was grandson of the emperor Louis II, and had Carolingian legitimacy
thereby. Crowned in 900, he was blinded (and thus disqualified from ruling) in 905.

33. The author of this filthy crime was Adalbert, margrave of the city of Ivrea, to whom the same Berengar had married his daughter, called Gisela; with whom Adalbert even had a son to whom he had given his grandfather's name.[38] It is this one, I say, he is the Berengar by whose immense tyranny all Italy is made mournful, and by whose pimping Italy is not helped but oppressed by all peoples. But for now let that be enough to have said, so that we may return to our subject.

34. Especially that same Adalbert, who was a menace to all good folk, had very evil ways. For while he lived his life with his youthful blood coursing through his veins, he was of admirable kindness and holiness, so clearly that if a pauper ran up to him when he was returning from the hunt, and he had nothing else at hand to give him, he would give without hesitation the horn that hung from his neck with golden clasps, and would buy it back from the same beggar for whatever sum he asked. Afterwards, however, he became such that his reputation was so dire that this accurate song was recited about him both by adults and by boys—and since it sounds better that way, let us say it in Greek: Ἀδελβερτος κόμις κουρτης μακροπαθης γουνδοπιστις; by which is meant and declared that he uses a long sword but is very short on trustworthiness.

35. The aforementioned Louis came to Italy through his invitation, and that of many other Italians. As soon as Berengar discovered this he set out against him. And when Louis realized Berengar was coming against him and had great numbers of troops, while his were few, impelled by fear he made a promise to Berengar by swearing that if Berengar would let him off then, he would not come back to Italy, even if summoned by other promises. For Berengar made the very mighty margrave of the Tuscans, [another] Adalbert, very loyal to himself, having given him many gifts, and on account of this Louis was driven out so easily.[39]

---

38. Adalbert of Ivrea (900–29) later married Ermengard, daughter of Adalbert of Tuscany, the rival of King Berengar I (see 1.40–43 and 3.7). Berengar never created aristocratic consensus in Italy, despite clever marriage policies.

39. Adalbert II (886–915). See 1.39, above.

36. Once a small interlude of time had passed, King Berengar was perceived to be tiresome by this same Tuscan margrave Adalbert; Bertha his wife, who was the mother of that King Hugh who later, in our times, ruled in Italy, fed no small kindling into this situation. Whence it happened that, on the advice of this same margrave Adalbert, the other Italian princes sent to Louis saying he should come; and he, having forgotten his oath through his lust for power, came quickly to Italy.

37. Thus Berengar, seeing that Louis was being well received by both Italian and Tuscan princes, set out for Verona. Louis, not hesitating to follow him there with the Italians, actually chased him from Verona and subjugated the whole kingdom to himself in a manly way.

38. Once these things had been done in that way, it seemed good to Louis that he see Tuscany just as he had seen all Italy. Leaving Pavia at last, he headed toward Lucca, where he was received honorably and with wondrous pomp by Adalbert.

39. And when Louis saw there were so many elegant soldiers in Adalbert's house, and observed so much pomp and such great expenditures, pricked by the longings of envy he secretly said to his men: "This fellow could more appropriately be called king than margrave; he is not inferior to me in anything except in his title alone." This matter could not escape Adalbert; and hearing of it, Bertha, since she was a clever woman, not only disengaged her husband from his fidelity to Louis but also turned the other princes of Italy into betrayers of the king. Whence it happened that while he returned to Verona from Tuscany, and he stayed there without hesitation, suspecting no evil, King Berengar corrupted the city guards, having paid out a sum, and after assembling some very valiant men he entered the city under the cover of night.

40. Like the Tiber in Rome, the river Adige runs through the middle of Verona; across it was built a big marble bridge, of marvelous craftsmanship and marvelous length. From the left side of the river, which lies to the north, the city is protected by a difficult, steep hill in such a way that, if that part of the city which the

aforesaid river laps on its right were seized by enemies, still Verona could be vigorously defended from there. On the top of this hill a church was built with precious workmanship, consecrated in honor of the most blessed prince of the apostles Peter, and there resided Louis on account of both the pleasantness of the church and the fortification of the site.

41. At length, Berengar, having entered the city at night as we said, crossing the bridge with his soldiers while Louis was unaware, came up to him at the very breaking of dawn. Awakened by the clamor and the shouting of soldiers and informed of what the uproar was, Louis fled into the church, and no one discovered where he was except a single one of Berengar's soldiers. This man, moved by pity, wanted not to reveal him, but to hide him; but fearing lest Louis, discovered by others, might be revealed and pay with his life, he went to Berengar and spoke to him thus: "Since God holds you so high that he has placed your enemy in your hands, you should uphold his warnings, indeed his precepts. For he says: 'Be therefore merciful, as your Father is merciful. Judge not, and you shall not be judged. Condemn not, and you shall not be condemned.'"[40] Thus Berengar, who was a clever man, understood that this soldier knew where Louis was hidden, and tricked him with this sophistic reply: "Do you think, you idiot, that I want to kill the man, indeed the king, whom God placed in my hands? Did not even holy David have the chance to kill King Saul, given into his hands by God, and yet desist?" The soldier, won over by such phrases, revealed the place to which Louis had escaped. When Louis was captured and led into his presence, Berengar thundered against him with such phrases: "Up to what point do you intend to abuse our patience, O Louis? Can you deny that occasion in the past when, hemmed in by my guards and my diligence, you could not even move against me?[41] And when I, inclining to pity, which was not owed you at all, let you go? Do you not feel, I say, that you are chained by your own

40. Lk 6.36–37.
41. Cicero, *Against Catiline* 1.1 and 1.7.

perjury? You clearly confirmed to me that you would never re-enter Italy. I grant you your life, as I promised that soldier who revealed you to me; however, I not only order but demand your eyes to be gouged out." Once these things were said, Louis was deprived of sight, and Berengar assumed the kingship.[42]

42. Meanwhile, the rage of the Hungarians, since they could not succeed with the Saxons, Franks, Swabians, and Bavarians, rampaged through all Italy, with no one resisting. In fact, since Berengar could not make his soldiers firmly loyal, he made the Hungarians not a little friendly to himself.

43. But also the Saracens who, as I said, inhabited Fraxinetum, after the destruction of the Provençals, quite thoroughly devastated those upper parts of Italy close to them; to such an extent that, having depopulated many cities, they reached Acqui, which is a city some 40 miles from Pavia, called by that name because of a bath complex for washing built there in a marvelous rectangular fashion. Such great fear had filled everyone that there was no one who would await their arrival unless in very heavily defended places.

44. At that same time, the Saracens, leaving Africa by boat, so occupied Calabria, Apulia, Benevento, and almost all the cities of the Romans, that the Romans everywhere held only half of the city and the Africans the other half. Indeed, they built a fortification on Mount Garigliano in which they kept, quite safe, women, children, prisoners, and all stolen goods.[43] Also, no one could travel from the west or the north to pray at the thresholds of the most holy apostles in Rome without being captured by them or released at the cost of no small ransom. Although wretched Italy

42. Blinded, Louis returned to Burgundy, where he was able to rule until 928. Blinding was an Italian and Byzantine political tradition. It prevented more dangerous rivals from replacing the defeated victim and creating new threats to the victorious blinder. Physically impaired in a world where physical prowess mattered enormously to leadership, the victim suffered a reduction of her or his sphere of influence and power, but not a removal of all legitimacy.

43. There are hefty hills at the estuary of the river Garigliano (the Liris of antiquity), south of Gaeta. After 882 a Saracen base nestled there, which has left no archaeological traces but may have occupied the site of the ancient city of Minturnae.

was oppressed by many misfortunes of the Hungarians and of the Saracens from Fraxinetum, still it was shaken by no devastations or epidemics like those brought by the Africans.

45. It is said, however, that they left Africa and came to Italy for this reason. Once Leo and Alexander, the august emperors, had departed mankind, Romanos, as we say in Latin, along with that Constantine who reigns to the present day, the son of Emperor Leo, ruled the Constantinopolitan empire.[44] And as usually happens, within the first year that Romanos assumed the emperorship several peoples, especially among the *Anatolikai*—meaning "the easterners"[45]—attempted to rebel against him. Moreover, while the emperor sent the army to defeat them, it happened that Apulia and Calabria, two regions which at that time were subject to him, rebelled. And since the emperor, having sent most of his troops to the east, could not direct a large army there, he first asked that they of their own free will return to their original allegiance; and when they refused this and said that they were not about to do so, the emperor, inflamed, quickly sent to the African king, asking him with a bribe to help him and to subdue Apulia and Calabria for the emperor with his forces. The African king, having received this message, sent numberless troops to Apulia and Calabria by boat and very vigorously subdued both regions to the power of the emperor. But when in the course of time they abandoned those regions, they turned their line of battle toward Rome, and they claimed for themselves as the greatest protection Mount Garigliano, and, doing battle, they took by force many strongly fortified cities.

46. Indeed, our Lord Jesus Christ, co-eternal and consubstantial with the Father and the Holy Spirit, of whose mercy the earth is

---

44. Romanos I Lakapenos ruled, 920–44, but had been influential at Constantinople since 913. Constantine VII Porphyrogenitus ruled, 945–59, but his marriage to Romanos's daughter Helena in 919 lent legitimacy to the regent. It is unclear what the boy-emperor (born in 906) had to do with fomenting Arab incursions in southern Italy (see 3.22–30, below).

45. The first of the military districts created in the 600s to defend Byzantium, Anatolikon occupied much of the Anatolian plateau in modern Turkey.

full, who wants no man to die but "will have all men be saved, and to come to the knowledge of the truth,"[46] invites some by his kindnesses to love him and their own fatherland. Others, however, he compels to love him with fear, lest that creature might perish which God alone foresaw before the world's creation and which he fashioned after making every other creature, like a lord using and dominating all other creatures, man, that is, whom through the shedding of his own blood the true man and true God, who is not two but one, redeemed for the end of time. Christ does this for our benefit, not for his own, for he can neither take profit from our goodness—as the prophet testifies, saying: "You have no need of my goods"[47]—nor lose from our wickedness. Thus it pleased him, we know not to what advantage, to chastise us in our time with this kind of terrors. But in order that the Saracens not insult all the more and say: "Where is their God?" God converted the hearts of the Christians in such a way that they desired more to fight than to flee in advance.

47. In that time John of Ravenna held the highest office in the venerable Roman see.[48] This man obtained the pontifical pinnacle by a wicked crime against law and custom, as follows.

48. Theodora the shameless harlot, grandmother of that Alberic who recently left mankind and whose very mention is most foul, was holding the monarchy of the city of Rome, and not in an unmanly way.[49] She had two daughters, Marozia and Theodora, not just her equals but if anything even faster in the exercise of Venus. Of these two Marozia, by a wicked affair with Pope Sergius, of whom we made mention above, gave birth to John, who, after the death of John the Ravennan, obtained the leadership of the Roman church; and with Margrave Alberic she had that Alberic who

46. 1 Tm 2.4.
47. Ps 15.2.
48. Pope John X (914–28).
49. A rare bit of praise for a member of the Roman clan of the Theophylacts, dominant in the 900s. Theodora died in 914, having benefited from her husband Theophylact's rise to power in Rome. Her grandson Alberic died in 954.

later, in our times, usurped the lordship in the Roman city. In that same time, in the see of Ravenna, which was the second archbishopric [in Italy] after the Roman one, Peter held the pontificate; this latter man, on account of the due subjection of his see, would often and repeatedly send to the apostolic lord in Rome the aforementioned Pope John, who in those times was still a priest of the Ravennan church. Theodora—as I testified, a quite shameless prostitute—inflamed with the heat of Venus, lusted ardently because of the beauty of John's appearance, and not only desired but actually forced him—O shame!—to fornicate with her over and over again. While they were shamefully doing these things, the bishop of the Bolognese church died, and this John was elected in his place. A little later, before the day of his consecration in Bologna, the aforementioned archbishop of Ravenna died, and this same John, swollen with the spirit of ambition, usurped his place by the inspiration of Theodora, having abandoned his prior church of Bologna, against the canons of the holy Fathers; and coming to Rome he was quickly ordained bishop of the Ravennan church. After a small interval of time, at the summons of God, the pope who had unjustly ordained him died, too; thus Theodora, with the perverted mind of Glycerium,[50] lest she should enjoy her lover by very rare beddings on account of the length of the two hundred miles that separate Ravenna from Rome, pushed him to desert the see of the archbishopric of the Ravennans—O wickedness!—and to usurp the highest pontificate at Rome. Therefore, with this sort of vicar of the holy apostles in charge, the Phoenicians,[51] as I explained earlier, miserably mangled Benevento and the Roman cities.

49. Meanwhile it happened that a certain young Phoenician, tired of his crimes, deserted the Phoenicians and came to this Pope John, and, touched by divine inspiration, he addressed the

50. Glycerium was a female character in Terence's play *Andria*, a text to which Liudprand made repeated references in his writings: see Chiesa, *Liudprandi Cremonensis Opera*, p. 231.

51. Ancient inhabitants of coastal North Africa. Liudprand means the Maghribi Saracens here (see 2.45, above).

pope as follows: "Great priest, if you were wise, you would not allow the Phoenicians so gravely to mangle the people and land subject to you. Select, therefore, some young men of great swiftness, like birds, who will obediently listen to me as general, teacher, and lord. I permit them to bring nothing except a single shield, a single spear, and a single sword apiece, and simple clothes, with a little food."

50. Once sixty youths of this description were found and sent to him, he set out against the Phoenicians, and he hid next to the roads that were the Phoenicians' preferred route. And when the Phoenicians returned, having depopulated the area often and repeatedly, charging on them by surprise from their hiding places suddenly and with a very huge clamor, they easily butchered them. The battle cry from their mouths and the blow from their hands came at the same time; and neither could the Phoenicians learn who or what it was before the ambushers' swords slashed their bodies. And at last several of the Romans were impressed through the fame of this exploit and by these tactics, and they killed the Phoenicians in many places; and worn out by this clever plan, the Africans abandoned the cities, having broken their alliances, and retained for themselves only Mount Garigliano as a defense.[52]

51. Once John was made pope as we said, a certain Landulf, a vigorous man and one learned in the ways of war, shone as prince of all the Beneventans and Capuans.[53] With the Phoenicians shaking the state of the republic not a little, Pope John consulted with this outstanding Prince Landulf about what should be done concerning the kind of thing the Africans were doing. When the prince heard the question, he answered the pope thus, through intermediaries: "This matter, my spiritual father, ought to be worked out through great assemblies. Therefore, send to the emperor of

52. As Liudprand notes, the collapse of the raiders' system of local alliances was the precondition of their elimination.

53. Prince Landulf I of Capua and Benevento (†943) alternately allied and fought with the Byzantines during a long reign he shared with his father (to 910), his brother (after 910), and his son (after 933).

the Argives,[54] whose land across the sea the Arabs never cease to depopulate, just like our own. Invite the Camerinans and even the Spoletans to our aid; with God as our protector, let us keenly go to war. If we win, let the victory be ascribed not to our numbers but to God; if instead the Phoenicians win, let it be imputed to our sins, not to our lack of enterprise."

52. Having heard these words, the pope quickly sent messengers to Constantinople, humbly asking that the help of the emperor be given to him.

In fact, the emperor, as a very holy man and one fearing God, without delay sent troops transported with ships. And when they disembarked across the Garigliano River, Pope John was there with Landulf, the most potent prince of the Beneventans, and also the Camerinans and Spoletans. Finally quite a hideous battle developed between the two sides. When the Phoenicians observed that the Christian side was prevailing, they fled to the top of Mount Garigliano and tried to defend only the settlement's narrow access roads.

53. On the very same day the Greeks established their camp on that side of the mountain where ascent was more difficult and the Phoenicians' escape routes easier; staying there, they maintained vigilance lest the Phoenicians escape, and fighting them daily they killed many.

54. Therefore, with the Greeks and Latins fighting every day, by God's mercy not one of the Phoenicians survived who was not put to the sword or captured alive. Moreover, in that battle the most holy Peter and Paul were seen by the pious faithful, and we believe that it was by their prayers that the Christians deserved that the Phoenicians should flee and that they should obtain victory.[55]

---

54. An archaic name for Greeks, by which Liudprand means Byzantines.

55. The battle of the Garigliano (915) was notable for the martial role of the pope, and for the concert of central and southern Italian powers against intruders with whom they often had allied. Liudprand overlooked John X's leading role, perhaps because his view of Ottonian intervention in Italy required a helpless and worthless papacy.

55. In those same times Adalbert, the mighty margrave of the Tuscans, died, and his son Wido was appointed margrave in his father's place by King Berengar. And after her husband's death Bertha, his wife, became no less powerful than her husband had been, alongside her son Wido; by craftiness, gifts, and the sweet exercises of copulation she made several men loyal to her. Whence it happened that, when a little later she was captured with her son by Berengar and led off into custody at Mantua, still she did not turn over all her castles and cities to King Berengar, but stoutly held them and shortly thereafter freed herself with her son from imprisonment.

56. As rumor has it, she generated three children with her husband: Wido, whom we already mentioned, and Lambert, who lives on until now, blinded, and her daughter Ermengard, her equal in the sweetness of Aphrodite,[56] whom she coupled in marriage with Adalbert, margrave of the city of Ivrea, once the daughter of Berengar, Gisela (that is, the mother of the current king Berengar), had died.[57] Ermengard bore him a son named Anscar, and a subsequent book will describe of what great virtue and bravery he was.[58]

57. In those times Adalbert, son-in-law of the king, margrave of the city of Ivrea, and Odelric the count of the palace, who traced his origin to Swabian blood, and also Gislebert, a very rich count and strong, and even Lambert archbishop of the Milanese, with no few other princes of Italy, rose in rebellion against Berengar. The reason for their rebellion was this. While Lambert, once his predecessor had died, was supposed to be ordained archbishop of the Milanese, King Berengar demanded no small sum from him, against the rules of the holy Fathers, and he ordered to be written in stone, once the money was given to him, how much of it the chamberlains, how much the doorkeepers, how much the peacock-wardens, and even the chicken-keepers should receive. Therefore Lambert, strong-

56. The ancient Greek goddess of love and patroness of eroticism. In 2.48 Liudprand calls her by her Latin name, Venus.

57. See 2.33–36, above.

58. See 4.8, below.

ly aroused by love of the see, paid whatever the king demanded with pain so great that you may understand it from this tale, which the following reading will discuss.

58. Berengar kept in chains that Odelric, the count of the palace whom we mentioned before; and, when he had made Lambert archbishop, the king entrusted Odelric to him while he decided what he would do with him. But the archbishop, mindful of the many coins he had paid out for his archbishopric, began to discuss Berengar's perfidy with the prisoner.

59. After a few days, through messengers he had sent, King Berengar instructed Odelric to come to him. The irony of the response that they received is not in doubt: "I must deeply betray my priestly office if I shall hand over anyone into someone else's hands to be killed." Therefore the messengers understood he had openly rebelled when they learned he had set free without the king's permission a man entrusted to him by the king; and having returned straight to the king, they gave this line of Terence as an answer: "Entrust it to him, if you want something properly cared for!"[59]

60. At that time King Rudolf ruled over the very haughty Burgundians; it happened that, to increase his power, he married a daughter called Bertha of the mighty duke of the Swabians Burchard.[60] Therefore, the Italians, having sent messengers, sought that he should come and expel Berengar.

61. While this was going on, it happened that the Hungarians, whose two kings Dursác and Bugat had been very friendly with Berengar, reached Verona, ignorant of all this. While Margrave Adalbert, and Odelric, count of the palace, Count Gislebert, and many others held a meeting about the removal of Berengar in the mountains near the city of Brescia, which is fifty miles distant from Verona, Berengar asked the Hungarians to rush against his enemies if they loved him. These Hungarians, since they were avid for kill-

---

59. Terence, *Adelphoe* 372.

60. Rudolf II (912–37), who ruled Italy, 922–26, and Burchard I (911–26), who led aristocratic opposition to east Francia's kings. Their alliance took place in 922. Burchard appeared in 2.18, above.

ings and desirous of fighting, as soon as they had obtained a guide from Berengar, came up to the rebels from behind through hidden tracks and struck them with such rapidity that they did not have time to take up their weapons. Thus, with many already captured and killed, the count of the palace, Odelric, who had defended himself in quite a manly way, was killed, while Margrave Adalbert and Gislebert were taken alive.

62. Actually Adalbert, as he was not a warlike man, but one of great wisdom and craftiness, when he saw the Hungarians rushing from every direction and all hope of fleeing was taken from him, cast off the belt and golden armbands and all his precious gear and put on the cheap clothes of his soldiers, lest who he was be recognized by the Hungarians. Captured and asked who he was, he answered that he was a soldier of a certain soldier, and asked to be led to a nearby castle called Calcinaria, in which he maintained he had relatives who would ransom him. Thus, led there, since he was not recognized, he was redeemed for a very low price: for one of his own soldiers, named Leo, bought him back.

63. Gislebert, however, since he was recognized, was led half-naked, whipped, and in chains before the presence of King Berengar. In truth, when he was led before him without leggings, wearing a short tunic, and he quickly fell prostrate at the king's feet, all nearly died from laughter at the revelation of his genital appendages. Yet the king, as he was a lover of mercy, tending toward that pity of which he owed Gislebert none, did not return evil for evil (as the people hoped), but instead, after Gislebert had been quickly washed and dressed in excellent clothes, allowed him to go. He even said to him: "I demand no oath from you: I commit you to your own fidelity; if you do evil to me, you shall receive retribution from God."

64. The king's son-in-law Adalbert and the others who were rebels along with him at the same time, sent Gislebert, when he returned to his lands forgetting the kindness he received, to Rudolf so that he would come. Having departed to him, before thirty days had elapsed, Gislebert convinced Rudolf to come to Italy. Rudolf, welcomed by all, left nothing of the entire kingdom to Berengar

except Verona, and he held the whole kingdom in a manly way for three years.[61]

65. Since in the twelve hours of a day a man likes himself and dislikes himself, and first loves this but soon despises that, who can manage to please everyone equally? Therefore, within those three years King Rudolf seemed good to some, burdensome to others. Whence it happened that half the people of the kingdom wanted Rudolf, half Berengar. They prepared no mean civil war; and since Wido, bishop of the Placentine city, favored the faction of Berengar, they prepared for battle near Fiorenzuola, twelve miles away from Piacenza.[62]

Then what a horrible civil war
Arose, alas, and mournful,
Four times four days before the calends
of August! But as Phoebus's
Rays appear,
When the loud horns of Mars sound,
The father himself gives his son
Eternal burial, and the offspring
Kills the father. What kind of deep pain?
Here the forefather prepares the nephew's
Death, only to be laid low by him;
Impelled by the dire furies
A brother kills another from afar.
King Berengar himself gallops
Quickly through the midst of the enemy
Hurrying like a lightning bolt from above;
The dark star of Cancer casts the new ears of grain
Down with a sickle
No differently than that wild and cruel
King Rudolf himself
Mows down the miserable populace with his sword.[63]

61. He was acknowledged as king of Italy in February 922.

62. On July 17, 923. By tenth-century standards, the battle of Fiorenzuola D'Arda was exceptionally bloody.

63. Prudentius, a late antique Christian poet, was one of this poem's inspirations, but Virgil and Boethius echo in it, too.

66. King Rudolf gave his sister Waldrada, a lady as honest in appearance as in wisdom, who still lives today, as a spouse to the very mighty Count Boniface, who later, in our times, became margrave of the Camerinans and the Spoletans.[64] This man, having gathered a host, came to the aid of Rudolf along with Count Gariard, and, as he was a man both crafty and bold, he preferred to await the outcome of the encounter in hiding places with his men rather than sustain the first attack of the battle. Almost all Rudolf's troops had run away, and those of Berengar, having sounded the victory signal, were occupied collecting the spoils, when Boniface and Gariard, suddenly leaving their hiding places, cut them down all the more easily because they were unexpected. Gariard spared some, striking them with the wood and not the iron part of his spear; Boniface, instead, sparing none, caused a huge massacre. Boniface therefore sounded his victory signal; and those of Rudolf's side who had fled regrouped, and, chasing the Berengarians, they forced them to take flight. Berengar reached his well-known haven of Verona. Such a great massacre of soldiers occurred on that occasion that there is a great scarcity of soldiers lasting until today.

67. Once these things had happened in this way, King Rudolf very effectually subjugated the kingdom to his rule; and coming quickly to Pavia, having assembled everyone he said: "Since I was allowed to reach the threshold of the kingdom by the generosity of the gift from on high, with my enemies vanquished, now it is my intention to commend the Italian kingdom to your fidelity and to go to see my old Burgundian fatherland." To which the Italians soon replied: "If it seems good to you, we are ready."

68. Then, after the departure of King Rudolf, the Veronese, having taken bad advice, plotted against Berengar's life; this did not escape Berengar. A certain Flambert was the author and deviser of

64. Between 947 and 950, under the youthful King Lothar, the larger territorial lordships in the Italian kingdom were overhauled. Hugh's son Humbert lost the duchy of Spoleto to Boniface, member of a local clan, but he retained the margravate of Tuscany. Waldrada was aunt to Adelheid, Otto I's wife, who played a role in Italian politics when Liudprand was writing *Retribution*.

this so cruel crime, someone whom the king had made his spiritual kinsman, since he had taken his son as his godson at the baptismal font. The day before he died he ordered Flambert to come to him;[65] and he said to him:

69. "If until now I had not had many and just reasons to love you, in some way the things they say about you could be believed. They claim you scheme against my life, but I do not believe them. I want you to recall what great advances in fortune and office there have been that you could not have obtained except through my good graces; whence you ought to keep this same spirit toward us, so that my standing may rest assured of your love and fidelity. I do not think anyone's health and fortune was ever as dear to them as your career was to me, a career for which I exerted every effort, act, care, industry, and thought while in this city. Hold onto this one thing as certain: if I shall perceive that you have preserved intact your allegiance to me, my concern for my own health will not be as intense as my gratitude in return for your steadfastness shall be pleasant."

70. Once these things were finished, the king held out to him a gold cup of no small weight and added: "Drink what it contains to my health and love, and keep the container." Truly and without ambiguity, after the drink Satan entered Flambert, just as it is also written about Judas, the betrayer of our Lord Jesus Christ, since "after the morsel, Satan entered into him."[66]

71. Forgetful of his past and present advantages, Flambert passed a sleepless night instigating the people to murder the king.[67] That

65. Presumably April 6, 924. Godparenthood made Berengar and Flambert kinsmen, adding to Flambert's treason. For a recent overview see B. Jussen, *Spiritual Kinship as Social Practice; Godparenthood and Adoption in the Early Middle Ages* (Cranbury, NJ: Associated University Presses, 2000), 15–45. J. Lynch, *Godparents and Kinship in Early Medieval Europe* (Princeton: Princeton University Press, 1986), ranges more widely in geographical and chronological terms.

66. Jn 13.27. Aside from the anti-eucharistic overtones, Flambert is reprehensible because exchanging gifts was a basic mechanism of tenth-century friendship, which he betrayed.

67. Berengar's murder took place on April 7, 924.

night the king, as was his wont, stayed in a very pleasant tiny hut close to the church, not in the palace, which could be defended; and he did not even place any guards that night, suspecting no evil.[68]

> Shaking himself, first the cock
> Crows who awakens
> All mortals; as usual resounds
> And, struck, sings out to God
> That bronze mechanism
> And invites all, teaching well,
> To push back heavy sleep,
> And to give praises quickly to him
> Who gave us life and gave us
> The task of properly seeking out
> Our heavenly fatherland.
> This king seeks the church
> And sings praises to the Lord;
> Flambert, advancing, flies
> And with him a big company
> To kill the good king.
> The king, awake but ignorant of their scheme,
> When he hears the uproar,
> Suspecting nothing, hurries forth
> To see what it is; he sees
> The armed group of soldiers.
> He calls to Flambert from afar,
> "What is this group, my good
> Man? What now does the people want
> With armed men?"
> He answered: "Fear nothing:
> This group rushes not to kill you
> But wants to fight
> With that faction that seeks
> To snatch your soul away."
> Deceived by trust, the king

68. Terence, *Andria* 116.

Hastened into their midst.
Then, captured, he is evilly dragged;
The impious one wounds him from behind
With a sword; he falls, alas! the pious one,
And to his God
Commends his happy soul, piously.[69]

72. Finally, while we fall silent, the stone that is placed before the door of that church, showing to all who pass Berengar's blood, suggests how innocent was the blood they spilled and how perversely the perverse ones acted; indeed it will not vanish, whether scrubbed or sprinkled with any liquid.

73. King Berengar had raised in a generous and familial spirit a certain young man, a hero even, named Milo, quite worthy of memory and praise. If the king had heeded his advice, he would not have experienced all the fates only as adversaries; unless, perchance, it was the suggestion of divine providence, so that he could not do otherwise. For on that very same night when King Berengar was deceived, that youth, having gathered to himself some troops, wanted to set them night watches; but the king, deceived by the assurances of Flambert, not only did not allow Milo to guard him, but actually forcefully forbade it. Thus Milo, as a loyal and upstanding man and mindful of the advantages granted to him by the king, soon took care to avenge bitterly the man whom he could not defend, since he was absent: on the third day after the murder of the king he ordered that Flambert and those who connived in such a wicked crime, taken by force, end their lives by hanging. Clearly, in this man Milo there were several perfect virtues that, if God favors the project, with life accompanying us, will not be shrouded in silence in the right place.

HERE ENDS THE SECOND BOOK OF RETRIBUTION

69. Prudentius was Liudprand's main inspiration for this composition. Berengar here becomes a Christ figure.

Book Three

HERE BEGINS THE THIRD BOOK

1. About the title of this book, and why it is called *RETRIBUTION*.

2. That the Hungarians mangled Italy once Berengar was dead and Rudolf was leaving Italy.

3. A poetic description of the lamentable burning of Pavia.

4. That the sword of God did not utterly destroy Pavia, but his mercy wonderfully freed it from the Hungarians.

5. That it was freed by the merits of Saint Syrus, patron of the city.

6. That the same Saint Syrus, coming to Pavia, by prophetic intuition predicted its affluence and Aquileia's demise.

7. Why Ermengard remained so powerful after the murder of her husband Adalbert.

8. Once King Rudolf had returned from Burgundy, after a little while Ermengard rose in rebellion against him and, along with the Italians, held Pavia.

9. King Rudolf besieges Pavia with an army.

10. That Ermengard, through her craftiness, arranged it so that Rudolf deserted his troops by night and ran away to her.

11. That, having discovered this thing, the morning after, Rudolf's soldiers fled to Milan.

12. The Italians send for Hugh.

13. Rudolf again goes to Burgundy and leads back his father-in-law Burchard to help him.

14. For what reason Burchard set out for Milan, and why, though lavishly received there, his death was agreed upon.

15. Returning from Milan, Burchard reaches Novara, where he is killed by the Italians together with all his men.

16. After Burchard's killing, Rudolf escapes to Burgundy, and Hugh comes to Italy across the Tyrrhenian sea.

17. Several Italians hasten to meet him at Pisa, where also the messengers of Pope John come, by whose encouragement he is made king upon coming to Pavia.

18. About Wido, brother of King Hugh, who then held Tuscany and who had the Roman harlot Marozia as his wife.

was appointed archbishop of Milan and Rather bishop of Verona by King Hugh.

43. How Pope John was captured, taken into custody, and died there, and who was ordained after him; and that Wido died and Lambert was appointed margrave.

44. Marozia invites King Hugh into her bed.

45. About the fortification placed at the entrance of the Roman city, in which King Hugh was received, and from which just a little afterwards he was foully cast by Alberic.

46. That this was done by divine ordination.

47. How and why King Hugh seized his brother Lambert and, following the advice of his brother Boso, to whom he also gave a march, blinded him.

48. King Hugh accepts an oath from King Rudolf and by gifts makes King Henry a friend.

49. Through the invitation of Count Milo and Bishop Rather, Arnulf, duke of the Bavarians, heads for Italy, and King Hugh quickly sets out against him.

50. About the Bavarians killed by King Hugh's soldiers.

51. Why Milo deserted Arnulf and joined King Hugh.

52. Arnulf, having stormed the fortification that was at Verona, returned to Bavaria.

53. About Verona, returned to King Hugh, and about its captured Bishop Rather and his book, written in a quite amusing way.

HERE END THE CHAPTER HEADINGS

HERE BEGINS THE THIRD BOOK, Βιβλος Γ[1]

1. I do not doubt, most holy father, that you wonder quite a bit about the title of this work. Perhaps you say: "Since he demonstrates the deeds of illustrious men, why does he insert the title *Retribution?*" To which I answer: the purpose of this work is this: namely, to depict, make public, and complain about the deeds of this Berengar who nowadays does not so much rule as tyrannize in Italy, and of his wife Willa, who is appropriately called a second Jezebel

1. "Book C."

on account of the immensity of her despotism and a child-eating witch on account of her insatiable desire for robbery. For without a good reason they let loose at me and my house, my lineage and family such great missiles of lies, such great losses of plunder, and such great machinations of impiety, that neither is the tongue capable of uttering them nor the pen of writing them down. Therefore, let this page be *antapódosis*, that is, retribution, when in return for my calamities I will lay bare for present and future generations their την ασεβεῖαν.[2] Nor will it be any less *antapódosis* for some very holy and fortunate men on account of the advantages they extended to me: of those recalled, or about to be recalled, none, or very few, can be found (except one, that is, the impious Berengar)[3] whom my forefathers or I, their offspring, do not have to thank fervently for favors. Finally, that this written booklet was composed εν τη εχμαλοσία, that is, in captivity or peregrination, my present exile demonstrates. Indeed, it was begun in Frankfurt, a place twenty miles distant from Mainz, and up to today it is still being worked on in the island of Paxú, nine hundred and more miles away from Constantinople.[4] But let us get back to the issue.

2. With King Berengar dead and Rudolf absent, under their leader Salard the rage of the Hungarians spread over all Italy, until they surrounded the walls of the Pavian city with an earthwork, and, having planted tents all around, they hindered the citizens' ability to leave.[5] The citizens, deserving this for their sins, could not resist these men, nor assuage them with a gift.[6]

3.
Noble Phoebus, departing from the wet constellation,
As usual begins to climb toward the first constellation of the zodiac,
And to melt the frigid frosts on the hill,[7]

2. "Shameless sacrilege."
3. Liudprand added this clause after the passage's first composition.
4. Paxos is an Ionian island off Epirus. Liudprand seems to have been there in 960, though the reason is unclear.
5. Actually Berengar died a month after the sack.
6. This sack of Pavia occurred on March 12, 924.
7. Virgil, *Georgics* 2.263.

And Aeolus, too, sends his double breath twice;
Then the furious band of Hungarians rejoices
To spread flames in the city, aided by the breezes of Aeolus:
The tiny fire is spread by strong breezes.
Nor are the Hungarians content simply to burn with these flames:
They come from every side and threaten to bring death,
They kill with weapons those terrified by the hot fire.
Once beautiful Pavia burns, unhappy,
And Vulcan, drawing churches into his arms with a breath,
At the same time climbs over the whole fatherland.[8]
Mothers are killed, boys and unmarried girls;[9]
Then the holy band of novices dies;
The holy priest and bishop dies in his city,
That John who by an appropriate nickname is called Good.
The gold that for a long time was closed in chests
Lest an outsider's hand might touch it, now lies scattered
And melts by fire, gushing through the vast sewers.
Once beautiful Pavia burns, unhappy!
You could see shining bowls turned into a rivulet of silver,
Bodies of the ancestors thoroughly burned.
Green jasper, precious, and red topaz
Are spurned, and expensive sapphire and beautiful beryls,
Alas, no merchant now turns his face toward gold.
Once beautiful Pavia burns, unhappy.
Nor does the shiny Ticino save the vast keels with its water,
At the same time the fire spreads through their bilge water.
Once beautiful Pavia has burnt, unhappy,[10]

in the year of the Lord's Incarnation 924, four days before the ides of March, in the twelfth indiction, the sixth day of the week, the third hour. I strongly exhort you and any who read this to uphold, with the love of pious recollection, the memory of those who were burned there.

4. Truly the sword of the very pious and almighty Lord, to whom

8. Liudprand was born in Pavia.
9. Virgil, *Georgics* 4.456–57.
10. In this poem Liudprand included partial citations of Paulinus of Aquileia, Boethius, and Juvenal.

the prophet ascribes mercy and justice and whose mercy fills the earth, did not rage to the point of annihilation. For although the land was burned because of sins that deserved it, still it was not handed over to the enemy; what the prophet-king sang of was fulfilled: "Will God then cast off forever? Or will he never be more favorable again? Or will he cut off his mercy forever, from generation to generation? Or will God forget to show mercy? Or will he in his anger shut up his mercies?"[11] And another prophet says the same thing to him: "When you are angry, you will remember mercy."[12] Indeed the remaining survivors resisted quite manfully against the Hungarians so that they could sing joyously with the prophet: "This is the change of the right hand of the Most High."[13]

5. The glorious intercession of that most holy father of ours and outstanding scholar, Saint SYRUS, whose remains rest in the aforesaid city, aided in this outcome, and gave great help.[14] And lest his prophecy be disproved, the aforesaid city Pavia was struck down but also was mercifully liberated by the Lord. For, after being sent to Pavia to preach by the blessed Hermagoras, disciple of the evangelist Mark, the most holy father honored the city with this prediction, given in a prophetic spirit:

6. "Rejoice in delights, city of Pavia, since exultation will come to you from the mountains outside. In the nearby cities you will not be called small, but abundant." And in order that this prophecy of his be believed more firmly, at the same time he announced the fall of the not unknown city of Aquileia with words to this effect: "Woe to you, Aquileia, since, when you shall be attacked by a band of impious men, you shall be destroyed, nor shall you rise again, rebuilt."[15] Through the testimony of sight the mind discovers that

11. Ps 76.8–10.   12. Hab 3.2.
13. Ps 76.11.

14. Syrus was Pavia's first bishop, before 381. In the ninth century his relics were translated into the cathedral from the suburban church of Sts. Gervase and Protase, signaling his rising importance in local devotions.

15. Aquileia, a flourishing Roman and late antique center in northeastern Italy, declined rapidly in the late fifth century after barbarian incursions. But it was evidently defensible in Liudprand's day: see 2.9, above. *Embassy* 39 shows that Liudprand could be skeptical about such prophecies.

it has turned out this way. For Aquileia, once a very rich and vast city, was taken by that most impious king of the Huns, Attila, and thoroughly demolished and never rose again, as is visible in present times; Pavia, instead, just as that most holy man had said, is both thought to be and called rich: in fact it not only surpasses in wealth all neighboring communities, but also cities located far away. Why do I mention these other places, when Rome itself, celebrated and the most famous city in the whole world, would be inferior to Pavia if it did not have the bodies of the most holy apostles? It is clear, therefore, that Pavia was rescued through the intercession of our most holy patron SYRUS, who honored it with so truthful and precious a prediction. At last, once Pavia was burned and no small booty was taken throughout all Italy, the Hungarians returned to their lands.

7. At that very same time, once Adalbert, margrave of the city of Ivrea, was dead, his wife Ermengard, daughter of the mighty margrave of Tuscany Adalbert and Bertha, obtained primacy in all Italy. The cause of her power was this: that—and it is most hideous even to say it—she exercised carnal transactions with one and all, not just princes, but even with ordinary men.

8. At that time King Rudolf, returning from Burgundy, came to Italy and vigorously seized the kingship, as Berengar was dead. After a few days all the Italians began to disagree among themselves: in fact they were drawn by no small longing on account of Ermengard's beauty in terms of fleshly corruption, especially as she granted sex to some and denied it to others. Whence it came about that the very rich archbishop of Milan and several others favored the faction of King Rudolf; at the same time the same number of rebels arose alongside Ermengard and quite manfully kept the king out of the very capital of the kingdom, Pavia.

9. So it happened that King Rudolf, having assembled troops, headed for Pavia. Once the king had encamped a mile from the city, in that place where the river Ticino comes together with the great river Po—about which Virgil sang these praises: "The Po, king of rivers," and again "The fertility-bearing river Po, sover-

eign over all waters"[16]—as she was quite crafty, at night Ermengard transmitted the following message to King Rudolf, along the banks of the aforementioned river:

10. "If I had wanted to kill you, you would be long dead by now. Indeed, your men all strive to desert you and ardently to join me, if only I wish them to. For you are in places where you would be captured and put in chains if I were only to organize it through some suggestions." The king, not only believing but actually becoming terrified by such statements, replied through messengers he would do whatever she advised. Without delay, the following night King Rudolf, secretly and having eluded all his guards, made up his bed nicely and abandoned his tent, and, having boarded a boat, he deserted his men and headed as quickly as possible to Ermengard.

11. Thereupon, in the morning the soldiers of the king circled his tent in great silence. With princes arriving there, there was no small wonder among them as to why the king should sleep to such an unusually late hour. And when they tried to rouse him with a noise such as the eunuch once made for Holofernes, he gave absolutely no reply, as Holofernes did.[17] Entering and finding nothing in the tent, some cried out that he had been kidnapped, others that he had been killed; however, no one could figure out by any means what the fugitive had done. Truly, as they wavered in their wonderment, a messenger arrived who said that King Rudolf intended to attack them, along with their enemies. And they, suddenly bewildered in their spirits, began to leave with such a swift movement that if you had seen them you would have said they did not run but actually flew.

12. And when they reached Milan, that is, a protected place, with the consent of all Archbishop Lambert sent to Hugh, most powerful and wise count of the Provençals, the message that he should come to Italy and should snatch the kingdom from Rudolf

16. *Georgics* 1.482 and *Aeneid* 8.77.

17. The Assyrian general whom Judith decapitated, as related in the biblical book of Judith.

and powerfully take hold of it for himself.[18] For he had himself
for a long time been weighing, through many debates, whether he
might perchance be able to obtain the kingdom of Italy. For this
man also in the time of the aforementioned King Berengar had
come to Italy with many men; but since his time for ruling had not
yet come, he was scared and chased off by Berengar.

13. At last Rudolf, since he could not overcome his previously
mentioned adversaries on account of the infidelity of his men,
went to Burgundy and asked Burchard, duke of the Swabians,
whose daughter he had married, to come to his aid;[19] the duke,
having gathered troops, quickly set out for Italy. And when they
reached Ivrea, Burchard addressed Rudolf in this way:

14. "It will not seem senseless if I depart for Milan myself with
the pretext of a message; and on this occasion I will be able to
reconnoiter the city and learn their intentions." Finally departing,
as soon as he reached Milan, before he entered the city, he turned
aside to the church of the blessed and precious martyr Lawrence to
pray; but actually, as some say, not so much to pray as to do something else. For they say—as the church is close to the city, built
with wondrous and precious craftsmanship—he wanted to build a
fortification there in which he was determined to imprison not just
the Milanese but many princes of Italy. And so exiting from there,
as he rode along the wall of the city, he spoke to his men in his
own language, that is, in German, as follows: "I am not Burchard if
I do not make all the Italians use only one spur and ride a shapeless
mare.[20] I esteem as nothing the strength of this wall of theirs and
its height, by which they count on protecting themselves. I will cast

18. Being related to the Bosonid king of Italy Louis (above, 2.36–41), and having
acted as his loyal agent in Provence (even supporting Louis after his blinding), Hugh
of Provence, or of Arles, had claimed the Italian throne since 920. He had opposed
Rudolf's rise to power in Burgundy, and after 924, with Rudolf in difficulty in Italy,
Hugh's military intervention seemed logical.

19. In early 926. He had married Bertha in 922 as part of a truce with the Burgundians (2.60, above).

20. Splendid horses, skillful riding, and aristocratic virility went together. Liudprand's Burchard is thus being as insulting as possible.

my adversaries down from the wall, dead, with a blow of my spear." He said this since he thought that no one of his enemies was present who knew his language. Actually a certain man was there, by Burchard's bad luck, who, though ragged and despised, nevertheless knew the language and quickly reported all these things to Archbishop Lambert. Lambert, who had a sharp mind, did not treat Burchard rudely, but admirably honored him while suspecting him of having evil intentions; indeed, among other things he granted the duke this, almost by the privilege of love: that he might hunt any stag in Lambert's hunting preserve, something he never granted to any save great and very dear friends. Meanwhile Lambert incited all the Pavians and several of the princes of Italy to kill Burchard; and he only detained Burchard until he felt hopeful that it was possible to assemble all who were supposed to kill him.

15. Thus it happened that Burchard, leaving Milan, reached Novara the same day. And when the night had passed and he rose from bed heading for Ivrea, suddenly there appeared the Italian phalanxes rushing against him; he did not turn against them like a warlike man, but he soon took flight. And since he could not escape the end that had been ordained for him, according to Job's sentence,[21] and since "vain is the horse for safety,"[22] his horse, tripping up, threw him into the ditch that circles the walls of the city. There, also pierced by pressing Ausonian spears, he exchanged death for life.[23] His men, seeing this scene, since they could not do otherwise, fled into the church of Christ's most holy confessor Gaudentius. The Ausonians, however, indignant and inflamed quite a bit by Burchard's threats, broke down the church doors and killed all whom they discovered in there, even under the very altar.

16. When Rudolf heard of this, he left Italy and very hastily went to Burgundy. And while these things were happening, Hugh, count of Arles and of the Provençals, boarded a ship and hastened

21. An allusion to Jb 14.5.

22. Ps 32.17.

23. April 29, 926. Following Virgil, Liudprand calls the inhabitants of north-central Italy by their archaic name.

to Italy across the Tyrrhenian sea. For God, who desired him to rule in Italy, in a short time by favorable breezes led him to Alphea—that is, Pisa, which is the capital of the Tuscan province, about which Virgil said, "Pisa, at its origin Alphea."[24]

17. And when he arrived there, the messenger of the Roman pope, that is, of John of Ravenna, was present; and also present were messengers from almost all the Italians who by all means invited him to rule over them. That man, therefore, since he had yearned for this for a long time, came quickly to Pavia and took the kingship, with all assenting. After a little while he went to Mantua, where Pope John, too, hastening to meet him, drew up a treaty with him.

18. At that time, with the mother of this same King Hugh dead, her son Wido, whom she had with Adalbert, as we said above, held the Tuscan march;[25] and Wido took the Roman harlot Marozia as his wife.

19. King Hugh was of no smaller wisdom than boldness, nor of smaller strength than craftiness; also a worshiper of God and a lover of those who love holy religion, solicitous for the needs of the poor, very caring toward churches; he not only loved but also deeply honored religious and philosophical men. Hugh was a man, though, who, even if he shone with virtues, besmirched them through his passion for women.

20. He took a wife of Frankish and German descent named Alda, who gave him a son by the name of Lothar. In those same times, from a certain very noble woman called Wandelmoda, he also had a son named Hubert, who is still alive and now is a mighty prince of the Tuscan province, whose deeds, God willing, will be explained in the appropriate place.

21. Once Hugh was ordained king, like a prudent man he began to send his messengers everywhere throughout all lands and to seek the friendship of many kings and princes, especially the very famous King Henry, who, as we said above, ruled over the Bavar-

24. *Aeneid* 10.179. Count Hugh added Italy to his Provençal possessions, 926–947.
25. 2.55, above.

ians, Swabians, Lotharingians, Franks, and Saxons.[26] This Henry also subjugated the countless Slavic people and made it tributary to himself; also, he was the first who subjugated the Danes and compelled them to serve him, and through this he made his name renowned among many nations.

22. Thus King Hugh, when he had made friends of the neighboring kings and princes, strove to make his name known among the Achaeans living far from us.[27] In those times the emperor Romanos, quite worthy of memory and praise, ruled them, a generous man, human, prudent, and pious, to whom Hugh sent my father as a messenger, both on account of his upright morals and of the smoothness of his speech.[28]

23. When my father reached him, among the various things that King Hugh sent as gifts to the emperor Romanos he included two dogs of a kind never seen before in that region. These two, when they were led before the emperor, would certainly have mangled him with their bites if the arms of many had not restrained them. And I think it was because, when they saw the emperor covered in a tunic after the Greek fashion and dressed in an unusual costume, they thought he was not a man but some monster.[29]

24. At last he was welcomed with great honors by the same emperor; nor was this so much because of the novelty of the thing or the grandiosity of the gifts as it was because, when my aforementioned father reached Thessalonica,[30] certain Slavs, who were rebels against the emperor Romanos and were depopulating his land, fell upon him; but truly it happened by the mercy of God that two of their leaders were taken alive after many had been killed. When he presented the prisoners to the emperor, the latter was filled with

26. 2.20, above.

27. An archaic name for Greeks, by which Liudprand means Byzantines.

28. For the accession of Romanos I Lakapenos, see 2.45, above. Liudprand's father traveled in 927.

29. An early warning of Liudprand's distaste for Byzantine fashions, most evident in the *Embassy*.

30. An important port in the northern Aegean Sea, an obvious stopping point on the route between Italy and Constantinople.

great glee and, my father, having received a great gift from him, returned happy to King Hugh, who had sent him there. After his return, only a few days having passed, seized by sickness, he sought a monastery and put on the habit of holy conversion; he died wearing it, after fifteen days, forsaking me, a small boy, and passed on to the Lord. Now, however, since the emperor Pομανος[31] was mentioned, it does not seem senseless to me to insert something here about who he was and how he reached the imperial office.

25. In the reign of Leo, father of the present emperor Constantine, that emperor Pομανος, although πτοχος,[32] was considered χρησιμος[33] by all. He came from one of those lowly families that took pay from the emperor for naval battles; since he often and repeatedly εις την μαχην[34] rendered several χρησιμοτατα,[35] at length he deserved to be made ετημιθη, ὁπως προτοκαραβος[36] by his commanding officer. On a certain night, when he went to spy on the Saracens and in that place there was quite a big swamp and reed bed, it happened that a very ferocious lion leapt from the reeds and mired a multitude of deer in the swamp and seized one of them and with it mitigated the ravenous rage of its stomach. Pομανος δε τον ἁυτων ψοφον ακουων εδειλιασεν σφοδρα,[37] for he thought it was a horde of Saracens who, having noted him, wanted to kill him off by some trick. Arising ορθρου δε βαθεως[38] when he very carefully thought through everything, having studied the remains he recognized ἐυθέως[39] what it had been. Since the lion was hiding in the reed bed, Pομανος ordered that Greek fire be shot throughout the reed bed, which cannot be extinguished by any liquid except vinegar.[40] Within the reed bed, however, there was a hillock full of reeds, and by escaping onto it the lion was saved

31. Romanos.   32. "Poor."
33. "Useful."   34. "In battle."
35. "Services."   36. "Honored."
37. "Romanos, hearing their noise, was terrified."
38. "Very early."
39. "Immediately."
40. Greek fire, a petroleum-based combustible substance, was a "secret weapon" of the Byzantine navy.

from the fire. In fact, the wind, spreading the fire in the opposite direction, removed it from the area, preventing it from reaching as far as this hillock. So after the fire was out, Ρομανος, criss-crossing the whole site with only one servant, holding only a sword in his right hand and in his left hand a cloak, checked to see if by chance he might find a bone of the lion or any trace of it. Indeed, as he was at the point when he could go back, as he had found nothing, he decided to see by what prodigy it happened that the hillock had been spared by the fire. And when the two fellows sat down nearby and were chatting about many things among themselves, the lion only heard them, as it could not see because of its watering eyes παρα τῶ καπνω.[41] And as the lion desired to spew forth onto them the rage of its spirit, which it had conceived because of the fire, with a very quick leap toward where it heard their voices, it appeared in their midst. Romanos was not quaking like his servant, but rather evaluating the situation in his mind, so that, even if the world should fall apart, the wreckage would leave him fearless;[42] he cast the cloak that he held in his left hand between the paws of the lion. And while the lion tore it to shreds as if it were a person, Romanos struck it from behind with his sword with all his strength, between the joints of the hindquarters; and since the lion could not stand with disjointed and divided legs, it slowly fell. Once the lion was dead, Romanos saw his servant prostrate on the ground, half dead, and he began to call him with a loud voice; but as he gave no response at all, the same Romanos stood next to him, and, kicking him with his foot, "Ἔγειρε," ειπεν, "ἀθλιε κἀ ταλεπορε, μη φοβοῦ!"[43] Upon rising, when he saw the immensity of the lion, he was breathless with admiration. Ἐξεπλισσοντο δὲ πάντες πέρι τοῦ Ρομανοῦ τάυτα ακουσαντες;[44] whence a little afterwards it came about that, both for other deeds and for this outstanding deed, very great honor was accorded to him by the emperor Leo,

41. "On account of the smoke."
42. Horace, *Odes* 3.3.7–8.
43. "'Get up,' he said, 'you wretched and miserable one, fear not!'"
44. "They marveled, all who heard of these exploits of Romanos."

οπως παντα τὰ πλοια[45] were entrusted to Romanos's hands and obeyed his orders.[46]

26. At last Leo, most pious emperor of the Greeks, about whom we made mention above, paying the debt of his human body and entering the path of all flesh, left his brother Alexander as heir to his kingdom, along with his son Constantine, who now lives and happily rules, who was then still small and, as the Greeks say, αλα- λον.[47] To them, to mind the palace and protect the family property, he entrusted a eunuch in the position of head of the imperial bed- chamber, as the custom is there, and he made Phocas δομεστικον μεγαν, that is, commander of the land forces. He, however, ap- pointed Romanos δελονγαρην της πλοως, that is, commander of the naval forces, despite the fact that he had not arisen of noble stock, but because of the generosity of his heart. Alexander died a little after this and left the empire to little Constantine alone.[48] Fi- nally, at the time when the great Emperor Leo moved on to Christ, the aforesaid commander Phocas, general of the land army, led the troops against King Symeon of the Bulgarians, who wanted to come to Constantinople, and repulsed him quite manfully.[49] Romanos, who was not foolish, was not at all far from the city with the naval forces when he heard of the emperors' deaths—that is, Leo's and Alexander's—and, having assembled the ships, he came to a small island near Constantinople, located so that it could almost be seen from the Great Palace. He hardly ever crossed over, however, to the palace and almost never sang the customary praises to the *porphy- rogenitus*.[50] This behavior caused no small fear and bewilderment to

45. "So that all the ships."

46. Lions were royal animals, and hunting them was the prerogative of kings in the Near East. In Europe such animals were known through literature and art.

47. "Not speaking."

48. Alexander was co-emperor with Leo VI, his brother, after 879, but ruled alone for just over a year, 912–13. Though Leo's son Constantine was titular emperor after 908, Alexander's coinage ignored him.

49. The Bulgarian tsar Symeon (893–927) successfully campaigned in the Balkans against the empire. Liudprand recalls his attack of 913 against Constantinople, which won him Byzantine recognition of his imperial status.

50. *Porphyrogenitus*: see 1.6–7.

the eunuch who was head of the imperial bedchamber and to all the Constantinopolitan magnates; so by intermediaries they asked what this portent might be, that Romanos did not attend to the king and render the due praises. Romanos answered these messengers that he avoided the palace because he feared for his life; and he added that if the head of the imperial bedchamber along with the other magnates did not come to him and promise with an oath to preserve his life and honor, he would soon hand himself over to the king of the Cretan Saracens, who would defeat the kingdom of the Argives by the vigor of his aid.[51] The outcome of the episode will prove how astutely he spoke these words. For, impelled by fear and ignoring that a snake lurked in the grass,[52] all the magnates we spoke of before went trustingly to visit him, seeking graciously to do what he demanded. He, having formed a good plan, cast them all into the ship's hold and bound them; and, feeling confident on account of this, he hastened to the city with a large retinue. He purged the palace of those whom he considered suspicious, and put there, in their places, the supporters of his cause. He made his own men the rector, generals, patricians, the prefect, the financial minister, wardrobe-keepers, chamberlains, first swordsmen, swordsmen, swordsmen-in-training, and naval overseers. The rest, as we said, he deposed. And he joined himself in sexual sweetness with the mother of the *porphyrogenitus*, named Zoe, so as to secure even more firmly the work he had undertaken.[53] The whole city was soon decked out in crowns, and Romanos was called "father of the emperor"[54] by everyone.

27. Meanwhile, what had been done by Romanos was announced

51. Liudprand sometimes used archaic names for "Greeks"; here he thereby belittled Byzantine imperial pretensions. Crete fell to Arab attacks in the 820s, and until its reconquest in 961 served as a launching pad for raids throughout the Aegean.

52. Virgil, *Bucolics* 3.93.

53. Alexander had expelled Zoe (widow of Leo VI, mother of Constantine VII) from the palace upon his accession. Oddly, given his interest in female authority, Liudprand overlooks Zoe's years as regent (914–19). Leo Phocas, like Zoe a member of the highest Byzantine aristocracy, was her essential supporter, and his defeats by Tsar Symeon caused Zoe's downfall.

54. In effect, a regent.

to the domestic Phocas, who was at that time fighting the Bulgarians and who himself ardently desired to be made father of the emperor, and who was just then obtaining a triumph in war over the enemy. He immediately became dejected in spirit and afflicted by great anguish, and he cast down the sign of victory with which he was chasing the enemies, turned his back, and made his men take flight. The Bulgarians then restored their spirits through Symeon's exhortation, and those who at first, with Mars contrary to them, had fled, now, with the war god turned favorable, did the chasing; and such a great massacre of Achaeans took place that the field was seen to be full of bones for a long time afterwards.

28. With all possible haste the aforementioned Phocas, the domestic, returned to Constantinople and wanted to enter the palace, and he strove to become "father of the emperor" by force if not by craft. But since, as Horace says, "force, deprived of wise counsel, collapses under its own weight," and "the gods advance a tempered force,"[55] he was captured by Romanos and deprived of both eyes. No small force of Bulgarians arose, and doubly paid back the Greeks through a depopulating raid.

29. And they used to say Symeon was half-Greek, on account of the fact that since his boyhood he had learned the rhetoric of Demosthenes and the logic of Aristotle in Byzantium.[56] Afterwards, however, having abandoned his studies of the arts, as they relate, he put on the habit of holy living. Truly, deceived by his lust for power, a little later he passed from the placid quiet of the monastery to the tempest of this world, and preferred to follow Julian the Apostate rather than the most blessed Peter, the heavenly kingdom's doorkeeper. He has two sons, one named Baianus, and the other, who is still alive and powerfully leads the Bulgarians, by the name of Peter.[57] They report that Baianus learned magic, so that

55. *Odes*, 3.4.65–67.

56. Symeon the Great studied at the Magnaura school in Constantinople before 886. The death of his elder brother Vladimir, Boris I's heir, caused him to abandon monasticism in 893 and assume power.

57. Tsar Peter I (c. 927–69). Unlike his father he sought conciliation with Byzantium.

you could see him quickly transform himself from man to wolf or any other beast.

30. Moreover, Romanos, in the same year during which he was made "father of the emperor," gave his daughter Helena as a wife to his small imperial lord Constantine Porphyrogenitus.[58] I call any *porphyrogenitus* who is born in the house called Porphyra, as we wrote above, and not who is born into a purple cloth. And as this matter came up here, it will not be displeasing to relate again what we heard about the birth of this Porphyrogenitus, just as you will find it also written in the earlier book with the same words, under chapters 6, 7, 8, 9, 10.

31. The august emperor Constantine, from whose name emerged the name of the city Constantinople, ordered τὸν οικον τουτον[59] to be built, on which he imposed the name Porphyra; and he desired the lineage of his noble progeny to see the light there, in such a way that any who were born from his stock would be called by the magnificent name of Porphyrogenitus. Whence several people claim that also this Constantine, son of the emperor Leo, traces his origin from his blood. Της γενεσεως δὲ αυτοῦ η αληθεῖα αυτῆ εστην.[60]

32. The august emperor Basil, his forefather, was born into a humble family in Macedonia and went down to Constantinople under the yoke of poverty so as to serve a certain abbot. Therefore, the emperor Michael, who ruled at that time, when he went to pray at that monastery where Basil served, saw him standing apart from all others in shapeliness and quickly called the abbot so that he would give him that boy; taking him into the palace, he gave him the office of chamberlain. And then, after a little while he was given so much power that he was called "the other emperor" by everyone. Truly, as almighty God visits just censure on his servants wherever he wants, he did not allow this emperor to be of sound mind to the end, so that the one he more heavily tested in this low-

58. In May 919.
59. "This very house."
60. "This is the truth about his birth." This phrase does not appear in 1.7, above.

ly world he may more mercifully recompense in the heavens. For, as is related, at the time of his fits he ordered even his intimates to undergo the death sentence; but, returning to his senses, he wanted them restored so that unless those he had ordered killed returned, those who had done it would be condemned with a matching sentence. With this fear, those he ordered condemned were spared. But when he did this often and repeatedly to Basil, the latter accepted the following advice—how hideous!—from his servants: "Lest by chance the insane order of the king be carried out one day by the zeal of those who dislike you or feel hatred, instead kill him and take the imperial scepter." This he carried out without delay, partly impelled by fear, partly deceived by lust for power. And so, after he was killed, Basil was made emperor.

33. Then, once a little time had passed, our Lord Jesus Christ appeared to him in a vision, holding the right hand of the lord emperor whose murderer he was, and addressing him thus: "Basil, for what reason did you kill your lord Emperor Michael?" Awakened, he realized he was guilty of a great crime, and, barely returning to his senses, he pondered what he should do about this.

34. And then, comforted by the healthful and truly acceptable promise of our Lord through the prophet, that on whatever day the sinner repents he shall be saved, with tears and moans he confessed to being a sinner, a spiller of innocent blood. Having accepted good advice, he made friends for himself by the mammon of iniquity so that he might be freed from the eternal fire of hell through the prayers of those whom he had consoled in this world with material subsidies. He built close to and to the east of the palace, with precious and marvelous workmanship, a church in honor of the archangel Michael, prince of the highest and heavenly militia, who is called *archistrategos* in Greek, meaning "leader of the militia." This church some call Nean, or "new," and others Ennean, which may be rendered "the church of nine-times" in our language, because there a machine for keeping the liturgical hours sounds when struck with nine taps.

35. Thus in the second year after Romanos was appointed "fa-

ther of the emperor," having summoned the magnates to himself, he spoke in this way: "Nobles of the Roman authority, since I was not only appointed 'father of the emperor,' but even associated with the most holy emperor's trust by the marriage of my gray-eyed daughter Helena through your decision, I judge myself worthy to show on my body some sign of imperial decoration so that I may be celebrated by the foreign peoples through the name of this dignity." It was judged and then declared by the unanimous counsel of the people that, since he had such great authority and had joined his *leucolenon*[61] Helena to the imperial dignity, he should use the red suede shoes which until today it is the custom of emperors to use; but not even that seemed enough to him. Therefore, a year later, since then his power was greater, he addressed the same magnates with words like these: "Since by your unanimous decision it was agreed for me to use the imperial shoes, περιφανέστατοι ηρωαις,[62] the kindnesses which by your authority you bestowed upon me appear to be αγλαα απινα;[63] but, more carefully considering things, I seemed to myself to make my entrance in the manner of actors and mimes who paint themselves with various colors so that they may easily induce the masses to laughter. In the end I move to laughter not just others but myself, too, when I am seen imitating the emperor with my feet and the common populace with my head; for what comedy, what mime could be better? Therefore, either offer me the crown or deprive me of the imperial shoes by which I am rendered ridiculous before the people." Having said this plainly enough, especially since he outstripped everyone in the authority of his power, by the verdict of all he received the crown and did not lose the honor of the shoes.[64] Let no one marvel at his prudence, but let him give praise to God from his deepest heart, who "lifts up them that are cast down, who looses

---

61. A Greek word that Liudprand transcribed in Latin letters, meaning "white-armed."

62. "You noble heroes."

63. "Precious gifts."

64. Romanos's investiture took place on December 17, 920.

them that are fettered . . . for in the hand of the Lord there is a cup of strong wine full of mixture, and he pours out from this to that."[65]

36. This man was of a lowly family, and originated from the nation of the Armenians, and never did he dream that one day he alone would be in the royal hall, and even less that he would hold the royal scepter. But what does the prophet Hannah say? "The Lord makes poor and makes rich, he humbles and he exalts, he raises up the needy from the dust, and lifts up the poor from the dunghill, so that he may sit with the princes and hold the throne of glory. For the poles of the earth are the Lord's."[66] Therefore, let honor and glory through all the centuries of centuries go to God alone, immortal and invisible. Amen.

37. At length, once Romanos was emperor, he appointed as co-emperor Christopher, whom he had had before assuming the imperial authority. But after his elevation to the emperorship his wife bore him a son called Stephen; and soon, having conceived a fetus, she bore him another named Constantine. Appointing all of them emperors, he accorded to himself and his eldest son Christopher more honor than even to his emperor, lord Constantine Porphyrogenitus, against law and decency; for it was clear when they were processing *is tin prolempsin*, that is, in public, to Haghia Sophia or to the Blachernai Palace or to the Church of the Holy Apostles, when Romanos and his eldest son would go first, Constantine Porphyrogenitus and the other two sons would follow. Exactly how the just Judge took this as improper, his later vengeance will show:[67] for after a little while Christopher died. Thereupon Constantine Porphyrogenitus, when he was done with his prayers and readings, commended himself wholly to the Lord, earning his keep by the work of his hands: certainly he used to execute τὴν ζογραφιαν[68] very beautifully.

38. At that same time the Bulgarian Symeon began vigorously

---

65. Ps 145.7–8; 74.8–9.   66. 1 Sm 2.7–8.
67. See 5.22–23, below.   68. "Painting."

to afflict the Argives.[69] Romanos, having given the daughter of his son Christopher as a wife for Symeon's son Peter,[70] who is still alive, restrained him from the rampage he had launched, and allied him to himself with a treaty. Whence the girl was called Irini, by a changed name, because through her a very solid peace was established between Bulgarians and Greeks.[71]

39. In those times Walpert and Gezo, whose first name was Heverard, were very powerful judges in Pavia.[72] The reason for Walpert's power was this: that he had made his son Peter bishop in that very wealthy place, Como, and joined his daughter Roza in marriage to the count of the palace Gislebert. At that same time both Peter and Gislebert had died. All the people of Ticino, that is, the Pavians, had come to Walpert and were debating all cases and controversies before him. In addition, mindful of his share of the power, Gezo, whose first name was Heverard, because he was joined to him by a certain affinity, was regarded as the powerful one; but Gezo spoiled his own nobility by his wicked ways. For he was very ambitious, avid, envious, seditious, a corrupter of the law, forgetful of God's teachings—something which God does not tolerate without vengeance; and, lest I drag out my speech any longer, Gezo was in every way similar to Catiline and, just as Catiline was trying to kill the consul and defender of the Roman Republic Cicero, similarly this Gezo schemed to put King Hugh to death.[73]

---

69. Symeon exploited Byzantine political turmoil during the second decade of the 900s, after Romanos I's accession, by pursuing his attack. Romanos tried to restrain him by creating a coalition of Balkan powers, but it had limited success.

70. Irene Lekapena married Peter in 927, as part of the new Bulgarian policy of détente that also obtained land, tribute, ecclesiastical independence, and an imperial title.

71. Her name means "peace" in Greek, though she had been christened Maria.

72. Since Lombard times Pavia had been the preeminent center of legal studies in Latin Europe. By the tenth century, judges trained there administered royal justice throughout the Po basin: F. Bougard, "Public Power and Authority," in *Italy in the Early Middle Ages*, ed. C. La Rocca (Oxford: Oxford University Press, 2002), 50–53.

73. The Roman aristocrat Catiline organized an unsuccessful coup against the Roman Republic in 62 B.C. His fame, disproportionate to his significance, derived from Cicero and Sallust's eloquent accounts of his deeds.

certain day, while King Hugh, suspecting no evil, stayed
with a few followers, this Gezo, having organized a re-
... nted to rush upon him; but with Walpert, who was not of
... savage spirit, lagging behind, the plan was postponed.

40. Nor did King Hugh play a lesser role in restraining them
from the rampage they had launched with his rhetorical and honey-
sweet praises. For when he learned that a revolt against him had
broken out and the rebels had assembled in the house of Walpert, through intermediaries he addressed them all with a speech like
this: "Why, O strong men, are you so suddenly aroused against
your lord, your king, even? If something was done that displeased
you, let it be compensated for. For it is not usual that a late correction is despised, especially if no negligence has been overlooked."
Having heard these words, all the rebels mitigated their wrath. Only
Gezo remained, clinging to the original wickedness, and urged that
all should rush upon the king and torment him with a most dishonorable death; but truly, with God disposing it thus, his wicked
desire could not take effect. Once the messengers returned to the
king, they related exactly what they had seen and heard.

41. Therefore, King Hugh mulled over all these events in his
subtle mind while pretending they were insignificant. Having left
Pavia, he hastened to go far away, and, having sent around written
orders, he instructed his soldiers to come to him. Among them
came the mighty count Samson, who was especially hostile to the
aforesaid Gezo. When he saw the king, he spoke to him thus: "I
observe that you are worried by the things that were done against
you in the city, tumultuously and harmfully, during these past days;
truly, if you listen to and obey me, they shall be caught in their
own nets. Another man who could give you better advice than I
could not easily be found; certainly no one will hand them over to
you more skillfully. I ask only one thing: namely, that, when they
have been captured by my endeavors, Gezo be given over into my
hands with his whole entourage." When he heard that Gezo would
indeed be surrendered by the king, he added: "Leo, the bishop
of the city of the Ticinans, is not a friend of Walpert and Gezo:

clearly they oppose him by all means whenever they can. You know it to be the custom for the greater citizens to come out of the city to welcome the king arriving in Pavia from other parts. Therefore, send a message secretly to the bishop so that, when you shall come to Pavia at the appointed time, and they shall advance toward you from the city, he have all the gateways of the city closed and keep the keys himself. In this way, when we begin to capture them, they may neither flee back into the city nor expect any help from within it." And this was done. For when the king headed towards Pavia at the appointed time and the aforementioned people went out toward him, the bishop obligingly did as he had been instructed; then the king ordered all to be captured, as Samson had advised. Thereupon, with Gezo quickly handed over to Samson, he was deprived of both eyes, and the tongue with which he had spoken blasphemies against the king was cut out. O, how well done if he had lived out all his time as a blind man, and mute! But—O wickedness!—he did not lose his speech with his tongue cut out, and, as in the fables of the Greeks, by the removal of his eyes he extended his life, so that until the present day he has not faltered in many wickednesses. We insert here, exactly as it is, a fable, indeed a joke, about why blind people live long, according to the clumsiness of the Greeks: Ζευς καὶ Ηρα ηρισαν περι αφροδισιῶν, της πλειονα ἐχει ηδομας εν τη συννουσία, και τότε Τιρεσίαν Εβρου υιον εἰήτησαν. Ὀυτος γὰρ εν ταις αμφοτέραις φύσεσοι μεταμορφώθη επιδι δράκοντα επατησεν. Ὀυτος οὖν κατα της Ηρας απεφκυνατο, καὶ Ηρα οργισθεῖσα ἐπήρωσεν αυτὸν, Ζευς δὲ εχαρίσατο ἀυτῶ πολοῖς ζῆσαι ετεσι, και ὀσα ελεγεν μαντικα λεγειν.[74] But let us get back to the issue. Once Gezo had been severed from his organs, as we said above, his wealth was seized; most

---

74. This is Liudprand's longest Greek passage: "Zeus and Hera disagreed about love, specifically, about who had more pleasure in sex, women or men. And then they inquired of Tiresias, son of Everes. For he had already been transformed into both genders, since he had stepped upon a dragon. He therefore pronounced against Hera, and she, angered, blinded him. So Zeus gave him the gift of living for many years and that everything he should pronounce, he should pronounce as an accurate prophecy."

of the other men were handed over to guards; Walpert was quickly beheaded; his boundless treasure was scattered; his wife Cristina was seized and tormented with various tortures so that she hand over the hidden treasures. From this time there grew great fear of the king not only at Pavia but throughout the territories of Italy; nor was this one treated as a nonentity, like other kings, but was honored in every way.[75]

42. At that same time Hilduin, bishop of the church of Lüttich, expelled from his rightful see, came to Italy to King Hugh, to whom he was related by family lineage; and he was honorably received by him, and the king granted him the Veronese bishopric for his sustenance. It happened, however, that after a little while Archbishop Lambert died, and this Hilduin was ordained bishop of Milan in his place.[76] There also came a certain monk called Rather along with this Hilduin, who, on account of his religious observance and knowledge of the seven liberal arts, was appointed bishop of Verona, a city where Milo was count, as we stated above.[77]

43. Meanwhile Wido, margrave of the Tuscan province, along with his wife Marozia, began fervently to plot the expulsion of Pope John, and this on account of the envy they felt for Peter, the pope's brother, since the pope honored him as his own brother. It happened that, with Peter residing in Rome, Wido had secretly gathered many soldiers; and so on a certain day, when the pope was at the Lateran Palace with a few others and his brother, the troops of Wido and Marozia, rushing upon them, killed his brother Peter in front of the pope's eyes, and, seizing the pope, they locked him up in custody, where he died not much later: for they claim that they placed a cushion over his mouth by which they most wick-

75. This episode underlines the autonomy and authority of royal judges in the tenth-century Italian kingdom, as well as Liudprand's ideas of how proper subordination could be reinstated.

76. Hilduin (†936) lost his bishopric in 921, caught in a power struggle between western and eastern Frankish kings. Lüttich was strategically important because close to Aachen, the Carolingian "capital."

77. The prolific writer and polemicist Rather of Verona (†974), formerly a Lotharingian monk, was one of Liudprand's literary role models.

edly suffocated him. Once he was dead, they appointed John, the son of this same Marozia, as pope, whom that prostitute had conceived with Pope Sergius.[78] Wido died a little later, and his brother Lambert was ordained his successor.

44. After the death of her husband Wido, Marozia, a quite shameless harlot, sent her messengers to King Hugh and invited him to come to her and take for himself the most noble city of Rome; and she affirmed that it could not be done in any other way unless King Hugh made her his bride.[79]

> Why, Marozia, do you rage, urged on by Venus's stings?
> Now you expect the sweetness of your spouse's brother
> And to marry two brothers, equaling Herodias.[80]
> You are blind, forgetful of John's teachings
> Who forbade brothers to violate brothers' spouses!
> The songs of the prophet Moses do not support you
> That ordered the brother to take the brother's wife
> If the first one could not engender a son:
> Our times know you to have borne offspring to your husband.[81]
> I know you will retort: "Venus, drunk, cares not a whit for this."
> Now there comes, like a desired bull led to you under yoke,
> King Hugh, moved more by the Roman city.
> What does it profit you, O wicked woman, to ruin such a holy man?
> While you hope through such a great crime to seem a queen,
> Actually you shall lose great Rome, with God judging you.

Even insensate creatures, not just the sentient, can tell that this actually happened this way.

78. Peter's murder took place in 928; John X earned Marozia and Wido's enmity through his alliance with King Hugh. He died in 929.

79. Though Marozia earned Liudprand's repeated jibes (2.48, 3.18, and here), her tough-minded and wily marital policy gave her public standing in Rome and secured her children's inheritance. Alberic's successes in Rome (3.46) were exactly what Marozia had sought to achieve through her serial monogamy. See P. Skinner, *Women in Medieval Italian Society, 500–1200* (London: Pearson Educational, 2001), 105–6.

80. Sister-in-law and concubine of Herod Antipas, who obtained John the Baptist's execution: see Mk 6.14–20.

81. A reference to Bertha, a daughter whom Marozia bore to Wido of Tuscany.

45. At the entrance of the Roman city there is a certain fortification, built with wondrous craft and of wondrous strength; before its gateway there is built a very precious bridge across the Tiber, which can be crossed by those coming to and departing from Rome, and there is no other route except across it.[82] No crossing, however, can be made unless with the permission of those guarding the fortification. And so that I may leave out the other things, this fortification has such great height that the church visible on its summit, built in honor of the heavenly militia's highest captain, the archangel Michael, is called the Church of the Holy Angel in the Skies. At length the king, having left his army far away because of the security of this fortification, came to Rome with a few men; received there in a respectable fashion by the Romans, he retired to the bed of the prostitute Marozia in the fortification mentioned just now. When he had enjoyed her impure desires, he began to despise the Romans as if he were secure. Actually Marozia had a son by the name of Alberic whom she had generated with Margrave Alberic; and when Alberic, at his mother's request, was pouring water so that King Hugh, his stepfather, that is, could wash his hands, he was hit in the face by him as a reprimand because he would not pour the water moderately and carefully. Therefore this man, so that he might avenge the offense against himself, gathered together the Romans and addressed them with a speech like this: "The dignity of the Roman city is led to such depths of stupidity that it now obeys the command of a prostitute. For what is more lurid and what is more debased than that the city of Rome should perish by the impurity of one woman, and the one-time slaves of the Romans, the Burgundians, I mean, should rule the Romans? If he hits my face, that is, the face of his stepson, and, what is more, when he is a recently arrived guest, what do you think he will do to you as soon as he has settled in? Do you perhaps not know of the voracity and haughtiness of the Burgundians? Pay attention

82. The Roman emperor Hadrian's mausoleum was fortified in late antiquity and served as the main papal fortress, also because it dominated the main urban crossing point on the Tiber, Ponte S. Angelo.

simply to the etymology of their name: indeed the Burgundians are called that since the Romans, after having conquered the world and having led off many captives from that nation, ordered them to erect houses for themselves outside the city, from which they were expelled a little later by the Romans because of their haughtiness; and, as they call a group of houses which is not enclosed by a wall 'a burg,' they were called Burgundians by the Romans, meaning 'those expelled from the burg.' They are called by their natural name by others, that is, Allobrogian Gauls. But I, according to my own lights, call them Burgundians as if they were Gurglians either because they speak entirely gutturally because of their haughtiness or—and this is more likely—because of their gluttony, exercised through their greedy gullets, which they strenuously indulge." Without delay, after hearing these words, all abandoned King Hugh and elected this Alberic as their lord; and, lest King Hugh have an opportunity for mobilizing his soldiers, they quickly began to attack the fortification.[83]

46. It is clear that this was the decision of the divine dispensation: what King Hugh had sordidly seized by such a crime he could not by any means hold onto. In fact, he was overtaken by such fright that, lowering himself with a rope on that side of the castle where the city walls were attached to it, he abandoned Rome and fled to his men. Thus, with King Hugh and the aforementioned Marozia expelled, Alberic held the monarchy of the Roman city, with his brother John presiding over the bishopric of the highest and universal see.[84]

47. Certain people say that Bertha, mother of King Hugh, bore no son to her husband, Margrave Adalbert, but, having secretly taken them from other women, by a simulated birth she claimed

83. Alberic, who became "prince and senator of all of the Romans" with this putsch in 932, was the most successful member of the Theophylact clan; he ruled Rome and environs until his death in 954. Marozia's marriage to Hugh had put Alberic's succession-rights in jeopardy, and his reaction made sense in dynastic politics. Otto I, Liudprand's hero in book 4 below, confronted similar dilemmas in his family.

84. John XI was pope, 931–36. Liudprand claimed his father was Pope Sergius III (above, 2.48).

as her own Wido and Lambert in such a way that after the death
of Adalbert Bertha might not lack sons with whose help she could
acquire all the power of her husband.[85] To me, however, it seems
that this lie was invented for this purpose: namely, that King Hugh
might cover his own fornication with that excuse, and escape the
υβριν[86] of dishonor; [but] this claim which I am about to report,
about why this story was circulated, seems more likely to me. Lambert, who ruled the Tuscan march after the death of his brother
Wido, was a warlike man and daring in any adventure.[87] King Hugh
took a dim view of him on account of suspicions that he wanted
the kingdom of Italy: for he feared lest the Italians desert him and
appoint Lambert king. At last Boso, brother of King Hugh, born
of the same father, prepared snares and traps for Lambert because
he ardently desired to become margrave of Tuscany himself. Therefore, following Boso's advice, King Hugh threateningly announced
to Lambert that he must not dare any longer to call himself his
brother. Since he was of a truly ferocious nature and undisciplined,
Lambert answered like this, not moderately as he should have, but
without control: "Lest the king cast doubt on my being his brother, I want to prove in a duel with everyone looking on that we came
out into the light of day from one and the same body." When he
heard this, the king chose a certain youth called Teudinus, whom
he committed to single combat with Lambert over the issue. God,
however, who is just and whose judgment is fair, in whom there
is no iniquity, arranged that Teudinus might fall very quickly and
Lambert gain victory, so that ambiguity be shattered and the truth
be manifest to all. King Hugh was not a little embarrassed by this
outcome. Having taken counsel, he detained Lambert and held
him in custody; for he feared lest he should snatch the kingdom if
he let him go. Thus, once Lambert was captured, Hugh reassigned

85. Bertha had been married to Theobald (father of King Hugh and Boso of Arles). She bore Adalbert of Tuscany (†915), Lambert, and Wido III (see 2.55–56, above).
    86. "Turpitude."
    87. Wido died in 930 (see 3.44); his brother Lambert was blinded in 931. Hugh
resented the Tuscans' power over Rome and their consequent ability to control access
to imperial coronations.

the Tuscan marches to his brother Boso and deprived Lambert of his eyes a little later.[88]

48. In those times the Italians sent for Rudolf in Burgundy, that he might come. When King Hugh discovered this through some messengers that he sent to him, he granted Rudolf all the land in Gaul that Hugh had held before he took on the kingship, and he accepted from Rudolf an oath he would never come to Italy.[89] And by delivering many gifts he also made a friend of Henry, whom we mentioned above, a very mighty king, a ruler whose name was then resplendent among the Italians because he had alone overcome the Danes, previously subject to no one, and had made them tributary. For that is an untamed nation living at the Ocean in the north, because of whose savagery the nobility of many nations often have mourned. Navigating with fleets along the course of the Rhine, these people periodically devastated everything with their iron weapons and fire; besides, they took by force, conquering them, the very noble cities of Agrippa, now called Cologne, and Trier, located far from the Rhine, and several others in the kingdom of Lothar, and having taken everything, they burned whatever they could not carry away with themselves; they even burned the baths of Aachen and the palaces. But now, leaving aside these things, let us return to the order of the narrative.

49. Duke Arnulf of the Bavarians and Carinthians, of whom we have made mention above, as he was not very far from Italy, went there, having gathered troops with which he could take over Hugh's kingdom.[90] Passing through the march of Trent, the first in that part of Italy, he got as far as Verona. There he was welcomed kindly

88. Hugh strove to remake central authority in the Italian kingdom using the larger territorial principalities (Spoleto, Tuscany, Ivrea) as building blocks, with southern French relatives in positions of power. His elimination of his stepbrother, the Tuscan margrave Lambert, in 931, exemplifies both policies. Blinded, Lambert lived on, incapable of ruling according to tenth-century Italy's political conventions.

89. In 931–32.

90. See 2.17 and 2.21–23, above. This expedition took place in 933–34. It aimed at securing a kingdom for Arnulf's son Eberhard. The east Frankish king Henry I may have supported it.

by Count Milo and Bishop Rather, as they were the ones who had invited him. When King Hugh heard this, he set out against Arnulf, having gathered an army.

50. When he got there and sent out "the ridings," as the populace calls them, a quite large party of Bavarians exiting from the castle called Gossolengo began to fight with the Italians. Gravely beaten by them, scarcely one of the Bavarians' party escaped to announce their defeat to the others. On account of this, Duke Arnulf was filled with no small confusion; whence it happened that, after he received counsel, he wanted to capture Count Milo and, having abandoned Italy, to lead him back to Bavaria. In this way, after reinforcing his army he could return once more to Italy with Milo; and this plan did not escape Milo.

51. Milo, vacillating between different thoughts, did not know at all what he should do. He was afraid of going to King Hugh, as he clearly deserved to be; he thought that to be led to Bavaria by Arnulf was not just death, but hell. In the midst of his indecisiveness, since he knew that King Hugh would swiftly incline to mercy, he decided to go to him and to flee from Arnulf. Then Arnulf returned to Bavaria as fast as he could.[91]

52. But beforehand he assaulted the fortification that was in the city of Verona, and led off to Bavaria Milo's brother and his soldiers, who tried to defend it. When Milo's brother left, the city quickly returned to Hugh's allegiance, and Rather, bishop of the same city, having been captured by the king, was consigned to exile in Pavia; there he began to write a book reflecting on his exile with sufficient humor and urbanity. Anyone who reads it will find several polished things there about this condition that will please the minds of readers no less than it will uplift them.[92]

HERE ENDS THE THIRD BOOK OF RETRIBUTION

91. The rebellion enabled Hugh to justify the overhaul of northeastern Italian institutions. See 4.6, below. Arnulf needed Milo because local contacts were essential to outsiders' success in Italy.

92. Rather's *Praeloquia* have been translated into English by P. Reid, *The Complete Works of Rather of Verona* (Binghamton: Medieval and Renaissance Texts and Studies, 1991).

Book Four

HERE BEGIN THE CHAPTER HEADINGS
OF THE FOURTH BOOK

17. About the daughter of the king of the English, whom King Otto married before taking over the kingdom.

18. About Henry, who became a rebel against his brother, on the advice of perverted men.

19. A poetic, invective oration to Henry against the devil, by whose scheme he desired to fight his own brother.

20. About Eberhard, who, while Henry, still loyal to his brother the king, was staying in a certain castle, captured him at the inception of his rebellion and led him off to Francia.

21. For what reason Eberhard severed Gislebert from his loyalty to the king.

22. Gislebert and Eberhard free Henry from custody.

23. By what scheme Eberhard wanted to trick Henry and Gislebert in acquiring the kingdom.

24. About the admirable victory that King Henry obtained by praying, and about Henry, wounded in the arm.

25. How King Henry secured the Holy Lance.

26. An argument based on the Holy Scriptures that such a victory or battle came about not by chance but with God arranging it.

27. Concerning the fact that, while the king was besieging the castle of Breisach, many deserted him, on the advice of Archbishop Frederick.

28. About the admirable perseverance and response of King Otto.

29. In what way, with God fighting for the king, Gislebert and Eberhard were killed at Andernach by Udo and Conrad.

30. About the messenger who announced their deaths to the king while he was heading for mass.

31. King Otto informs Duke Berthold of the Bavarians about their deaths, and that he wants to give him his sister or his sister's daughter as a spouse.

32. About Archbishop Frederick, who earlier deserted the king and went to the city of Metz to assemble an army, where he, too, heard of their deaths.

33. About this same archbishop's capture and detention.

34. About Henry, who was forbidden by his sister from entering the fortification with hostile intentions against the king.

35. About the same man, who afterwards came to the king for mercy.

HERE END THE CHAPTER HEADINGS

HERE BEGINS AUSPICIOUSLY THE FOURTH BOOK

1. The events presented up to this point, most holy priest, I wrote down just as I heard them related by very serious men who had observed them; the rest of the events to be related I will explain just as I witnessed them.[1] At that time I was so prized because I obtained King Hugh's favor by the sweetness of my voice; for he loved good singing that much, a field in which none of the boys of my same age could outdo me.

2. Therefore King Hugh, when he observed everything going well for him, appointed his son Lothar, whom he had with his wife Alda, to be king after him, with all assenting.[2] Having appointed him, he pondered how he might acquire Rome, from which he had been shamefully cast out. Thus, having assembled a host, he set out for Rome; although he pitifully devastated the city's outlying sites and provinces, and attacked the city itself with daily sallies, he could not attain his goal of entering it.

3. At last, hoping he might deceive Alberic with his craftiness, Hugh intimated to him that he might take Alda in marriage, his daughter and sister of his son King Lothar, and that, having obtained peace this way, he could remain secure as if he were Hugh's own son. Thus Alberic, as he was not a foolish man, joined Hugh's daughter to himself in marriage, but he did not hand over Rome, for which Hugh so lusted, and he did not at all trust the king.[3] In truth, however, King Hugh would have ensnared and fished out

---

1. Here Liudprand clarifies for Recemund's benefit the distinction between learned and witnessed evidence (see 1.1, above), a stereotype much used by tenth-century contemporary history writers: see G. Arnaldi, "Liutprando e la storiografia contemporanea nell'Italia centro-settentrionale," *Settimane di studio del Centro italiano di studi sull'Alto Medioevo* 17 (Spoleto: CISAM, 1969), 508. Eyewitness accounts made the reader a co-witness and had special value: C. Leonardi, "Il secolo X," in his *Letteratura latina medievale* (Florence: SISMEL-Il Galluzzo, 2002), 164.

2. Lothar became co-ruler of Italy in 931. This signaled to magnates (accustomed in the tenth century to such cooperative rulership) that Hugh aimed at dynastic continuity.

3. The marriage took place in 936.

Alberic τουτω τῷ αγκηστρω[4] if the trickery of his own soldiers, who did not want him ever to enjoy peace with Alberic, had not done this: for if the king sought to punish any of his own men, the fellow would soon manage to flee to Alberic, and, generously welcomed by Alberic because of the latter's fear of the king, a deserter could stay in Rome, honored.

4. While these things were happening, the Saracens living at Fraxinetum, having assembled a multitude, reached as far as Acqui, fifty miles distant from Pavia; their πρωβωλος[5] was Sagittus, a very evil and impious Saracen. Yet since God was well disposed, having engaged in battle, the ταλέπορος[6] himself died with all his men.

5. At the same time, in the Genoese city, which has been built in the Cottian Alps, overlooking the African sea, eighty miles distant from Pavia, a spring flowed most copiously with blood, clearly suggesting to all a coming calamity. Indeed, in the same year, the Phoenicians arrived there with a multitude of fleets, and while the citizens were unaware, they entered the city, killing all except women and children. Then, placing all the treasures of the city and the churches of God in their ships, they returned to Africa.

6. At that time Manasses, bishop of the city of Arles, discerning the power of King Hugh, with whom he had kinship by bloodlines, having deserted the church entrusted to him, set out for Italy, ready to violate and even mutilate many churches, in a spirit of ambition. King Hugh, hoping to hold the kingdom of Italy more securely if he were to grant the high posts of the kingdom to his relatives, against justice and law commended the Veronese, Tridentine, and Mantuan churches to him or, more accurately, offered them up as sustenance. And, not content even with these, Manasses appropriated the march of Trent, where, with the devil instigating it, he ceased to be a bishop when he began to be a soldier.[7] It is

4. "With this hook."   5. "Leader."
6. "Miserable fellow."

7. In 935 Hugh combined secular and ecclesiastical authority in creating a new borderland district in northeastern Italy. To appoint relatives in the kingdom's main administrative districts had long been Hugh's policy. Later in his own life Liudprand would also add a secular office (count of Ferrara) to his episcopal authority.

pleasing here, holy father, to dwell a little on this matter, and, with God permitting it, to choke off, with my own, Manasses's explanation of why he did this.

7. "Blessed Peter," he says, "having established the Antiochene church, afterwards moved to the Roman city, which then ruled all nations by the enormity of its power. There, when according to God's dispositions he founded the holy church venerated throughout the whole world, he commended his first church, that is, the Antiochene one, to his disciple the blessed evangelist Mark; in just the same manner Mark himself first instituted the Aquileian church and then hastily set out for the Alexandrian one. We know that all who shall read their acts will not fail to note that it went this way."[8] But, O Manasses, let us answer so that you may learn that you do not understand the truth about these things, and may perceive that your parents had foresight with the etymology of your name: for Manasses is interpreted as "forgetful" or "forgetfulness" of God.[9] How could your parents more truthfully or openly reveal things than through this name? This, I say, is your forgetfulness: namely, that you do not remember you are only a man. Of course the devil knew the Scriptures, too, and yet, as a perverse creature, he interpreted them perversely, and when he used them it was for the sake of wickedness, not for health. Do you not know that when, with heinous daring, he tried to wound the Lord our Redeemer Jesus Christ with the arrows of temptation, he wrongly used the prophetic words, since "he has given his angels charge over you, that they lift you up in their hands, lest you ever dash your foot against a stone"?[10] This is written clearly in such a way that none of the faithful had doubts about the phrase. But you will be able to understand how deceitfully that Leviathan put forth these truths through the answer of the very One who outstrips not just the

8. Manasses's version of events derives from the apocryphal *Acts of St. Mark*; see *Acta Sanctorum* Apr. 3 (Paris: V. Palmé, 1866), 347–49. Bede, Rhabanus Maurus, and Notker were among the early medieval authors to chronicle Mark's movements.

9. According to the early medieval encyclopedist Isidore of Seville, *Etymologies* 7.6.73.

10. Lk 4.10–11, quoting Ps 95 (94): 11–12.

perception of mortals but also that of angels: he says, "You shall not tempt the Lord your God."[11] Thus you see, Manasses, you, too, use something true, but with deceitful interpretations assigned to it; in the same way the apostate Julian also is said to have answered the Christians, whom he robbed of their property through thievish greed: "Your master says, 'Do not possess gold nor silver.'[12] And also, Ἐυκοπώτερον γαρ εστην καμηλον δια τρυμαλίας ραφίδος εισελθεὶν η πλουσιον εις την βασιλεῖαν τοῦ θεοῦ.'[13] And again, 'so likewise anyone of you that does not renounce all that he possesses cannot be my disciple.'"[14] Therefore, I ask, should he be believed to have said anything more perversely or more treacherously than you? For what Peter carried out for the sake of justice you translate for the benefit of sin. I believe either you did not understand the Acts of the Apostles, or, what is more likely, you just did not read it. There you will find written plainly enough that the faithful used to sell their goods and lay the money at the feet of the apostles, for whom all property was held in common and no one called anything his own; rather, everything was divided according to each person's needs. If, therefore, Peter refused to touch gold, which in human estimation is most precious and is dearer to you than your own soul, as if it were something infected, for what reason do you assert he flew over to the Roman church, having deserted the Antiochene? If you bark out that he sought its income—which is above all things false—I shall prove that he sought a profit in souls and a glorious martyrdom. In fact, it had been foretold to him by the Master, indeed his Creator and Redeemer, saying that "when you were younger, you did gird yourself,

11. Lk 4.12 quoting Dt 6.16.

12. Mt 10.9. Julian (†363) was the sole Roman emperor after Constantine (†337) who was not Christian, and enjoyed a poor reputation in the Middle Ages in consequence.

13. Mk 10.25 (the famous passage about it being easier for a camel to pass through the eye of a needle than for a rich man to enter the kingdom of heaven).

14. Luke 14.33. Liudprand probably derived his image of Julian's doings from the late antique historical compilation, the *Historia ecclesiastica tripartita* 6.39.3, a translation into Latin of the Byzantine historian Socrates' work, which mentions the emperor's flippant treatment of Christian victims of his tax policies.

and you did walk where you would; but when you shall be old, you shall stretch forth your hands, and another shall gird you and lead you whither you would not go."[15] He said this intending that with his death he should add splendor to God. And finally in another passage it can be read that after the Resurrection the Lord answered Peter, who asked where he was going: "To Rome, to be crucified again." For Peter came there not puffed up with ambition, but inspired for martyrdom, seeking not gold but a profit of souls. O, happy are you, indeed blessed, if your conscience could testify you were the same! Nor can you deny, I say, that you sold the bishopric of Verona cheaply, something that we say never happened to Peter, not to just any Peter, I mean, but to the same apostle. On account of this act we recognize that you were deprived, not just of spiritual, but also of earthly honor by your desire for property. But as we return to our subject, for now let this be enough, until in the proper place we come, with God permitting, to how you usurped the episcopal throne in Milan.[16]

8. In that time the margrave of the city of Ivrea was the very same Berengar under whose tyranny now all Italy mourns.[17] King Hugh gave him his niece named Willa as a spouse, whom Boso, the margrave of Tuscany and brother of the king, had with his wife Willa. But Anscar, Berengar's brother, whom Ermengard, King Hugh's sister, had with Adalbert, outshone other men in audacity and power.

9. There was also a certain hero called Tedald, related by close family ties to King Hugh, who was margrave of the Camerinans and Spoletans.[18] This fellow went to the aid of the Beneventan

15. Jn 21.18.

16. Formosus's pontificate (above, 1.29) introduced to Italian politics the contentious issue of whether bishops could change sees. Canon law and practicality did not align.

17. By 929 Berengar II was margrave of Ivrea, about the only major territorial unit that King Hugh failed to subject to a close relative. Though also a cousin of Hugh, Berengar was the son of Margrave Adalbert (†929) and so had the local contacts that Hugh's relatives lacked. Together with his brother he came to dominate Piedmont, Liguria, parts of Lombardy, and the march of Spoleto and Camerino after 936.

18. Tedald (†936) had been appointed margrave by Hugh in 929.

prince against the Greeks, who had gravely afflicted him;[19] when he waged war on them, he enjoyed victory. At length it happened that he captured many of the Greeks who held not the fields but the castles of the area; and when he amputated their virile members, he announced the following to the *strategos* who led them:[20] "Since I discovered that nothing is more precious to your holy emperor than eunuchs, I respectfully endeavor to send him just these few for now, but will send him some more as soon as possible, with God favoring the enterprise."

10. The jest, indeed the wise deed, that a certain woman did, then, we shall insert into the narrative here. For when on a certain day the Greeks went with the men of that land to fight outside a certain castle against that Tedald we mentioned before, many of them were captured by him. While he was making them eunuchs and directing them to the castle, a certain woman, inflamed by love for her husband and not a little worried about his member, left the castle enraged, with loosened hair. When she lacerated her face with bloody fingernails and cried with a loud voice before Tedald's tent, he asked, "For what reason, woman, do you wail with such loud cries?" She responded this way (for it is the highest wisdom to simulate stupidity in the right context): "It is a new and unheard-of crime, O hero, that you wage war on unarmed women. No blood-line of ours leads back to the Amazons; in fact, given over solely to the activities of Minerva,[21] we are wholly ignorant of weapons." And when Tedald said to her: "What hero with sound mind ever waged war on women, except in the time of the Amazons?"[22] she answered: "What more cruel war on women could you wage, I ask, and how could you make it more uncomfortable for them, than to try to amputate the bulbs of their men, in which lies the replenishment of our bodies, and, what is most important of all, in which

---

19. During Landulf I of Capua's struggle against Byzantine overlordship of 929–34.

20. *Strategos* was the title of the military officer responsible for defense in Byzantine provinces.

21. The Roman goddess of handicrafts.

22. Mythic female warriors of antiquity.

lies our hope for future children?[23] For you remove not what is theirs but what is ours when you turn them into eunuchs. I ask you, does the quantity of cattle or sheep that you took from me days ago drive me to come to your castle? In fact, I praise the pillage of my animals you inflicted, but I shudder before, I flee, and I want to avoid by any means this particular great loss, as cruel as irreparable. Holy gods, all of you, avert such a plague from me!" Having heard these words, all present were stirred by great laughter, and the favor of the people for her grew to such an extent she merited to get back not just her husband, intact, but also all the animals that had been taken from her. When she left with the things she had obtained, Tedald sent after her a boy who asked what he should take from her husband if he were to come out of the castle to do battle with him again. "Those are his eyes," she said, "his nostrils, hands, and feet. If he needs it, let Tedald remove what is his; but let him leave alone what is mine, I mean, of his humble servant." Through the laughter and the gift of her husband she understood that the favor of the people was with her for her first speech, so afterwards she sent back that answer through the intermediary messenger.

11. In that same time Boso, brother of King Hugh, with his very avid wife Willa egging him on, schemed to pull off a novel and perverse thing against the king.[24] This fact did not escape Hugh; because of this Boso was captured and quickly placed under arrest. In the end the cause of his downfall was this. While Boso ruled the march of Tuscany, once Lambert was deprived of sight as we mentioned above,[25] his wife Willa began to burn with love of gold so that none of the noble matrons of the whole province of Tuscany would adorn themselves with jewels of any price. This Willa, though she had no male children, had four daughters, Berta,

---

23. Relying on Theophrastus, Pliny (*Natural History* 26.62.95) described the *orchis*, a plant whose "double root is like testicles." Liudprand called the husband's testicles *orchidia*, a usage obscure enough that he translated it (*testiculos*) interlinearly. Actually the orchid's tuberous root is not as distinctive as its flowers.

24. These events would have taken place in 936.

25. See 3.47, above.

Willa, Richilda, and Gisla; of these Willa, married to that Berengar who now still lives, managed things so her mother could not
be considered the worst of women. And in order not to record her
deeds in lengthy digressions, you will be able to understand what
and how enormous the others were when we have described this
most sordid deed.

12. Her husband Boso had a golden belt of wondrous length
and width, which glittered with the splendor of many precious
gems.[26] When Boso was captured, the king ordered that this belt
should be meticulously sought out beyond all his other treasures;
and, having confiscated his riches, he ordered that Boso's wife, as
an impious woman and author of the whole wicked plot, be dis-
honorably expelled from the Italian kingdom and led to Burgundy, the country whence she came. And when, having meticulously
searched everything, they had not found the belt, the messengers
returned to Hugh bearing the rest of the things. Then the king
spoke: "Upon returning," he said, "turn all the gear of her horses
inside out, even the pillow upon which she sits while riding. And if
you cannot find the belt even there, strip her of all her clothes, lest
she hide anything anywhere on her person: for I have learned how
crafty she is, and how greedy." Therefore, having gone back and
obeyed the king's command, since they found nothing after having searched everything, they deprived her of all her clothes. Since,
with eyes averted, none of the decent men would look upon this
filthy and unprecedented crime, one of the servants directed his
gaze and saw a purple string hanging below the sphere of her buttocks and, when he impudently grabbed it and pulled in a defiling
way, the belt they were seeking came out of the most intimate part
of her. Then the servant, not just shameless but rendered all the
more giggly by his dirty deed, burst out: "Ha! Ha! He! What an
expert midwife is this soldier! A red-headed boy was born to the
lady; I ask that you be my witnesses!"[27] O, how fortunate I would

---

26. Such items were signals of aristocratic stature (Fichtenau, *Living*, 32–33, 45) and
of military activity (though the *balteum* was also an item of clerical attire). Liudprand
mentioned them in 1.23 and 2.62, where they also play symbolic roles.

27. Terence, *Andria* 486–87.

be, indeed the happiest of men, if my wife bore me just two such children! Indeed, I would send them both as messengers to Constantinople since, as I learned when merchants told about it, the emperor graciously welcomes this kind of messenger!" Willa, hurt beyond compare by such words, revealed to all the pain hidden under her heart by shedding tears. But the servant, as is the nature of these people, was not just unmoved by her mortification, but he was actually stirred up by it, and added this to increase the pain of the wound:

"Willa, what madness is this? To hide gold in the dark
Recesses of your limbs? O, I think it unheard of!
By the name of the furies you hide gems in your body!
To produce such offspring is unusual for mothers:
From it the ten months' gestation brought you no discomfort.
Noble mother, do not hold back from us such offspring,
Who, once born, may overtake you, the mother, in age!"
One energetic man hit the neck of the one saying such things,
And reprimanded him with harsh words.[28]

When these things had been done in this way, the belt was taken to the king, and she was sent to Burgundy. It seems to me uncertain whether the one who hid it or the one who ordered the search acted more basely; however, it is clear that both were inspired by a great greed for gold and gems.[29]

13. Next, King Rudolf of the Burgundians died. As [his wife] Alda, mother of his son King Lothar, had died, King Hugh linked himself in marriage with Rudolf's widow, named Bertha; but he also secured for his son, King Lothar, the daughter of Rudolf and this same Bertha as a spouse, a girl named Adelheid, who was both most virtuous in form and gracious in the probity of her ways.[30]

28. Terence and Virgil provided some of Liudprand's inspiration here. Note the ambiguity in Liudprand's separation of prose (history) from poetry (literature) in the last two lines. The entire composition was inserted in the margin of the manuscript.

29. This famous "birth scene" may be a satirical play on the arrival of a boy in Virgil's fourth *Eclogue*. C. Villa, "Lay and Ecclesiastical Culture," in *Italy*, ed. La Rocca, 202.

30. Rudolf II died in July 937, Bertha remarrying in December. The double marriage alliance secured Italy's northwestern border and perhaps gave Hugh some rights

To all the Greeks this does not seem fitting, because if a father takes a mother as his wife, because the two are one, the son may not unite in marriage with the daughter without committing an offense.

14. At length Hugh, deceived by the attractions of many concubines, began no longer to love his aforesaid wife Bertha with conjugal love, and even began to hate her in every way; and in the proper place it will not be displeasing to write about how justly God punished this attitude. In truth, while there were several concubines, he burned with most sordid love for three above the rest: Pezola, whose origin was in the bloodline of lowliest servants, with whom he also generated a son named Boso, whom he ordained bishop of Piacenza's church after Wido's death; then Rosa, daughter of the beheaded Walpert we mentioned above,[31] who gave him a daughter of wondrous beauty; third was Stephania, a Roman, who also bore a son, by the name of Tedald, whom he later appointed archdeacon of the Milanese church for this reason: namely, that once the archbishop died, this man might become his successor there. If, however, life accompanies me, the order of writing will reveal that God would not allow this to take place. But the people called these three women by the names of goddesses on account of their sordid crime of promiscuity, with Pezola nicknamed Venus, Rosa Juno because of her quarrels and tenacious hatred (since, according to the corruption of the flesh *she* seemed more attractive), and Stephania Semele. And since it was not just the king who made use of them, their children take their origin from unknown fathers.

15. At that time King Henry passed on to the Lord, afflicted by a very serious illness in the castle called Himenlev, on the bound-

---

in Burgundy. Adelheid was sixteen when she married Lothar (947). She became Otto I's wife in 952, having been a widow a little over a year, which might explain Liudprand's unnecessary observation on Orthodox canon law, according to which the legitimacy of Adelheid and her son Otto II could have appeared dubious in Constantinople. On Adelheid see Sean Gilsdorf, ed. and trans., *Queenship and Sanctity: The Lives of Mathilda and the* Epitaph *of Adelheid* (Washington, DC: The Catholic University of America Press, 2004), 55–60, 128–43.

31. See 3.39.

ary between the Thuringians and Saxons.[32] His body, carried off to Saxony, was placed with immense veneration inside the church in a monastery of most noble and observant nuns, located on the property of the same king, called Quedlinburg.[33] There also his wife and venerable partner in rule, born of the same nation, named Machtild, does not desist from offering a living sacrifice to God and the liturgical office of the dead in expiation of past sins, beyond what all the matrons do whom I have seen or heard about. This woman bore her husband a son before he took on his kingship, whom she called OTTO, and this, I say, is the man by whose power the northern and western sections of the world are ruled, by whose wisdom they are pacified, by whose religious observance they are pleased, and by whose severity in just judgment they are cowed.[34] After assuming the royal office she bore two more sons, one named with his father's name, Henry, quite gifted and witty, acute in giving advice, handsome in the luminosity of his face, at ease with his vigilant eyes, on account of whose recent death we spilled quite a lot of tears. The third, by the name of Bruno, his holy father desired to strive for Utrecht's recovery, since the Norsemen utterly destroyed the church there.[35] But actually let us return to the issue, so that we may explain their deeds more profusely in the appropriate place.

16. You may ascertain how great was King Henry's prudence and how great his knowledge from this: namely, that he appointed the most accomplished and observant of his sons as king. For there loomed, O most prudent king, a chance for the extinction of your whole people, had not such a great successor to the royal office sprung up. For this reason we composed a poem of praise for both:

32. July 2, 936.
33. This great nunnery in Ostphalia (where the Ottonians owned most of their land) was, together with Gandersheim, the most important monastic foundation of the ruling dynasty.
34. Otto I, "the Great," ruled from his father's death in 936 until his own in 973.
35. Henry the Younger was duke of Bavaria for eight years before dying in 955. Bruno (925–65) was trained in the cathedral school of Utrecht between ages four and fifteen. He became Otto's spiritual advisor.

You, the very one who was accustomed to overcome impious
Peoples by brutal war,
We just learned, O king, how great a ruination
You gave to the populace by your own death!
Let the horde, suddenly orphaned of its dear
King, now stop weeping, when
Another arises, to be venerated the world over,
A son similar to the famous father:
King Otto, who will pursue the nations
With great authority and bring blessed peace.
Whatever ended with Henry's demise
This one offers back to the people by his high birth,
Kind and gentle and patient towards the holy,
Virulent and hard and rabid towards the savage.
There are wars for you to fight, Otto, with several enemies,
By which, bringing back a name known in all the galaxies,
You shall tread with your feet over the globe—
Wars which the late-shining Boötes pursues,
And to which the noble Hesper gives its name.
Lucifer is called back,
And, hurrying, there arises glittering Eos.[36]

17. This same King OTTO, before assuming the kingship, had
taken as a wife for himself a woman named Edith, from the very
noble English nation, daughter of a brother of King Hadelstan,
and with her he had a son named LIUDOLF.[37] Whenever we
evoke his memory, we fill our breast with tears[38] on account of the
recent misfortune.[39] O, if only he had never been born or had not
died so grown up!

18. In that time Henry, the brother of the king, at the instiga-

36. In practice, Otto is here assigned an empire over which the sun never sets.
The poem refers to the classical names of several constellations to make the point.
Liudprand's composition recycles elements from Catullus, Seneca, Boethius, and, as
always, Virgil.
37. Otto's first prestige-enhancing marriage took place in 929–30. Edith died in 946.
38. Virgil, *Aeneid* 4.30.
39. Liudolf died in 957, while Liudprand was in Germany.

tion of certain perverse people became very hostile to Otto.[40] But the one who, soon after the most noble dignity of his creation, wanted to make himself similar to his Creator, through his followers aroused Henry against the power of his brother, indeed against his king and lord, with words like these: "Do you think your father acted rightly in giving precedence over you, born into the royal station, to one not born into the same standing? Clearly he did not weigh this on the scales of discretion, and truly he erred through the greatness of his love. Act therefore—for you will not lack supporters—cast down your brother, seize the kingdom, and let there be a right to rule for you, to whom also befell birth into the same regal station by God's bestowal."[41]

19.
Why do you have such a youthful craving to rule,
You most high-born Saxon? God bars it,
Not just your father Henry; for he gave the scepter, and
Good, pious, star-moving God himself advised it,
Without whom neither is a kingdom taken, nor do the times subsist.
In the world, whatever God ordains takes place,
God by whom dukes decide the laws and kings triumph.
Do you now wickedly desire to make
The brotherly ranks fight, O wrong, cruel, and unfair one?
O impious one, Leviathan, behemoth, do you prepare
To re-initiate the ancient duel by your guile?
You shall suffer the punishments for the entire crime,
A double-cross forever because a number is committing this sin.
O wretch, you shall take the torture at the same time,

40. In 939. As Liudprand knew (see 2.45), kings' early years were often as unsettled as Otto's. (Presciently, his father had begun arranging the succession in 929—the so-called *Hausordnung*, a series of legal enactments for his family.) Between 937 and 941 Otto confronted a series of crises involving Saxon aristocratic resistance to the elevation of a peer family, disagreement with his brothers over inheritance, the Conradines' resentment over his family's settlement for Thuringia, Bavaria's uncertainty about its institutional position, and West Frankish rivalry over Lotharingia.

41. The importance of being "born in the purple" for Byzantine emperors was stressed in 1.6–8 and 3.30–32.

And whatever fiery chains are due to all the wicked
Are brought forth for you, miserable one. Nor,
Justly sunk in the shades of fire-belching Erebus,
Shall you drag the Christians with you forever
To be burned since, once they are washed by holy baptism
And remit their sins, there remains God's
Grace, which raised up the fallen by blood freely given.[42]

20. Count Eberhard incited that man to such a great and perni-
cious crime.[43] For until the time of the first rebellion Henry gave
aid to his brother and king and lord, as he should have, and with every effort harried the king's enemies. But since negligence frequently
prepares a fall not just for those dedicated to worldly things, but
also for those given over to eternal ones and those resolved on the
vision of inner contemplation, and, as Vegetius says in the book
about military affairs, as "a security greater than necessary usually
causes a crisis,"[44] Henry was staying in a certain town and handling
himself incautiously; so the aforesaid Eberhard, having gathered
a multitude, besieged that place and, before his brother the king
could come to his aid, he stormed it and carried Henry off to his
own lands, along with no little property. Therefore, the king, who
desired only to avenge the affront against his brother, and indeed
himself, began to hunt down this Eberhard and his accomplices
with all his zeal.

21. Eberhard had severed Gislebert, duke of the Lotharingians,
from his fidelity to the king, and with his help he resisted the king
quite effectively.[45] And although this Gislebert had a sister of the

---

42. Boethius is Liudprand's main model here, but there are also many Virgilian
echoes. The poem was written in the margin of the manuscript.

43. Eberhard, duke of Franconia (†939), who aided with Otto's coronation. The
Franconian rulers preferred Henry the Fowler's style of rule through "friendships" to
Otto's apparently more autocratic one. Liudprand fails to mention Thankmar, Otto's
half-brother, whose resentment over Henry's settlement gave the rebel cause added
legitimacy.

44. Vegetius, *Epitoma rei militari* 3.22.

45. Gislebert, duke of Lotharingia (†939), who had a major role at Otto's coronation in Aachen. He had married Otto's sister Gerberga.

king as his wife, still, encouraged by hope of acquiring the kingship, he preferred to resist the king rather than to help him against his rivals, as he was obligated to do. But when they observed they could not resist the king in this way, having taken advice that was not lacking in human cunning, but was quite vacuous by divine standards, they addressed Henry with words like these:

22. "If you promise with an oath to heed our advice, not only will we release you (remember you are a prisoner), but, what is more, if you want to become king we will appoint you our lord." They did not, however, say this to him with the intention of actually carrying through with it, but instead so that with his help they might more easily overcome the king.

23. The king actually had many very valiant troops, among whom were Hermann the duke of the Swabians and his brother Udo and Conrad surnamed "the Wise"; they, though related to Eberhard by bloodlines, justly preferred to fall with the righteous king, if it became necessary, rather than to triumph unjustly with their relative.[46] Therefore, Henry, deceived by the promise just mentioned, having quickly assembled his own troops, began to help the rebels with all his strength, and to fight against the king. Since, however, it is written: "iniquity has lied to itself,"[47] here it is useful to delay the narrative a little and explain exactly how iniquity deceived itself. Eberhard had barely managed to sever Gislebert from his fidelity to the king when he promised him that he would be made king. Gislebert, however, sought to deceive Henry by the same trick, proposing that, when he had defeated the king with his help, he would depose him and Henry would take the throne of the kingdom. Actually, Eberhard had organized things in a very different manner. For he wanted, if he could defeat the king, to deprive both his associates of the kingdom and usurp it himself, as we may deduce from his own words, which he uttered to his wife a little before he died.

46. Hermann I (†948) and his brother Count Udo, as well as their first cousin Count Conrad of Franconia (†948), were members of the Conradine lineage, like Eberhard.

47. Ps 26.12.

While he snuggled against her breast, he said: "Rejoice in the bosom of a count for now; soon you shall be elated in the embraces of a king." The current state of affairs proves that it did not work out that way and that iniquity deceived itself.

24. Thus, as we said earlier, encouraged by that promise, indeed deceived by it, having gathered an army with Gislebert and also with Eberhard, they prepared war on the king; against them the king hastened gladly, not afraid of their numbers but trusting in God's piety. But in order that you know how easy it is for God to overcome many with a few and that someone "shall not be saved by the abundance of his strength,"[48] listen to the ancient miracle, renewed by the Lord. The soldiers of the king reached the Rhine at the place called Birten and soon began to cross the bed of the river, unaware that Henry was already so very close to them, along with the counts mentioned earlier. At last, a few who had disembarked from the ships scarcely had time to mount their horses and don their armor when the legions of the aforesaid rebels were not so much announced as approaching but perceived by the senses as present. Therefore, they addressed each other with words to this effect: "The width of this river, as you can see, does not allow our allies to come to our aid nor us to go back across, even if we wanted to; nor is it hidden from us that to our nations it is laughable above all things for strong men to hand themselves over to enemies and, by not resisting, to escape death and gain life with eternal ignominy. Although both the lack of any hope of escape, which is not infrequently a nuisance to enemies, and the eternal ignominy of begging for our lives give us the confidence to fight, it is especially this which drives us to fight: namely, the cause of truth and justice. For if our earthly residence shall be dissolved while resisting injustice, we shall receive an eternal one in the heavens, one not made by human hands." Having said these things, encouraged, with a vigorous gallop they charged among the enemy. Thereupon the king, deciding that such great steadfastness on the part of his

48. Ps 32.17.

men did not lack divine inspiration, as he could not come to the aid of his troops with his physical presence, given the intervening river, was reminded of the people of the Lord, who by the prayers of God's servant Moses conquered the attacking Amalekites. He quickly got off his horse and along with all the people gave himself over to prayer, shedding tears before the victory-giving nails that pierced the hands of our Lord and Savior Jesus Christ, and which had been placed on his lance; and the outcome of the whole affair proved how much the prayer of a just man can be worth, according to Saint James's phrase.[49] For as he prayed, while none from the ranks of his army fell, the enemy all turned to flight, and not a few of them hardly knew why they were running since they could not see the enemy on account of the fewness of their pursuers. When many had thus been killed, Henry was violently struck on the arm, and, though the blow did not penetrate to the flesh, thanks to the strength of his triple shield, still his arm turned livid through the force of the cruel blow, so that it could not be cured by any of the doctors' remedies against his feeling very great pain all year long; they also acknowledged that he departed mankind on account of this wound, long after the occasion of his crime. But as we brought up the holy lance, let us here insert an explanation of how it came into the king's possession.

25. King Rudolf of the Burgundians, who ruled the Italians for several years, received that lance as a gift from Count Samson.[50] For this lance was of a different kind from other lances, with a novel style and also a new elaboration of shape, having openings on both sides of the flank section: in front of the thumb pieces, two very

---

49. Jas 5.16: "The prayer of the righteous man has great power in its effects."

50. Samson appeared in 3.41, above. The lance had been a symbol of royal authority in late antiquity and among the Lombards, though its royal-military associations were erased in this account in favor of more religious ones. It is uncertain whether Rudolf gave it to Henry in 926 or 935, but in Germany it became part of the royal insignia, not just a sign of lordship over Italy. This holy lance (there were others in medieval Europe) is now in the treasury of the Viennese Hofburg's Schatzkammer, today a national museum. See P. Schramm, *Herrschaftszeichen und Staatssymbolik* 2 (Stuttgart: Hiersemann, 1955), 492ff.

beautiful blades extend up to the middle slope of the lance. They claim this lance belonged to Constantine the Great, son of Saint Helena, the discoverer of the life-giving cross; it has crosses made from the nails driven through the hands and feet of our Lord and Redeemer Jesus Christ at its mid-point, which above I called the flank. When King Henry, who was a God-fearing man and a lover of all things religious, heard that Rudolf had such a priceless heavenly gift, he inquired through special messengers if he could acquire it at any price and thereby prepared for himself a most invincible weapon against, and eternal triumph over, visible and invisible enemies. When King Rudolf replied he would never by any means do such a thing, King Henry took great care to scare him thoroughly, since he could not mollify him by gifts; in fact, he promised that all Rudolf's realm would be depopulated by slaughter and fires. And since what he sought was the gift by which God united the heavenly and the earthly, that is, the keystone that makes one out of two, the heart of King Rudolf softened, and he personally handed over what was right to the righteous king who was rightly seeking it. Nor was there occasion for any quarrel, with peace prevailing; for by the agency of him who was crucified with those nails when he set out from Pilate to Herod, the ones who had been mutual enemies before became friends on that same day. Moreover, although it also has become clear from many other circumstances, the great love with which King Henry received this aforesaid priceless gift emerges through this circumstance above all: that he not only gave Rudolf gold and silver gifts, but also honored him with quite a large section of the province of the Swabians. God, however, perceives in what spirit anyone does anything, and is the inspector and repayer not according to the quantity of the gifts but according to the good will of the donor. Thus he gave signs of how great a reward in eternal time he granted to the pious king on account of the blessed exchange when the king always terrified and dispersed enemies attacking him with this victory-bringing symbol leading the way. By this means, indeed by the will of God, King Henry got the holy spear that upon his death he left to his son, about whom our text relates in the present context, along with the hereditary kingdom.

And with what deep veneration Otto adored the priceless gift the present victory is not alone in showing, but also the admirable giving of divine gifts, as we are about to tell. Having therefore terrified and scattered his enemies, King Otto returned not so much elated by his victory as exalted by God's compassion.

26. It is pleasing here to delay a little and explain that these things happened in this way not by chance but with God orchestrating them; that will be clearer to us than light itself if we now consider the apparition of our Lord and Savior Jesus Christ that was granted to the women and disciples after the Resurrection. Thomas knew perfectly well of Peter's faith and of John's love, who leaned on the breast of the Master at the Last Supper; he heard that they had run to the tomb and had found nothing beyond the cloth wrappings; he learned of the visions of angels that visited the women, in which they asserted he lived. But still: mindful perhaps of women's weakness he did not believe them. I ask you, Saint Thomas, if you do not believe two disciples hastening to the castle of Emmaus—to whom Jesus not only appeared but also taught about those scriptures that referred to him, and even blessed, broke, and gave bread as was his custom—why do you not lend credence to all his disciples, to whom he appeared when the doors were closed? I ask, do you not remember that your own Lord and Teacher, for whom you promised you would die, had predicted all of this before his passion? For he said: "Behold, we go up to Jerusalem, and all things shall be accomplished which were written by the prophets concerning the Son of Man. For he shall be delivered to the gentiles and shall be mocked, and scourged, and spit upon, and after they have scourged him, they will put him to death; and the third day he shall rise again."[51] Why therefore do you doubt that he rose again, when you see him handed over to the peoples, whipped, spat upon, and crucified exactly as he had foretold? It is not without good reason that you desire to touch your God with your own hands. For that King of ours who centuries ago brought salvation throughout the earth, who knows all things

51. Lk 18.31–33.

before they happen, had predicted many would perish through this same error; and, as he is merciful and clement, he said, "Put in your finger here, and bring here your hand and put it into my side, and be not faithless, but believing."[52] Ἔξαυδα δὲ Θομὰ ἁγιε,[53] and by your doubting root out all your own uncertainty. He said, "My Lord and my God!"[54] O hesitation most worthy of every praise! O doubt to be heralded throughout the ages! If you had not doubted I would not believe as firmly as I do. If we were to tell the heretics, who used to howl that our Lord Jesus Christ had not risen in body, only about the faith of the believing women and the disciples, they would throw against us many arguments with diabolical cunning. But when they hear that doubting Thomas touched the body and stroked the gashes of the wounds and, with all doubt suddenly removed, exclaimed, "God and Lord!" the ones who before were vociferous quickly become as dumb as fish, recognizing that it is real flesh, which could be touched, and the real God, who entered through closed doors. And it was not by chance but by divine dispensation that Thomas doubted.

Thus, O pious king, this victory, unexpected because of the fewness of your soldiers, came by the decision of divine Providence, since God wanted to indicate to men how dear to him was one who deserved to obtain such an immense triumph with so few troops, simply by praying. Perhaps, indeed for sure, you did not know beforehand how dear you are to God, something he caused you to learn afterwards, when he honored you with so great a victory. For holy men ignore until they have tested them what virtues they possess and how high they rank in the eyes of the divine Examiner, something we may also deduce from the words uttered by the angel to Abraham, when he wanted to sacrifice his son. For he said: "Lay not your hand upon the boy, nor do anything to him; now I know that you fear God,"[55] that is, I caused you and your posterity to learn. For the Lord knew, and this before Abraham wanted to sacrifice his son, with what pure love the holy patriarch loved him; but

52. Jn 20.27.
54. Jn 20.38.

53. "Confess it, Saint Thomas."
55. Gn 22.12.

he who loved did not know how perfectly he loved until he made it most patently clear through the sacrifice of his beloved son. We can also prove this with the promise of holy Peter. "Lord," he said, "I am ready to go with you both into prison and to death."[56] To which the Lord replied: "I say to you, Peter, the cock shall not crow this day till you thrice deny that you know me."[57] O Saint Peter, the One who made you knew you better than you yourself did! You declare the true faith, as you see it; but the One who knows all things before they happen foretold you would deny him three times. In fact, mindful of this sentence, when later he asked you if you loved him, believing him more than yourself, you declared your love by this mild response, saying, "Lord, you know all things; you know that I love you."[58] In my conscience I love you more than myself, unless by loving you I love myself. Whether, as I think, this is the truth you know better than I do, you who made me as I am and inflamed me with very righteous love so that I could love you. Therefore, my good king, this happened not because of your faith but because of those waverers who think victory depends on numbers and human affairs depend only on chance. For we know you would ascribe it not to yourself but to God, even if you were to march forth with twelve thousand legions and obtain victory. And this is the reason why he wanted you to win by prayer, with few troops, namely, that he might thereby more vigorously kindle to love him those who trust in him, and so that he might show the ignorant how much he loves you. But having dropped these matters, let us now return to the order of the narrative.

27. In the area of Alsace there is a castle called Breisach in the native tongue, fortified both by the Rhine, circling it like an island, and by the natural harshness of the site.[59] In consequence Eberhard placed in it a multitude of soldiers, by whose terror tactics he not only took his vengeance on a large part of the aforesaid prov-

---

56. Lk 22.33.   57. Lk 22.34.
58. Jn 21.17.

59. Though accurate accounts of this episode existed, Liudprand deliberately colored his version to give Otto a higher profile: see Sutherland, *Liutprand*, 68.

ince, but also pitifully mauled the nearby retainers of the king. The good king at last, considering not only his own interests but those of his followers as well, after assembling an army set out for Alsace to besiege the aforesaid castle. And when he reached there, by the encouragement of Frederick, archbishop of the see of Mainz, who was there with him at the time, very many bishops began secretly to desert the king and to flee to their own cities, having abandoned at night the tents set up all around; but Frederick slyly remained behind.[60] Mulling this over, the king's soldiers addressed the king with a speech like this: "O king, show consideration for your safety by leaving here and seeking Saxony. It is hardly hidden from you that your brother Henry strives to wage war on you; if he senses that there are so few troops with you, he will rush here so quickly that there will be no place to run. Therefore, it is better to retreat now, having saved the army, than either to die miserably or shamefully escape." Unmoved, the king spoke to them as once Judas Maccabeus did to his men: "Don't!" he said. "Do not utter such talk. 'And if our time be come, let us die manfully, and let us not stain our glory.'[61] For it is better to submit to death for the sake of true justice than to live shamefully by escaping from that justice. In the end, if our enemies, resisting God's ordering, trusting in the help of numbers alone and not in God, will fight unjustly, it will cause them to die and to descend to the relentless tortures of hell. On the other hand, let it please us to fight ever more zealously, since we fight confidently for justice, and in fighting, if the fate of all flesh befalls us, we may die more confidently. For those about to fight for justice to turn away before entering battle because of a paucity of troops is equivalent to not trusting in God." With these words he not only overturned their plan of fleeing but forthwith encouraged them to fight even more vigorously.

60. Though Frederick had been appointed by Otto in 937, he kept up his archbishopric's traditional alignment with the Conradine clan and resented the centralizing tendencies in the new monarchy.
    61. 1 Mc 9.10, without the detail that Judas wanted his men to die "for our brothers."

28. I want you, O outstanding father, to diligently heed this one single matter; when you hear it, you shall marvel about how he overcame the passions of the soul more than how he overcame the enemy.[62] Quite often even sinners can defeat enemies in this way, with God permitting it; but it is only for the perfect to keep the virtue of the soul uncorrupted, that is, not to be elevated in spirit in favorable circumstances nor to be shattered in adverse ones. Listen, then, upon what a rock of faith, which is Christ, his courage was based, even in this tempestuous instability. A certain very rich count was there with him, one whose vast number of soldiers adorned the king's line of battle. This man, however, observing that many became deserters and fugitives from the king's army, caring not for the inner man but for the outer one, began to quietly mull over things in his head: "In this mess without doubt I shall obtain whatever I shall demand of the appointed king, especially as a bitter fight looms over us and he fears that I might desert him." Therefore, having sent messengers to the king, he begged that he grant him a certain abbey called Lorsch, very rich in endowments, through whose properties he might serve himself and his soldiers with anything they needed. As the king, however, was stuffed full not just of snakish, but of viper-like guile, he could not fail to understand what the request actually implied. Wherefore he gave the messengers an apology like this: "Regarding what I feel about this matter, I will explain to the count more fully in words than through messages." When the fellow who had sent the messengers heard this, he was filled with an immense happiness of the soul, hoping what he had planned would come about; so, impatient of any delay, he went to the king and asked him to pronounce his sentence on the matter. With the people standing around, the king said to him: "'We ought to obey God rather than men.'[63] That is, could anyone with a sound mind ignore that you said what you

---

62. Liudprand behaves like the Byzantine functionary in *Embassy* 38 by seeking to impress Recemund with the virtue of the potentate whom he had visited as ambassador in Frankfurt in 955.

63. Acts 5.29.

said not with the humility of a petition but with the arrogance of a threat? It is written, 'Give not that which is holy to the dogs';[64] and, though the theologians say it is to be understood spiritually, nevertheless I estimate I would really have given that which is holy to the dogs if I were to take the properties of monasteries, which have been donated by actively religious men, and give them to people active in the world. With the whole people as witness, I testify to you, who so immodestly seek unjust things, that you will never receive this from me or any other grant, ever. If it is in your heart to fly away with the other faithless ones, the more quickly you do it, the better." After hearing these things, since the face is the mirror of the mind, the blush on his face laid bare the shame in his heart, and, rushing quickly to the feet of the king, the count confessed that he had sinned, and had gravely erred. Consider therefore with what steadfastness the athlete of God countered not just his visible enemies but also the invisible ones; for the ancient enemy thought he had not harmed Otto when he persuaded such mighty princes to rise in rebellion against him and also instigated his brother to take away his kingdom from him, since these were only external damages; therefore, the devil also incited the aforesaid count to ask for the endowment of the saints, so that when the king unjustly handed over to his soldiers the income of the servants of God, by such means he might more rapidly cause offense to God.[65] But since Otto refused, now, for the benefit of all, we shall relate how much the holy king improved himself on account of his steadfastness before temptation, with God fighting for him.

29. Holy David, speaking for the Lord, says: "If my people had heard me, if Israel had walked in my ways, I should have readily humbled their enemies and laid my hand on them that troubled them."[66] The event that I am about to describe makes clear that this was fulfilled in the case of our king, heeding God and walking

64. Mt 7.6.
65. The message that a good king protected ecclesiastical endowments from rapacious lay aristocrats showed up most tenth-century rulers as inadequate.
66. Ps 80.14–15.

in his ways. Having heard the king was in Alsace, since Eberhard and Gislebert feared no one who might resist them, after gathering a very large army, they crossed the bed of the Rhine at Andernach and proceeded to ravage the king's retainers in the environs. But in those same regions there was Udo, brother of the Swabians' Duke Hermann, along with Conrad surnamed "the Wise," both of whom, as we said above, were faithful to the king; yet they hesitated to march against Eberhard and Gislebert as their own troops were far fewer than the raiders. Still, with God ordaining it not by means of speech but by inspiration, they followed behind them as they returned with much plunder. And when they had advanced just a little, a certain priest came towards them, weeping and groaning; when asked by them where he was going and why he wept he said: "I come from those robbers, who increased the depth of my poverty after seizing the one and only mare I owned." When the aforesaid Udo and Conrad heard this, they carefully inquired if he had seen Gislebert and Eberhard. After the fellow answered, "Now that almost all their men have been sent across the Rhine with the loot, they are grabbing some food alone with their most trusted soldiers—and may it turn out badly for them," they rushed upon them with such speed that, if you had seen them, you would say they flew, not galloped. What happened next? Eberhard was killed by swords; Gislebert was submerged by the waves of the Rhine, and, since he could not soak them up on account of their number, with his soul departing, he died; truly not one of the rest escaped who was not bound up alive or killed by the sword.[67] Thus you see in what way the Lord lowered his hand on those who made trouble for a king whom he recognized as walking in his ways.

30. While these things took place, the king, unaware of them, was prepared to die in Alsace rather than take flight before his adversaries. Thus it happened that, as was his custom, since the church was far away, in the earliest part of the morning he mounted his horse, and with it he was going to his prayers fully clad in armor; then,

---

67. The Saxon contingent under Otto played no part in this decisive encounter of September 939, which proved the "friendship" of the Swabians to the new Saxon king.

having directed his glance there, in the distance he saw a man heading toward him with extreme swiftness, whom he understood on
the spot to be a messenger. And since the fellow who came brought
favorable news, as soon as he saw the king he offered some advance
signs of joy, an early prelude to the coming happiness. Thanks to
this clue those who were near there understand that things are propitious to the king and run with ears pricked up so they may hear
the messenger; his now slowed advance, his arranging of his clothes
and hair, his forthright greeting seemed to them to take a year. The
king perceived the people were impatient and that the messenger's
delay in talking was hard to bear, "Do," he said, "what you were
sent here to do. With an inversion of the proper order, first tell us
the facts, chase away the fear of those standing around, and fill their
spirits with joy; only *then* soften us up with long preliminaries and
the preambles of rhetorical greetings. The time is right for what you
say, not for how you say it, for we prefer to rejoice with rustic simplicity rather than try out Ciceronian witticisms."[68] Having heard
these statements, the messenger announced in a first rush of words
that Eberhard and Gislebert had departed mankind, and, though he
wished to go on with how this had happened, the king restrained
him with a gesture of his hand and quickly dismounted from his
horse and gave himself over to prayer, rendering thanks to God with
tears. Once the prayer was finished, he rose again and resumed the
trip he had begun to the church to commend himself to God.

31. At that time Duke Berthold of the Bavarians, brother of
Duke Arnulf, a vigorous man, supported the king's side with all his
strength.[69] Therefore, the king, desiring him to participate in the
present joy just as he had in the past tribulation, on the following
day revealed to Berthold through some messengers he sent what a
great favor the Lord had bestowed on him. To increase his joy Otto
also offered Berthold and gave him a promise by an oath that if he
were to capture his sister, that is, Gislebert's widow, he would unite

68. Ironically Otto quoted the fourth-century Latin grammarian Donatus (*Ars
maior* 4.402.10) while pleading for unadorned speech. This text about the virtues and
flaws of speech dominated postclassical grammar study.

69. Berthold ruled, 938–47. Liudprand discussed Arnulf in 3.49–52.

her to Berthold in marriage, since Berthold was bound by no conjugal ties at all; and if this did not work out, he would hand over
to him a daughter of the same Gislebert, whom he held in custody,
born to the same sister, now almost of marriageable age. Having
heard this, Berthold was filled with an immense glee, and he chose
rather to wait for the young maiden than to have the mother, who
had already married.[70]

32. At last Frederick, archbishop of the church of Mainz, according to whose advice several bishops had abandoned the king, as the
duplicity he had been nurturing discreetly now was evident to all,
deserted the king and went hastily to Mainz, ten days before the
death of the two characters mentioned above; without staying there
he went on to the city of Metz. For the king's brother Henry had
arranged with this same Frederick to gather the army there when
Gislebert and Eberhard returned, and there to organize a large-scale
war against the king, who was staying in Alsace. And when the archbishop reached the city, unexpectedly and inopportunely messengers
ran up to him who told him that the exalted princes no longer lived
because of death's intervention. Once he heard this, baffled in his
spirit, he was totally at a loss about what he should do.

33. Meanwhile, leaving Alsace, the king occupied Franconia; on
account of their fear of Otto the citizens of Mainz did not welcome the returning bishop within the walls of the city. Whence it
transpired that not much later he was captured by those loyal to
the king and led into the king's presence and sent into custody in
Saxony. Having remained there awhile, he was restored to his original standing through the king's mercy.[71]

34. At length Henry, mad with fear of the king, that is, of his
own brother, wanted to enter a castle called Chèvremont,[72] which
was fortified not only by the ingenuity of men but also by nature

70. This marriage never took place. Still, Otto's younger brother Henry succeeded
Berthold in 947 because he had married the latter's niece around the time of the
battle of Andernach.

71. Frederick was exiled to a monastery, 939–41. Thereafter he served Otto loyally,
and died while attempting to mediate between other rebels and the king in 954.

72. Near Liège.

itself. Foreseeing this, his sister, the widow, that is, of Gislebert, not only forbade him to do this, but also addressed him with a speech like this: "Woe! Will you not grow weary of adding to the miseries that I endure, now my husband has been killed, unless by occupying my fortifications you pour the wrath of the king over this region, as if it were water? I will not bear it, not suffer it, not stand for it.[73] For while I struggled in obedience to you, I ruined my husband's life;[74] now, however, there will not be such folly in me that you may claim your comfort through my discomfiture."[75]

35. When Henry heard these words, since he did not know what else to do, having brought along certain bishops by whose good offices he might be helped, on a certain day when the king was off his guard, barefoot, he made it through to the king's feet, and, prostrate, he begged for mercy. The king said to him: "Your unworthy crime does not deserve mercy; but since I see you humiliated before me, I shall not cause evil to befall you." Therefore, the king ordered him to be taken to the royal palace which lies at a place called Ingelheim in Franconia, and to be guarded with careful vigilance until, once the bitterness of anger receded a little, he might decide what to do with Henry, with the advice of wise men.[76]

HERE ENDS THE FOURTH BOOK, THANKS TO GOD

Book Five

HERE BEGIN THE CHAPTER HEADINGS OF THE FIFTH BOOK

1. How Duke Hermann of the Swabians gave his daughter named Ida as wife to Liudolf, the king's son.

2. About the solar eclipse and the appearance of a comet.

---

73. Cicero, *Against Catiline* 1.5.11.   74. Terence, *Andria* 822.
75. Ibid., 626–28.
76. The decision was benign: Henry was assigned major components of Otto's realm, beginning with Lotharingia.

3. About the fact that King Hugh oppressed Rome for years.

4. About the brothers Berengar and Anscar, of whom the latter was appointed margrave in Camerino and Spoleto.

5. About Sarlius, whom King Hugh sent against Anscar, and about Anscar's pronouncements.

6. About the good advice of the good soldier Wikbert, and the bad advice of the bad soldier Arcod.

7. About the first battle between Sarlius and Anscar, in which Wikbert was killed and Arcod fled.[1]

8. About another battle in which Anscar killed Count Hatto with his lance and afterwards, falling from his horse, was himself killed by the enemies, and Sarlius took over the [whole] march.

9. About King Hugh, who sent messengers to Constantinople for the sake of ships and Greek fire.

10. About King Hugh, who wanted to destroy Berengar but was unable because of Lothar, who revealed this to Berengar; and about the flight of Berengar and his wife.

11. A curse against the mountains that allowed Berengar and Willa to get through.

12. How Duke Hermann welcomed Berengar and led him into the king's presence.

13. About the fact that King Hugh sent his messengers to King Otto, promising money if he were not to receive Berengar; a goal which he was utterly unable to achieve.

14. About the fact that the emperor Romanos of the Greeks asked that Hugh grant his daughter as a spouse for his nephew, the son of Constantine.

15. About the naval battle in which Romanos engaged with Igor, king of the Russians, whom he marvelously vanquished.

16. About the fact that King Hugh, heading for Fraxinetum, directed the Greeks there with their ships.

17. About the fact that King Hugh could have destroyed Fraxinetum, but did not want to.

---

1. Liudprand added the headings for chapters 7–32 after February 962.

HERE END THE CHAPTER HEADINGS

HERE BEGINS BOOK V

1. It happened that after the deaths of Eberhard and Gislebert and also the imprisonment of the king's brother Henry, along with all the magnates rushing from all over to the king to congratulate him, there also came the very rich man Hermann, duke of the Swabians. After a surfeit of congratulations, he addressed the king with words like these: "It is no secret to my lord that I am without children, though rich both in the extent of my holdings and the amount of money I have; nor is there anyone who might be my heir when I die except a tiny daughter. Therefore, let it please my lord the king that I adopt his small son LIUDOLF as my own son, in such a way that, when I die, he, associated with me through a marital alliance with my only daughter, may become magnificent through the inheritance of my belongings." Therefore, since this advice pleased the king, what he had proposed was done without delay.

2. At that time, as you well know yourselves, the sun underwent a great eclipse, terrifying for all . . .[2] at the third hour of the sixth day, the very same day when your King Abd ar-Rhaman was defeated in battle by Radamir, the most Christian king of Galicia.[3] But also, in Italy for eight consecutive nights a comet of wondrous size appeared, emanating fiery rays of extreme length, portending the famine that would come not much later, which pitifully ravaged Italy with its severity.[4]

3. Also at that time, with King Hugh shamefully driven out, Alberic, about whom we have related earlier, was exercising sole rule over the Roman city.[5] For years King Hugh had heavily oppressed him, devastating by sword and fire everything that he could, to

---

2. There is a gap in the text at this point. The eclipse of July 19, 939, visible in the Mediterranean, was noted throughout Europe: see D. Schove, *Chronology of Eclipses and Comets AD 1–1000* (Woodbridge, England: Boydell Press, 1984), 226–28.

3. Ramíro II, king of León, surprisingly defeated the caliph's army at Simancas on August 8, 939.

4. Schove, *Chronology of Eclipses*, 297, records no such phenomenon, but had not read Liudprand.

5. See 3.45–46, above.

the point that he took from Alberic all his cities except that same Rome in which he resided. But without doubt he would have conquered the city itself, too, either by depopulating it or by corrupting the inhabitants with gifts, had the mysterious sentence of the just God not prevented it.

4. At the same time the brothers Berengar and Anscar became renowned in Italy. They were born of one father, that is, Adalbert the margrave of Ivrea, but not from one and the same mother. For Gisla, that is, the daughter of King Berengar, gave birth to Berengar, as we said earlier, but Ermengard, daughter of Adalbert the margrave of the Tuscan province—whom he had with Bertha, mother of King Hugh—gave birth to Anscar.[6] Of the two, Berengar was wise in counsel and crafty in mind, while instead Anscar was prepared to commit any crime; King Hugh held him in deep suspicion, fearing he might kill the king and take over the kingdom for himself. Thus, having taken counsel, since the margrave Tedald had departed mankind, Hugh appointed Anscar margrave of the Spoletans and Camerinans. Hugh imagined he might live that much more securely as he knew Anscar to be sequestered far from himself.[7] As he was impatient in spirit, when Anscar went there, he immediately made clear by the signals that his deeds sent everything his mind suggested to him in conjuring up evil for the king. This could hardly escape Hugh.

5. Therefore, meditating about what sort of remedy he might find for Anscar's bitterness, he summoned Sarlius to himself, born of the Burgundian nation.[8] And to him he said: "The trustworthi-

---

6. See 3.33 and 3.56, above, for genealogical details.

7. In 936. Hugh in effect strengthened Berengar II, who became the leader of aristocratic opposition to the king, by allowing his half-brother to rule the important marches of central Italy and by appointing relatives to rule elsewhere, depriving local magnates of opportunities to exercise power and alienating them. Perhaps Hugh thought Berengar controllable because he was married to the king's niece, Willa.

8. Sarlius was evidently trustworthy, though unrelated to Hugh. His successes in Spoleto contributed to the encirclement of Rome (see 3.45, 4.3, 5.3, above) and led to Hugh granting him control over central Italy's greatest monasteries (Farfa, Monte Amiata).

ness of the men of Camerino and Spoleto is not unknown to me;
for it is quite like the pen 'upon which, if a man lean, it will pierce
his hand.'9 So go and corrupt their minds with money taken from
me, shift them away from their love for Anscar, and unite them to
yourself. There is no one who can do it better or more easily than
you. For you have [an ally in] the wife of that excellent nephew of
mine, the dead margrave Tedald. Depending on her help, the whole
people will come over to you." At length he left and the people of
Camerino and Spoleto acted scarcely differently from how the king
had predicted they would; having gathered a host, Sarlius hastened
to set out toward the city where Anscar was. When Anscar heard
about it he addressed words like these to a standard-bearer of his
named Wikbert:

"The weakling Sarlius, trusting in the weapons of many,
  Heads out to fight, against whom men strong in heart and
    weaponry10
It is proper to dispatch and bring cruel war.
Let a select band of youths, experienced in many wars,
  That accompanies me, the lord, heading toward him,
  Reach there directly, adorned with dark metal."11

6. Having heard these words, Wikbert, a man filled not only
with audacity but also with understanding, said: "Wait and gather
troops as best you can, for it is very dangerous to rush against a
numerous army with so few troops. If you consider with whom
this encounter arises, you will note they are heroes, hardly lazy
men, and accustomed to war, like us." Now Anscar decided to
agree with Wikbert, who advised him rightly, and having sent out
messengers all over, he wanted to assemble an army, when a certain
Arcod, born of Burgundian blood, assailed Wikbert, who was giving good advice, with biting words: "You are like Chremetus," he
said, "who, on account of his fear of Thraso, gave advice to Thais

9. Is 36.6.
10. Virgil, *Aeneid* 4.11.
11. Liudprand here evokes Terence, Juvenal, and Virgil.

about blocking off the building until he might lead his helpers there from the forum, and when Thais prohibited it, said: 'It is stupid to subject yourself to something that for your own good you may avoid. I prefer us to take precautions rather than to take vengeance after having been harmed.'"[12] Wikbert replied: "I'd say you have most fittingly recalled the memory of the soldier Thraso, who, at first raging with rabid mouth, when he came to face the real thing, chose for himself a place behind the front line, placing Syriscus on the right wing and Symalio on the left. For the Burgundians are chatterboxes, big eaters, and unwarlike, and no one who has learned to know them doubts it. Even the scars on your back, which you received fleeing, show what you often have done ever so strenuously."

7. Thus Anscar and Wikbert, aroused by such speeches, strove to go quickly, with just a few soldiers, to the place where they heard Sarlius was encamped with his many troops.[13] Sarlius had six lines, of which he directed three against Anscar's one, the detachment in which was Anscar himself. Sarlius himself stayed behind with three lines, with a river between him and the battle, observing the outcome of the whole thing: for he worried that not even such a great multitude would serve to protect him if Anscar were to set his gaze upon him and lead his forces against him. Without delay a battle began in which Arcod was not seen, since he fled, while Wikbert was mortally wounded, since he behaved like someone who preferred to die rather than to take flight. But once the first three lines had been overcome by Anscar, Sarlius sent another two lines against him, retaining only one with himself. And when Anscar wanted to inquire about which of his men had fallen on the field, he ran across Wikbert, spattered not just with his own blood but with that of others as well. To Anscar Wikbert said: "Two lines of men very beautifully trained in weapon-handling are coming against us, which I beseech you to flee from, rather than to confront. As you

12. Terence, *Eunuchus* 761–62. Arcod is depicted citing the names of characters in Terence's play.
13. This battle took place in 940.

know well, Arcod was the instigator of this battle, and you saw how he ran. But I, having reached the end, do not now mull over battles, but pray God for mercy on my soul, lest God accuse me of the crimes I committed today out of love for you, giving death to the bodies of many men." Having uttered these words, he died.

8. Then, having gathered those he could, rushing towards the two phalanxes, Anscar leapt, raging, into their midst and created an immense massacre. A certain count named Hatto led those two lines, who ran up to Anscar confidently, since he saw only the shaft in Anscar's hand, with the spear having snapped. When Anscar recognized him, he said: "Are you not the one who, in contempt of the cross and the saints, perjured yourself by your oath in the name of God, deserted me, your lord, and went over to that fox Sarlius as a turncoat and traitor? There are certain afterworlds and subterranean kingdoms where perjurers are punished, and there are also boats and black-throated frogs of the Styx that until now you only dreamed about but soon will experience in reality!"[14] Saying this, forcefully throwing his lance-shaft, which he was holding without its metal point, through the count's mouth, he retrieved it spattered with blood and brains through the back of Hatto's skull, and, having drawn his sword, he began fighting anew, since many were rushing onto him. And accompanied by none of those who supported him, alone he sustained the attack of almost the whole army, rushing here and there until the horse on which he sat fell into a ditch in such a way that it lay on top of him with its neck below and its feet sticking out above, and he was killed by onrushing enemies who cast their projectiles at him. Once he was dead, Sarlius ruled the march safely, and King Hugh was filled with enormous glee.

9. While these things were taking place, the mountain districts that close Italy in from the west and north were most cruelly de-

---

14. In feudal circles betraying one's lord was a serious infraction. Sarlius's success in undermining Berengar's principal aristocratic support (Hatto came from near Ivrea), must have alarmed Berengar and motivated his hostility to Hugh. See G. Mor, *L'Italia feudale* 1 (Milan: F. Vallardi, 1952), 150–52.

populated by those Saracens who dwelt at Fraxinetum.[15] On account of this fact, having taken counsel, King Hugh sent messengers to Constantinople, asking the emperor Romanos to send him ships equipped with Greek fire, of the kind which the Greeks call warships[16] in their native speech. Indeed, Hugh did this so that when he set out to destroy Fraxinetum by the land route, the Greeks might set up a naval blockade on the side of the settlement that is defended by the sea, and burn the Saracen ships and most diligently prevent troops or additional food from reaching the enemy from Spain.[17]

10. Meanwhile Berengar, the margrave of Ivrea and brother of Anscar, whom we mentioned before, secretly began to scheme against the king. When this was revealed to the king, having simulated good intentions and hidden his anger, he arranged to deprive Berengar of his sight when Berengar came to visit him. Whereupon Hugh's son by the name of Lothar, himself also a king, small and ignorant of the things necessary to rulers, after the manner of all boys could not conceal such things, as he was present at the councils deciding them;[18] actually, having sent Berengar a messenger, he revealed what his own father wanted to do to him. As soon as Berengar heard about this, he quickly abandoned Italy and set out across Mount Jupiter[19] to Count Hermann in Swabia; and he instructed his wife Willa to come to the same province by another route.[20] I cannot marvel enough at the fact that she was able to make it through such steep and impassable mountains on foot, when at the time of her

15. By 940 the Saracens hampered communications across the western Alps, important to Hugh, whose family came from southern France. Their mountain base was at St. Maurice d'Agaune.

16. *Chelándia*, a transliteration.

17. In 940, as the Cordoban caliph's control grew, the inhabitants of Fraxinetum were enjoined to spare the inhabitants of southern France; this may have been part of Abd ar-Rahman III's policy of détente with Christian Europe, though from Liudprand's Italian viewpoint it had little effect on the raiders.

18. Born around 927, crowned co-ruler in 931, and married in 937 to Adelheid, the daughter of Rudolf II of Burgundy, Lothar was being groomed for the succession.

19. The Great St. Bernard, adjacent to the highest peak in the Alps, looms over an important pass between Piedmont and the Rhone valley.

20. In 941.

flight over the Mount of Birds[21] she was pregnant and close to delivery, unless I know for sure all the fates were against me. But ha! Lothar, unaware of the future, could not see what a trap he prepared for himself: for when he warned Berengar, he saved the one who would deprive him of life and kingdom. I curse not Lothar, however, who erred by the superficiality characteristic of youth and later bitterly repented of it, but rather those cruel mountains offering all the fugitives an easy passage, against their usual custom. Therefore, it now pleases me to declaim this invective against them:

11.

Wicked Mount of Birds, you are not worthy of such a name;
Why do you save that pest when you could dispatch it?
You are supposed to be pathless even when the fiery sun burns,
In the season when the reaper with curved sickle again asks Ceres
        for grain,
In the season when the star of Cancer roasts with the rays of
        Phoebus;[22]
Most evil one, are you now passable in the unheard-of season of stout
Mists? And would that my wishes could now come true
That you might be cast forth into the depths, cut off from the other
        mounts!
Now Mount Jupiter saves Berengar, and it tolerates
Him to pass along a straight path, and it's hardly surprising, as it is
        accustomed
To ruin the holy and spare the wicked[23]—the ones they alas call
        Moors by name,
Who delight in shedding men's blood and profit from a life of rapine.
Why should I speak? Now I want God to burn you with a lightning
        bolt
And, shattered, may you lie in chaos for all time.[24]

---

21. The Vogelsberg (2721 meters) dominates the Little St. Bernard pass (2065 m) that links Chur to central Lombardy.

22. Boethius, *Consolation of Philosophy* 1.6.1–2.

23. In 972 the abbot of Cluny was kidnapped on the Great St. Bernard by the Fraxinetan Saracens, but what other saints Liudprand might refer to when he wrote, a decade earlier, is unclear.

24. Boethius and Virgil were Liudprand's main models here.

12. Thus Hermann, duke of the Swabians, kindly received Berengar, who was coming to visit him, and he led him amidst great pomp before the presence of the most pious King Otto. My pen doubts it can record with what great devotion the king welcomed Berengar and how many gifts he gave him and how much he honored him; but actually the discerning reader may easily detect from the things written down how holy and humane the king was and how great Berengar's wickedness proved to be.[25]

13. King Hugh, having heard of Berengar's escape, sent his messengers to King Otto, promising he would give him a supply of gold and silver according to the decision of Otto's will if he were not to receive Berengar and not bestow support on him. To these offers the king gave a retort like this: "Berengar came to our piety not in order to depose your lordship, but, if possible, for reconciliation's sake. Because of this, if I shall prove able to rehabilitate Berengar before your lordship, I not only do not accept the payments promised to me by your lordship but will most freely give one of mine to your lordship. It would be the height of folly not to offer and to furnish aid to Berengar or to anyone else imploring clemency from our holiness." Note, therefore, with how much charity the pious king loved this man [Berengar], since he not only wanted not to accept money promised to him, but wanted to give some of his own on his behalf.[26]

14. While these things were happening, the Constantinopolitan emperor Romanos sent back his own along with King Hugh's messengers, declaring that he would supply the ships and all that

25. Berengar's association with Otto may have been decisive to his rise, as it added to his credibility for Italian magnates seeking an alternative to Hugh. Otto may have resented Hugh's influence in Burgundy, and seen Berengar as a convenient tool through whom to weaken a rival.

26. With Swabian help and the consent of Otto, in 945 Berengar returned to Italy (see 5.26–33, below). For Liudprand, and for Otto (especially after 962), the nature of the relationship between Otto and Berengar was a sensitive subject. Unlike some northern writers (Widukind, *Res Gestae Saxonicae* 1.31; Hrotswita, *De Ottone Rege*, lines 700ff), Liudprand mentioned no vassalic ties to justify Otto's later hostile actions against a rebellious liege man.

Hugh wanted if the king would give his daughter in marriage to his young nephew and namesake, the son of Constantine—I mean Constantine the son of the emperor Leo, not of Romanos himself; for these three ruled alongside Romanos, that is, his own two sons Stephen and Constantine, and also this fellow we are now talking about, Constantine the son of the emperor Leo. King Hugh, however, having heard this embassy and having again sent messengers to Romanos, claimed he did not have any daughters born of lawful marriage, but if the emperor wanted one of the daughters of his concubines, he could send one outstanding in shapeliness. And since in genealogies of aristocracy the Greeks examine who the father was, not who the mother, Emperor Romanos promptly prepared ships equipped with Greek fire, sent the greatest gifts, and asked that the girl be married to his nephew.[27] Truly, since my stepfather, a man adorned with dignity, full of wisdom, was the messenger of King Hugh,[28] it would pain me not to insert here what I often heard about the emperor's wisdom and humanity and how he defeated the Russians.

15. A certain people is established within the northern region, which the Greeks call Ρουσιος from the nature of their bodies,[29] and we instead call "Norsemen" from the location of their country. Indeed, in the German language *nord* means "north" and *man* means "people," whence we might call the Norsemen the "men of the north." The king of this nation was called Igor, who, having collected a thousand and more ships, came to Constantinople.[30]

27. More even than was traditional in Byzantium, Romanos pursued a careful marital diplomacy; his offspring married Macedonian dynasts and Bulgarian tsars, so this union with the family of Italy's most prominent ruler was part of a broader strategy. Liudprand (4.13, above) was sensitive to Byzantine marital theory.

28. This mission took place in 941, and continued a family tradition: see 3.22. The negotiations dragged out until September 944, when the marriage was celebrated at Constantinople (below, 5.20).

29. Liudprand's dubious etymology links Greek words for "red" and for Russians.

30. Constantinople's sea walls made such naval expeditions difficult. A Russian raid against Byzantium took place in 941, but focused on the Black Sea ports of Asia Minor. Igor (r. c. 913–45) vastly expanded the tribute base of the Kievan Rus and

When Emperor Romanos heard this, since he had sent his navy against the Saracens and to guard the islands, he began to bubble over with thoughts. And when he had passed not a few sleepless nights in his thinking and Igor had brutalized everything close to the sea, it was announced to Romanos that there were 15 half-sunk warships, which the people had abandoned on account of their age. When he heard this, the emperor ordered τοὺς καλαφάτας, that is, the shipbuilders, to come to him, and to them he said: "Starting without delay, prepare the warships that are left; but place the contraption from which fire is shot not just on the bow, but also on the stern and in addition on both sides of each ship." Thus, once the ships were refurbished according to his directive, he stationed very clever men on them and ordered that they steer toward King Igor. When at last they cast off, when King Igor saw them floating on the sea, he ordered that his army take the crews alive and not kill them. At last the merciful and mercy-giving Lord, who wanted not just to protect those who worshiped him, adored him, and prayed to him, but also to honor them with a victory, suddenly turned the sea calm by stilling the winds—for it would have been a nuisance to the Greeks to have contrary winds, on account of having to shoot the fire. Thus, placed in the midst of the Russians, they cast their fire all around. As soon as the Russians observed this, they cast themselves quickly from their ships into the sea, and chose to be submerged by the waves rather than to be burned by the fire. Others, however, burdened by breastplates and helmets, sought out the bottom of the sea, never to be seen again, while several, swimming between the waves of the sea, were burned, and on that day no one escaped who did not free himself by fleeing to the shore. For the ships of the Russians pass even where the water is very shallow, on account of their smallness; this the warships of the Greeks cannot do because of their deep keels; on account of this fact, Igor, freed with many of his men by flight

---

traded in Byzantium the furs, wax, honey, and slaves gathered in the north, thanks to a commercial treaty that his predecessor established, c. 911.

to the shore, afterwards in the enormous confusion returned to his country. Having obtained victory, the Greeks returned happy to Constantinople, leading off many live captives; Romanos ordered all the prisoners beheaded in the presence of the messenger of King Hugh, that is, of my stepfather.

16. Therefore, King Hugh, having gathered an army and sent the fleets to Fraxinetum across the Tyrrhenian Sea, himself headed there by the land route. When the Greeks reached there, they quickly burned all the Saracens' ships, having spewed out Greek fire. But the king, having entered Fraxinetum, forced all the Saracens to flee to Moor's Mountain, on which he might have captured them by a siege if this fact, which I am about to relate, had not prevented it.

17. King Hugh greatly feared lest Berengar, after assembling troops from Francia and Swabia, might rush upon him and snatch the kingdom from him. Whence, having accepted bad advice, King Hugh sent the Greeks back to their country and himself entered an agreement with the Saracens to this effect, namely, that they should stay in the mountains that divide Swabia from Italy in such a way that, if by chance Berengar should seek to lead an army through, they would by all means prohibit him from passing. And actually what a vast amount of blood of Christians heading to the thresholds of the blessed apostles Peter and Paul was spilled by this treaty God alone knows, who keeps their names written in the book of the living. How unjustly you attempted to defend your kingdom, King Hugh! Herod killed many innocents lest he be deprived of his earthly kingdom; you, so that you might hold onto it, let off the guilty and those deserving of death; if only the guilty had then lived on condition they would not later murder the innocent! I think, or, to be more truthful, I believe that you did not read, nor even hear, how the king of Israel Ahab incurred the Lord's wrath when he sent away as an ally Ben-hadad, the king of Syria, a man deserving death. For one of the sons of the prophets said to Ahab: "Thus says the Lord: 'Because you have let go out of your hand a man worthy of death, your life shall be for his life, and

your people for his people'";[31] this duly happened. Truly, our pen shall narrate more appropriately in the designated place how much you harmed yourself by this act.

18. At the time when Berengar ran from Italy, he led away with himself a certain soldier named Amedeus, who was a noble to begin with and, as later events clarified, not inferior to Ulysses in craftiness and audacity. The very mighty King Otto, both prevented by many events and mollified each year by the immense gifts from King Hugh, could not supply Berengar any troops, so the same Amedeus, of whom I made mention above, addressed Berengar thus: "It is not unknown to you, my lord, how King Hugh has rendered himself unpopular with all the Italians through his harsh rule, especially as he granted offices to the sons of his concubines and to other Burgundians, and no Italian can be found who was not either expelled or deprived of every office. And the reason why no one has schemed against the king is that they do not have anyone whom they might elect as their leader. Therefore, if one of our men, having donned a different costume lest he be recognized, should travel to Italy and inquire after the locals' will, without doubt he would draw out from his inquiry good advice for us." Berengar said to him: "As you could do this most easily, no one could do it better than you." Thus Amedeus, having changed his attire, pretending to be heading to Rome with the paupers who travel there to pray, went to Italy, assembled the magnates, and inquired as to what each had in his heart. For neither did he reveal himself to all in the same costume: he was seen as a black man by some, as a ruddy-haired one by others, as a freckle-face by others still. But rumor, the evil than which none moves faster,[32] brought it to the king's ears that he was in Italy. And while Hugh ordered him to be searched-for carefully, that fellow deeply blackened with pitch his flowing and most beautiful beard, changed his golden hair with soot, made his face ugly, pretended to be demented to the point that he showed himself half-naked to the king, among the

31. 1 Kgs 20.42.
32. Virgil, *Aeneid* 4.174–75.

paupers eating [a charitable meal] in the king's presence, and actually accepted clothes to wear from him and heard what the king said about Berengar and himself.

Finally, having most meticulously examined everything in this way, he returned not in the same way in which he had come, with those going to pray, for the king had ordered the guards of the "closures" not to allow anyone to pass unless they had first discovered who he was by a most thorough investigation.[33] Hearing this, Amedeus crossed the Alps by certain pathless and unguarded places and reached Berengar with the message he wanted to hear.

19. At that time King Hugh, having given ten measures of coins, made peace with the Hungarians; after accepting hostages from them, he expelled them from Italy, and, after giving them a guide, he directed them to Spain.[34] In truth the reason why they did not reach Spain and the very city of Córdoba, where the king resides, is this: that they crossed through a vast, waterless region for three thirsty days; considering, therefore, that their horses and they themselves would die of thirst, having beaten to death the guide granted by King Hugh, they returned at a quicker pace than that with which they had advanced.

20. Also at the same time, King Hugh sent his daughter Bertha, whom he had generated with the prostitute Pezola, to Constantinople with Sigefred the venerable head of the church of the Parmesans, to be united in marriage with Romanos, the small son of Constantine Porphyrogenitus. Romanos the elder held the highest imperial power with his two sons Constantine and Stephen; in or-

33. Though early medieval territorial boundaries were vague and porous, Liudprand stresses the efficacy of such closures (e.g., 1.13, above). The "closures" in the Alps were fortifications at the strategic passes, some of which dated back to Roman times. See N. Christie, "The Alps as a Frontier (AD 168–774)," *Journal of Roman Archaeology* 4 (1991): 410–30; A. Settia, "Le frontiere del regno italico nei secoli VI–XI," *Studi storici* 1 (1989): 155–69.

34. Liudprand suggests that instead of fighting the Hungarians in 943, as at least he had begun to do with the Saracens in 941 (5.17), Hugh negotiated a settlement. This depiction of King Hugh accommodating both non-Christian enemies (Hungarians and Saracens) in the space of a few years delegitimizes him. It also suggests that Hugh was increasingly unable to muster the Italian magnates.

der of rank, after Romanos came Constantine, the son of the emperor Leo, whose small son—born from Helena the daughter of the elder Romanos, the emperor—took the aforesaid Bertha as his wife, whom the Greeks called Eudochia, having altered her name.[35] Thus, with these four ruling, the brothers Stephen and Constantine devised a certain σφάλματα[36] against their father Romanos, while Constantine the son of Leo remained unaware of it. For it troubled them, subject to the severity of their father, not to be able to do whatever they wanted; wherefore, having also taken some bad advice, they were pondering how they might overthrow their father.

21. The Constantinopolitan palace surpasses all the buildings that I have ever seen not just in beauty but also in security, and it is also guarded by no small crowd of soldiers. It is the custom there to open the palace to all after the break of day, but after the third hour of the day, having sent everyone away by a given signal (that is, *mîs*), to prohibit access to everyone until the ninth hour.[37] Thus Romanos was most overbearingly staying in the *chrysotriclinon*, which is the most opulent section of the palace, and had assigned to his son-in-law Constantine and his sons Stephen and Constantine the other sections of the palace.[38] But at length these latter two, unable to stand the just strictness of their father, as we said before, having gathered many troops in their private quarters, chose a date when they would depose their father and could rule alone. When the longed-for day arrived, once everyone had left the palace according to custom, having formed their assembly, Stephen and Constantine rushed upon their father and evicted him from the pal-

35. She died in 949.

36. "Foul play."

37. The third hour ended about 180 minutes after sunrise. The ninth hour came in late afternoon, about 180 minutes before sunset. But hours had variable length, according to the season, latitude, and consequent extent of daylight.

38. Such spatial segregation, as Liudprand himself experienced in Constantinople (see *Embassy* below), was a political tool much used in Byzantium. The "golden hall" had been built by Justin II, an octagonal domed hall whose symbolic and architectural centrality within the Great Palace grew thereafter. See P. Magdalino, *Constantinople médiévale* (Paris: De Boccard, 1996), 40–41.

ace though the citizens were unaware of it. Then, after shaving his head as is their tradition, they sent him to love wisdom at a nearby island where a crowd of monks practiced the love of wisdom.[39] Very quickly there arose a multifarious rumor among the Constantinopolitan people: some said Romanos had been deposed; others claimed his son-in-law Constantine had been killed. Without delay the entire people crowded around the palace. Romanos was not found there, almost like an imaginary emperor, and whether Constantine still lived was the question discussed by all. And when, in the course of this inquiry into Constantine's fate, there broke out no small unruliness, Constantine the son-in-law, by the order of Stephen and Constantine, showed his head, with his hair hanging down through the gates, from that side whence the immensity of the Zucanistrium is seen.[40] By this exposure he quickly calmed the tumult of the people and induced everyone to walk home again. This fact caused deep pain to the two brothers. "What was the use," they said, "if after ridding ourselves of our father we now must put up with another lord, who is not even our father? For we would suffer a paternal domination in a more even-tempered and dignified way than an external one." "Who is this fellow," they continued, "to whose aid come not just the locals but even foreign nations? Indeed, Bishop Sigefred, the messenger of King Hugh, having assembled the nations of his language, namely, the Amalfitans, Romans, Gaetans, came to undo us and save that man!"[41]

22. Having said these things, they filled their private chambers

39. Romanos, about whose career Liudprand wrote also in book 3, was exiled to the island of Prote in the Sea of Marmara in 944 and died there in 948. "Philosophizing," or loving wisdom, was a late antique expression for entering the monastic life.

40. Liudprand was the sole early medieval Latin author to refer to the "Zucanistrium." This τζυκανιστήριον was a stadium reserved for the court, and used mostly to play polo. It was rebuilt in the ninth century, grander than the late antique original. It lay to the south of the Great Palace, connected to it. See R. Janin, *Constantinople byzantine* (Paris: Institut francais d'études byzantines, 1969), 118–19.

41. Evidently there was an expatriate community of Italian origin in Constantinople, and King Hugh's emissary could count on their "Latin" solidarity at times of crisis like this. See *Embassy* 46 for another reference to a resident Latin community.

with groups of armed men, just as they had in the case of their father. A certain Diavolinus commanded these men. He was the instigator of all the brothers' deeds and after a little while became their betrayer too. For he addressed Constantine, who was reading a book, like this: "That old-style religiosity that lives on in you could not fathom the troubles that your brothers, I mean your enemies, Stephen and Constantine, are brewing for you. For if you were to learn what misfortunes are planned for you, you would begin thinking about your survival. The brothers of your wife,[42] Stephen and Constantine, after gathering armed bands and locking them in their private chambers, are planning not to expel you from the palace as they did with their father, but to kill you here. The occasion of your murder will be this. After three days Stephen and Constantine will invite you to dinner. And when you attempt to take the middle seat as is the custom of your excellency, suddenly, at the sound of a shield being struck, the holed-up men will leap from the private chambers and end your life with bloodshed. If you wonder, however, about the credibility of these revelations, I shall affirm it by the present evidence, since I will show you the hidden men through some cracks in the wall; then, what is more important for your safety, I will give you the keys to the doors." Having heard these words, Constantine said: "As you revealed the duplicity of the plotters, utter a word now about how I may overcome it. For my own safety is not as dear to me as will be my devotion in rendering joyful thanks." Diavolinus replied to him: "It is not hidden from you that the Macedonians are as devoted to you as they are tough in combat; send for them and stuff your own rooms with them, leaving Stephen and Constantine ignorant of it. And when the designated day for the dinner arrives and the moment comes for the ceremony of seating, at the giving of the signal, that is, when the shield is struck as I said before, while their bands of armed men will not be able to protect them, let your men suddenly and quickly sally forth and capture the brothers as easily

42. To legitimize his role at court, Romanos had married his daughter Helena to the young Constantine Porphyrogenitus in May 919. See 3.30, above.

as unexpectedly, and with their hair shaven as the custom is, pack them off to love wisdom at the nearby monastery to which they sent their own father, meaning your father-in-law. Indeed, the rectitude of divine justice, whose retribution did not scare them off from sinning against their father, and which prevented you from offending, will abet your endeavor." That this took place exactly in this manner by God's just judgment not just Europe, but nowadays both Africa and Asia declare, too. Indeed, on the designated day, when the brothers Stephen and Constantine invited the other Constantine to dinner after counterfeiting peace, and when a tumult broke out over the ceremony of seating, and when the shield was struck as we said, the Macedonians unexpectedly sallied forth and, as soon as they captured them, packed off the two brothers Stephen and Constantine with shaved heads to the nearby island to love wisdom, the same one to which they had sent their father.[43]

23. When their father, Romanos, heard of their arrival, he gave thanks to God, and, hastening towards them outside the monastery with a joyful face, he said: "What a holiday it is that brought your imperial highnesses to visit us in our humble condition! I imagine that the same love that expelled me from the palace did not allow you, my sons, to stay there long? O well done, that you sent me ahead a little time before! My fellow brothers and monks, minding only the loftiest love of wisdom, might not have known how emperors are welcomed had they not had me here beforehand, weakened but wearing imperial regalia. Now here is some boiled water colder than Gothic snow;[44] there are broad beans for dessert, and fresh leeks; here seafood delicacies do not cause you any discomfort, but instead continuous fasts do. Our modestly positioned self does not receive such a great and elegant horde of visitors here; it only welcomes your majesties, who came lest you desert your father in his old age." It is not necessary to recount in detail, but just to imagine, with Romanos deafening them in this way and his sons

43. Constantine VII Porphyrogenitus's restoration of the Macedonian dynasty's rule took place in 945.

44. Juvenal, *Satires* 5.50. The temperature of drinking water mattered to Byzantine connoisseurs: see *Embassy* 63.

Stephen and Constantine shamefacedly casting their gazes on the
ground, how unwillingly they headed toward the monastery. After
this, Romanos, having extended his hands and prostrated at the
base of the altar, amidst his tears offered prayers to God like this:

24.
"Christ God, who are one with the Father and Spirit,
    Word, by the pronouncement of the Father, through whom the Father
    Made all things known to the world, revealing the mystic secrets of
        the earth's extremities,
    Look upon this image created by your own goodness.
    Do not permit me, I pray, to perish by the deceits of demons,
    A man whom you wished to return to life through your holy blood!
    Grant, O God, that I may still be able to tread upon
    The ferments of the world; and keep far away the unjust corruptor
    Whose purpose it is always to defile blessed souls.
    What was pleasing when I took up the scepter now, of course, is not
        pleasing.
    Let it be so!
    You deigned by your grace to cast down the unjust ones
    Lest they unjustly hold their father's post."

25. When these things had taken place in this way, Stephen and
Constantine were watched under close guard, with their father
bearing what had happened to him with equanimity. For they say
and confirm under interrogation that, when he was reproached by
the unfeeling brothers for his expiation, he answered that one who
served the humility of God's servants would rule more splendidly
than one who commanded mighty sinners in the world.

26. Meanwhile the long-awaited Berengar, accompanied by a
few men from the Swabian regions, journeyed to Italy from Swabia
along the Val Venosta, and approached the fortified castle called
Formicaria, which had been entrusted to the vigilance of his cleric
Adelard by Manasses—as we just said, archbishop of the see of
Arles and usurper of those of Trent, Verona, and Mantua.[45] And

45. Upon returning to Italy in 945 (see 4.14, above), Berengar received protection
from the lord of the northeastern march, Manasses (see 4.6–7, above), and Bishop

while Berengar pondered how he could capture this stronghold with no siege equipment and no war band, knowing Manasses's ambition and vainglory all too well, he ordered Adelard to come to him; and he said to him: "If you hand over into my power the fortification and convince your lord Manasses to aid my cause, after taking power in the kingdom I will give him the archbishopric of Milan and you the office of bishop of Como. And so that you may accept the trustworthiness of my promise, I confirm by oath what I offer in words." When this was told to Manasses by Adelard, he did not just order the fortification given to Berengar, but also invited all the Italians to come to his aid.

27. Therefore rumor, the evil that none surpasses in speed,[46] most quickly conveyed news of Berengar's arrival to all; and soon many began to join Berengar, having deserted Hugh.[47] The first among them was Milo, very mighty count of Verona; and as he was watched by guards, secretly dispatched through Hugh's suspicion, he pretended he did not understand he was being watched and dragged out his dinner almost into the middle of one night. So when all consigned their bodies to rest, burdened both with sleepiness and wine, accompanied only by the man who bore his shield, Milo went very swiftly to Verona, and by sending messengers he roused Berengar, whom he then met in Verona, so that he could resist Hugh more firmly. Actually, no infidelity divided him from Hugh, but instead he suffered several damaging decisions from the king, with which he could put up no longer. Wido, bishop of the Modenese church, followed him, not provoked by any offense but desirous of the mighty abbacy of Nonantola, which he later acquired; he not only deserted Hugh but brought along a multitude of other mules. When Hugh

---

Wido of Modena. Hugh had dismantled his old base, the march of Ivrea, allowing "new" Piedmontese lineages to appropriate the margrave's main rights and titles.

46. Virgil, *Aeneid* 4.174–75.

47. Though Hugh favored his (Burgundian) entourage, and appointed relatives over the larger districts of the kingdom, the dissatisfaction of the Lombard aristocracy derived mostly from his attempt to undermine heritability of office, one of the bedrocks of aristocratic power: G. Sergi, "The Kingdom of Italy," in *Italy*, ed. La Rocca, 355.

heard about this, having gathered troops, he came to Wido's castle of Vignola and there attacked it manfully, but uselessly; the following story will show how far from falsehood this statement is. For while he stayed there, Berengar, prompted by Archbishop Arderic, left Verona and came quickly to Milan.[48] Having heard this, King Hugh returned, disconsolate, to Pavia. All the magnates of Italy meanwhile began to desert Hugh, under no good star, and to join needy Berengar. I say a man is needy not when he owns nothing, but when nothing is ever enough for him. Indeed, crooked and avaricious men, who have insecure properties based on luck, always hunger for more—nor has anything yet been found that it would satisfy them to possess—so they should be considered not only *un*-abundant in wealth, but even poor and wanting.

For only those men are rich and possess fruitful and eternal things who, content with their own things, consider what is to be enough. Not to be greedy is true wealth; not to be a buyer is itself an income. Indeed, let us judge who is richer: the one for whom things are always wanting or the one for whom there are too many? The one who pines, or the one who finds abundance? The one for whom the greater his possessions, the more he wants things to possess, or the one who supports himself by his own strength? The one who is satisfied with his things has the greatest and most secure riches. Truly, now let what has been said about this suffice. Let the intent of the pen return to Berengar, at whose advent all promised the golden century was nigh and squealed the blissful times had begun.

28. Therefore, with Berengar staying at Milan and handing out Italian offices to those who supported him, King Hugh sent Lothar, his son, not just into the presence of Berengar but to the entire people, asking that, since they rejected him as non-compliant with their wishes, at least for the love of God they should accept his son, who had committed no crime against them, and turn him into a ruler compliant with their wishes. Then, with Lothar heading

48. The archiepiscopal see was probably the largest city of the Lombard plain; its fall was a mortal blow to Hugh's regime. Arderic may have been worried about his prospects, since Hugh had designated an heir for the Milanese see (4.14, above).

to Milan, after having left Pavia with all the treasure, King Hugh was thinking of abandoning Italy and going to Burgundy. But this fact held him back, for the magnates, inclined to be merciful, lifted up Lothar, who was prostrate before the cross in the church of Ambrose's blessed martyrs and confessors, Gervase and Protase, and appointed him their king, soon after which event they sent a messenger to Hugh, to whom they promised he would again rule over them.[49]

Not all of them, but Berengar alone obviously dreamed up this plan, or rather trick, as he was stuffed full of cunning, not so that it might allow Lothar and Hugh to rule but, as later became clear, lest Hugh might leave and, with the immense fortune he had, incite the Burgundians or other peoples against Berengar.[50]

29. At that time a certain Joseph, an old man in his ways, a youth in years, shone as the bishop of the Brescian city. Because Joseph feared God, and on account of the probity of his ways, Berengar deprived him of his bishopric and appointed Anthony in his place, who still lives now, with no council being held, no decision by the bishops. But then he also appointed as bishop of Como, not Adelard as he had promised, but a certain Waldo, on account of his love for the archbishop of Milan. And both people's groans and outward signs like the pillaging of subjects, the slashing of vines, the girdling of trees, the gouging of many eyes, and the very frequent repetition of quarrels, prove how well he acted in this regard. He also made Adalhard leader of the church of Reggio.

30. In truth he thought of expelling Bishop Boso, bastard son of King Hugh, from the Placentine see, and Bishop Liutefred from

49. Liudprand exaggerates Berengar's success. Initially Berengar was content to serve as Lothar's chief adviser. Hugh, satisfied with his son's succession, did not abdicate but returned to Provence in mid-945. Lothar soon recalled him to Italy, where he watched the overhaul of the kingdom and the demotion of many of his own men. After his definitive return to Arles, he died in 948.

50. By the tenth century, treasure was not as vital a political tool as it had been, and land was the preferred gift (a distinction Liudprand understood: see 5.1, above), though the ability to give splendid presents remained an important component of successful and legitimate rule. Liudprand, however, feared the corrupting power of movable wealth (e.g., 4.12, 5.31).

the church of Pavia; actually, with a bribe intervening, he pretended to have let them off for the love of God. How immense was then the joy of the Italians! They howled that another David had come, and with blinded minds they preferred him to Charlemagne. For although the Italians raised up Hugh and Lothar as kings, in fact Berengar was margrave in name alone, and in real power he was the king while they, kings in name, in deed were not even worth what counts are. What happened next? My parents, struck by Berengar's great reputation, by his humanity, by his generosity, handed me over to him for service; and having donated immense gifts to him, they made me his private adviser and the signatory of his letters. When I had served him faithfully for a long time, as repayment he granted me this which—what anguish!—I will relate in the appropriate place.[51] Really this retribution would drive me almost to desperation if he had not produced many fellow victims in similar situations. For we accept very approvingly this saying regarding him: "The feathers of the ostrich are like the feathers of the sparrowhawk and the heron . . . when the time arrives, she raises her wings on high, she scorns the horse and its rider."[52] For, with Hugh and Lothar still living, this fellow, Berengar the great voracious ostrich, though not good, seemed to be like a good man; however, when they were deceased, and with all promoting him to the pomp of kingship, how he raised his wings and scoffed at us all I narrate not so much with words as with sighs and moans. But leaving these things aside, let us return to the order of the narrative.

31. King Hugh, as he could not avoid the divine opposition and outshine Berengar, having left Lothar behind and entrusted him to Berengar's care through a counterfeit peace, set out for Provence with all the wealth.[53] Having heard this, the prince of the Aquita-

51. The text does not contain an explanation of the harm Berengar II did to Liudprand, but see 3.1 for some hints. It seems clear that after launching his career at Hugh's court (see 4.1, above), Liudprand's family, like the dynasts described in chapter 27, above, sensed that Berengar's fortunes were waxing and changed allegiance.

52. Jb 39.13 and 18.

53. In 947. Thus Berengar was unable to prevent the exportation of Hugh's treasure, though Liudprand claimed that had been his reason for accepting the compromise of 945–47 (above, 5.28).

nians, Raymund, went to him, and both gave himself to Hugh as a soldier for a thousand coins and affirmed his faithfulness to him by oath, promising that he would protect Hugh. But he also promised that he would enter Italy and overcome Berengar, after gathering troops; and what great giggles this caused us all the paucity of his men makes clear. And even if such a promise might have been a protection, still he hardly made it effective at all since shortly thereafter, with the Lord summoning him, King Hugh took the way of all flesh, having left the wealth with his niece Bertha, widow of Boso the count of Arles. After a small interlude of time, the aforesaid Raymund, most impure prince of the most impure nation, made her his spouse, though elegant connoisseurs of physical appearance thoroughly confirm that he was unworthy not only of bedding her but even of a single kiss.[54]

32. At that time his sister, that is, Berengar's wife Willa, became guilty of the crime of infidelity.[55] That it happened in the following way not just courtiers and chambermaids, but even bird-hunters and gluttons affirm. She had a chaplain, a small priest, Dominic by name, short in stature, sooty in color, crude, bristly, restless, rough, a barbarian, harsh, hairy, endowed with a tail, shameless, mad, rebellious, unfair, to whose instruction Willa had entrusted her daughters, that is, Gisla and Girberga, so that he might imbue in them knowledge of letters. Therefore, using the excuse of the girls, whom the priest Dominic, hairy and unwashed, taught amusingly, the mother seduced him, giving him delicate food and costly clothes. Everyone wondered why a woman so unlikable, unpleasant, and unyielding to all should be so generous to him. That truthful saying, however, which goes: "For nothing is covered that shall not be revealed, nor hidden that shall not be manifest,"[56] did not allow men to wonder about it for long. For on a certain night, with Berengar absent, when that hairy fellow sought to get into the lord's bed as usual, a dog

---

54. Liudprand advertised his distaste for Provence and its inhabitants at the beginning of his account (1.2, above).

55. When Raymond married Bertha, Willa (the other daughter of Boso of Arles) became his sister-in-law.

56. Mt 10.26.

was at hand who awakened those sleeping nearby with its horrible barking and mauled the priest with a fierce bite. Whereupon those who were in the house arose, and when they seized him and asked where he was going, the mistress, anticipating him, gave this answer: "He was going, a lost soul, to visit our maids." Thus the priestlet, hoping he would be dealt with more leniently if he supported the lady's affirmation, said: "I declare it is so." Thereafter the mistress began to make attempts on his life, and to promise a reward if there were anyone who would take his life. But as all feared God, his death was postponed, and the whole story reached Berengar. Willa began to make inquiries of diviners and witches so that she might be helped by their incantations. Whether she was aided, however, by their incantations or by Berengar's softness, regardless his mind was so inclined that he spontaneously placed his head back in the marital muzzle. Thus the priestlet, since he neighed at the servants of the mistress, was sent away with his manly attributes cut off; and the mistress was loved all the more by Berengar. Those, however, who made him a eunuch said that the mistress had loved him for a good reason, as he proved to carry massive priapic weapons.[57]

33. In that same time Taxis, king of the Hungarians, came to Italy with a large army. Berengar gave him ten measures of coins not from his own money, but from an exaction on the churches and paupers. Yet he did this not so that he might take care of the people, but so that, with this excuse, he might assemble a large sum, as indeed he did. Every person, of either sex, whether already weaned or still suckling, gave a coin for himself, and, mixing bronze with these coins, Berengar obtained ten measures from just a few coins; he kept for himself the other part and what he extracted from the churches.[58]

HERE ENDS THE FIFTH BOOK. Thanks to God.

---

57. Priapus was a pagan divinity usually represented with a disproportionately large, erect penis.

58. This chapter was written after February 962, when Otto became emperor, along with all of book 6: see Chiesa, *Liudprandi Cremonensis Opera*, lv, lxxx.

Book Six

HERE BEGIN THE CHAPTER HEADINGS
OF THE SIXTH BOOK

1. The nature of the present time would turn me into a writer of tragedies instead of histories, unless the Lord "set a table in my sight against those who trouble me."[1] For I cannot explain by how many losses I am battered, having set out as a pilgrim, and it would suit my external persona better to weep than to write. Instead my inner self, encouraged by the apostolic statutes, is glorified by such tribulations, "knowing that tribulation works patience, and patience trial, and trial hope; and hope does not confound, because the charity of God is poured forth in our hearts by the Holy Spirit who is given to us."[2] Therefore, let the external persona imitate the inner self and not only stop lamenting its misfortunes but actu-

1. Ps 22.5.
2. Rom 5.3–5.

ally acquiesce to them; and while hard at work writing, when one describes the wheel of fortune lifting these, lowering those, let one feel one's present loss less and, rejoicing in fortune's mutability, let one not fear worse things—which, frankly, there cannot be, unless death or debility of the limbs were to strike—but let one always expect favorable things. For if one's present condition changes, it will bring that health that is now absent, and chase off the misfortune that now prevails. Let me write, therefore, and add to what is written above the true events that follow.

2. With King Hugh dead in the region of Provence, the name of Berengar, celebrated among several nations, presently became so among the Greek ones, too. For he excelled all the Italians in strength, while Lothar was king in name only. Therefore, having heard that Berengar outstripped Lothar in power, Constantine, who held the empire of the Constantinopolitans, having cast down Romanos and his sons, sent letters to Berengar through a certain Andrew, who was called "count of the manor" from the nature of his office, and in them it was said that he strongly wanted to see a messenger of Berengar's, upon whose return to Italy Berengar would learn in what deep affection Constantine held him. He also wrote recommendation letters to him for Lothar, so that Berengar would be a faithful administrator for him since, with God granting it, he was his executor. Indeed, Constantine had no small solicitude for Lothar's health, piously thinking of it on account of his love for his daughter-in-law, who was Lothar's sister.[3]

3. So Berengar, pondering, with all the craftiness of which he was stuffed full, the question of whom he could send, to whom he would pay no expenses for the duration of the journey, summoned my stepfather, under whose tutelage I lived, and then said: "How useful it would be to me if your stepson were not ignorant of Greek letters!" And when he answered: "If only I could shell out half my wealth to attain that goal!" Berengar replied, "It is not necessary for you to spend even a hundredth part of it. Through

3. The details of this marital alliance are in 5.20, above.

letters the Constantinopolitan emperor prays that I send him one of my messengers; on account of his steadfastness of spirit, no one could do the chore better, and, on account of his eloquence, no one could do it more easily. Why need I state how much more easily a lad who drank down Latin teachings at such a young age would imbibe Greek ones?" My stepfather, readily encouraged by that hope, underwrote all the expenses, and sent me to Constantinople with great gifts.

4. In fact, leaving Pavia on the day of the calends of August, after three days of following the course of the Po, I reached Venice, and there I also found Salemon, the envoy of the Greeks, a palace butler and a eunuch, who had returned from Spain and Saxony and intended to depart for Constantinople, bearing great gifts and taking with him the messenger of our lord, then king, now emperor, the most wealthy prelate of Mainz, Liutefred. Leaving Venice at last on the eighth day before the calends of September, we arrived at Constantinople on the fifteenth before the calends of October; it will not be a nuisance to write about the unheard-of and wondrous way in which we were received there.[4]

5. For at Constantinople there is a palace next to the Great Palace, of wondrous beauty and size, that is called Magnaura by the Greeks, having inserted a "u" in the place of the digamma, as if it were *magna aura*.[5] And so Constantine ordered this mansion to be prepared in due fashion both because of the messengers of the Spaniards, who then were coming there for the first time, and because of Liutefred and me. In front of the emperor's throne there stood a certain tree of gilt bronze, whose branches, similarly gilt bronze, were filled with birds of different sizes, which emitted the

4. Liudprand left Pavia on August 2, 949, and Venice on the 25th, reaching his destination on September 7th. Liudprand returned to Italy in early 950.

5. "Great Breeze" (Latin). The ceremonial hall (*magna aula*) on the edge of the Great Palace was basilican in plan. In the 900s it was already a venerable four hundred years old. See C. Mango, *The Brazen House* (Copenhagen: I Kommision hos Munksgaard, 1959), 57–59. On the automata favored by Byzantine rulers, see G. Brett, "The Automata in the Byzantine 'Throne of Solomon,'" *Speculum* 29 (1954): 477–87.

songs of the different birds corresponding to their species. The throne of the emperor was built with skill in such a way that at one instant it was low, then higher, and quickly it appeared most lofty; and lions of immense size (though it was unclear if they were of wood or brass, they certainly were coated with gold) seemed to guard him, and, striking the ground with their tails, they emitted a roar with mouths open and tongues flickering. Leaning on the shoulders of two eunuchs, I was led into this space, before the emperor's presence. And when, upon my entry, the lions emitted their roar and the birds called out, each according to its species, I was not filled with special fear or admiration, since I had been told about all these things by one of those who knew them well. Thus, prostrated for a third time in adoration before the emperor, I lifted my head, and the person whom earlier I had seen sitting elevated to a modest degree above the ground, I suddenly spied wearing different clothes and sitting almost level with the ceiling of the mansion. I could not understand how he did this, unless perchance he was lifted up there by a pulley of the kind by which tree trunks are lifted. Then, however, he did not speak at all for himself, since, even if he wished to, the great space between us would render it unseemly, so he asked about the life of Berengar and his safety through a minister. When I had answered him reasonably, and when his interpreter gave a sign, I left and was soon received in the hostel assigned to me.

6. But let it not be a nuisance to recollect what I did then for Berengar, in such a way that it might be acknowledged with what great kindness I loved him, and what manner of recompense I received from him for my good deeds. The messengers of the Spaniards and Liutefred, whom I mentioned above, the messenger of our lord Otto, then still king, had brought the emperor Constantine large gifts on behalf of their lords. Instead I had brought nothing more than a letter on behalf of Berengar, a letter full of lies. My spirit was therefore not a little agitated because of the shame of it, and carefully pondered what it should do about this situation. In my agitation and great hesitation my mind suggested that the gifts for

the emperor that I had brought on my own behalf I should present as coming from Berengar, and that I should adorn the slight value of the gifts with words as best I could. I offered, therefore, nine excellent breastplates, seven excellent shields with gilt bosses, two gilt silver cups, swords, spears, skewers, and four *carzimasia* slaves, to this emperor the most precious of all these things. For the Greeks call a child-eunuch, with testicles and penis cut off, a *carzimasium*. The merchants of Verdun do this on account of the immense profit they can make, and they are accustomed to bring them to Spain.

7. Once these things had been accomplished in this way, after three days the emperor ordered me to be called to the palace. And having spoken to me with his own mouth, he invited me to a meal, and after the meal he gave my retainers and me a great gift. Truly, as the opportunity for telling about it presents itself, I consider it good not to be silent but to write down what his table is like, especially on feast days, and what games are performed at table.

8. There is a residence near the hippodrome, toward the north, of wondrous height and beauty, which is called Decanneacubita. This name did not emerge from the structure itself but for quite obvious reasons; for in Greek the Latin "ten" is *deca* and "nine" is *ennea*, while we may say *cubita* derives from incubating, or lying, on a slope, or something slightly curved. All the more so since on the birthday, according to the flesh, of our Lord Jesus Christ, ten and nine tables are placed inside the residence, at which the emperor, and equally his guests, do not eat sitting up, as on other days, but reclining on curved couches; and on those occasions they are served not with silver but only from gold dishes. After the food, apples are brought in three gold dishes that, because of their immense weight, are not carried on the arms of men but are brought on purple-veiled carts. Only two of these, however, are placed at table. Through three holes in the roof there are [three] ropes wrapped with gilt leather, and they have been positioned with gold rings. Placed through the handles that project from the vessels, these rings allow such bowls to be lifted onto the table and lowered in the same way by means of a jointed device above the ceiling, with

four or more men helping below. Finally, I omit the shows I saw there, since it is a very long thing to write about; but one alone, on account of its astonishing quality, it will not be unpleasant to insert here.

9. There enters some fellow sustaining on his forehead without the help of his hands a wooden pole that is twenty-four and more feet long, which had, a cubit below its tip, a crosspiece two cubits long. Then two naked boys were led in, but girt with short knickers, that is, wearing brief costumes, who climbed up the wooden pole and played around there, and then, clambering back down it with their heads turned upside-down, they maintained the pole so motionless that it appeared rooted to the earth. Finally, after the descent of one, the other, who remained there alone, cavorted up there and left me stunned with even greater admiration. For in some way it seemed possible as long as both played, since, although that was marvelous, too, actually by their not unequal weight they steadied the pole they had climbed up. But the one who, by balancing his weight, stayed on the top of the pole, where he even played, and then came down unscathed, left me so agape that my admiration did not escape the emperor himself. Wherefore, having invited an interpreter, he asked which seemed to me more wonderful: the boy who moved so circumspectly that the pole remained steady, or the fellow who held it with his forehead so resourcefully that neither the boys' weight nor their playing tipped the pole even a little. And when I replied that I did not know which seemed *thaumastoteron*[6] to me, he swelled with loud laughter and said that he did not know, either.

10. But I reckon that this ought not to be passed over in silence, namely, what else I saw there that was novel and marvelous. During that week that comes before the *vaiophóron*—which we call "palm branches"[7]—the emperor makes a payment of gold coins both to

6. Liudprand's Greek for "more marvelous," transliterated into Latin characters here.

7. The penultimate week of Lent, leading up to Palm Sunday and a holy time in the Christian calendar.

the soldiers and to those appointed to the various offices, according to what their rank deserves. Since he wanted me to be present at this pay day, he ordered me to come. It happened in this way. A table ten cubits in length and four in width had been set down, which supported the coins, bound in bags according to what each was owed, with numbers written on the outside of each bag. Thereupon, they entered before the emperor not in a jumble, but in an order, according to the summons of the herald who recited the written names of the men according to the dignity of their rank. The first of them to be called in is the rector of the palaces, on whose shoulders, and not into whose hands, the coins are placed in four military cloaks. After him are called *o domesticos tis ascalonas* and *o delongaris tis ploos*,[8] of whom the former commands the army and the latter the navy. These two, taking an equal number of coins and cloaks, as their dignity is equal, because of the volume could not carry them away on their shoulders but dragged them off with an effort, aided by others. After them twenty-four generals are admitted, to whom are issued pounds of gold coins, twenty-four to each, according to his number, with two military cloaks. Lastly, right after them the order of the patricians follows and is given twelve pounds of coins and one military cloak. And since I do not know the number of the patricians, I do not know the number of pounds either, except that given to each. After that is summoned the immense horde of first swordsmen, swordsmen, swordsmen-in-training, chamberlains, treasurers, first headsmen, of whom the first received seven, and the others according to their dignity received six, five, four, three, two, and one. Nor do I want you to think that it was all accomplished in a single day. Having begun on the fifth day of the week at the first hour of the day, it was finished by the emperor at the fourth hour of the sixth and seventh days;

---

8. The Greek titles were transliterated into Latin characters by Liudprand. Perhaps the author sought to make his text more user-friendly, realizing that his northern European contemporaries knew even less Greek than might his Italian ones. If this is true, then Liudprand was recalibrating his style for a new, previously unexpected audience.

for to those who receive less than a pound, the chief of the imperial bedchamber, not the emperor, makes payment throughout the
whole week before Easter. Thus with me standing by and considering the procedure with admiration, the emperor asked through the
minister what had pleased me about the whole matter.[9] To this I
answered: "Of course it would please me, if it profited me, just as
the repose given to Lazarus would have benefited the rich man as
he suffered the heat, if it had come his way; since it did not happen to him, how, I ask, could it please him?" Chuckling and a little
embarrassed, the emperor signaled with a nod of his head that I
should come to him, and I gladly accepted a large cloak with a
pound of gold that he gladly offered.[10]

9. Constantine knew that Byzantine administration was more complex than what
a young courtier from Pavia had ever witnessed, and displayed its bureaucratic workings precisely to evoke wonder. Royal administration in Europe, even in the relatively
sophisticated kingdom of Italy, relied more on personal relationships between ruler
and aristocrats, and less on money.

10. This witticism, worthy of that of the Byzantine wife in 4.10 above, brings a
happy ending and prevents *Retribution* from being tragic, as Liudprand had promised
(6.1). But the joke is also transgressive (Liudprand represents himself as a blasphemer,
making fun of the story in Lk 16.23–25 of the poor man Lazarus) and thus contradictory of the high moral standards that Liudprand espouses elsewhere in this text.
The abrupt end to *Retribution* may reflect the interruption that the journey of 949–50
brought to Liudprand's life and career (Vinay, "Oltre il giardino delle maschere," 27).
By accepting the emperor's largesse, Liudprand confirmed his family's traditional cli-
entage towards the Macedonian dynasty (Leyser, "Ends and Means," 128), which may
have displeased Berengar II enough to cause a rupture that launched Liudprand's years
as exile and historian.

⊛ HOMILY OF LIUTSIOS
THE ITALIAN DEACON

1. Most beloved brothers, we preach to you[1] about Jesus Christ
and him crucified, something that is "to the Jews indeed a stum-
bling block and to the Gentiles foolishness."[2] For indeed we confess
that the Lord Jesus is at once God and Son of God, coequal with
God the Father, consubstantial, equally omnipotent, and God's co-
operator, that he for our salvation at the end of time took on flesh
from the Virgin, mounted the cross, died, was buried, arose on the
third day by his own powers, and ascended to God the Father in

1. The title was written in Greek (Ὁμιλεῖα τοῦ λιουτζιου ιταλικοῦ διάκόνου).
The fine Greek miniscule in the single manuscript copy of this text indicates that
Liudprand wrote it (and presumably reviewed the rest of the writing) himself. Such
manual labor was unusual for high-ranking authors until the tenth century: see
G. Arnaldi, "Il secolo X," in his *Letteratura latina medievale* (Florence: SISMEL-Il Gal-
luzzo, 2002), 161. It was necessary as few in the West knew Greek characters: see B.
Bischoff, "Ein Osterpredigt Liutprands von Cremona (um 960)," in his *Anecdota no-
vissima* (Stuttgart: A. Hiersemann, 1984), 23; P. Chiesa, "Introduzione," in *Liudprandi
Cremonensis Opera Omnia*, CCSL 156 (Turnholt: Brepols, 1998), lxxxv.

As with most early medieval sermons, it is not certain that this one was delivered
in public (in this or a less literary form). Despite the direct address, it may have existed only as a written exercise: T. Hall, "The Early Medieval Sermon," in *The Sermon*,
ed. B. Kienzle (Turnholt: Brepols, 2000), 228–37; C. Muessig, "Sermon, Preacher,
and Society in the Middle Ages," *Journal of Medieval History* 28 (2002): 77–78.

2. 1 Cor 1.23. At certain times of the year the crucifix could become a target for
Jewish satire: Horowitz, "'And It Was Reversed,'" *Zion* 59 (1994): x.

heaven not as God alone or man alone, but as both at the same time, neither mixed nor separate nor anything else, and that he will return as judge at the end of time and will mete out to each according to how he has conducted himself. The Jew fears this, and the unhappy man refuses to hear it.

2. The idle listener to the law (rather than he who acts upon it) employs these arguments, increasing his own perdition: "If God is omnipotent, which I, too, admit, what need had the Uncreated One to take on a creature and, as a creature, to free a creature? Is it not written, 'He spoke and they were made; he commanded and they came into existence'?[3] If by his mere command, or rather by his will, God created everything, including that creature worthiest of angels (from whose rank and honor, through pride, that part fell by whose inducement to sin man fell, through disobedience), then surely and without taking on flesh he could free the creature above all from the power of the apostate angel whom he had cast out."

3. O unhappy Jew, who does not acknowledge God's omnipotence? For you sin gravely, as long as you preach his power while denying his true justice. As the king and prophet David said: "God is a righteous judge."[4] For if God were merely to free fallen man by his power, and not for any reason, where would the justice be, in reference to which the prophet asserts that God is a just judge? In a certain way it would be more just, following your flawed reasoning, for God to coerce with his power an angel who wanted to grow prideful, so as to arrest his pride, than it would be for God, purely out of his power and without any just and true reason, to free man from the jaws of a well-earned death, when we lapsed because of disobedience.[5] For if either case pertains to virtue, neither coercing angels nor saving mankind pertains to justice. I ask what fairness there may be in this case: to restrain from haughtiness a created angel, and against his own will to give him blessedness and fellowship with humble and blessed souls—a created angel unburdened by bodily weight, but called Lucifer "who didst arise in the

3. Ps 32.9.   4. Ps 7.12.
5. Augustine, *On the Trinity* 13.13.

morning"[6] on account of the special effulgence of his rank, who desired to be prideful out of his own will, not inspired from outside by someone else, and who wanted to make himself similar to his Creator? For those who acknowledged a Creator set over them and humbly praised him, venerating and adoring, refrained from sin not because they were incapable of it, but because within themselves they did not wish to sin. It was just to give the capacity to act to those who had the will to sin. For that reason God created the angels, so that by their own free will they could either enjoy eternal bliss or receive the punishment of eternal damnation.[7]

4. As the Lord wanted to replenish the order depleted of their unclean spirits, he created man from a bit of earth, so that not only would the devil's expulsion be his punishment, but also so that his punishment might be increased by the promotion of man into the devil's prior position of glory. Thus, impelled by envy, but also on account of his hatred for his Creator, by his own instigation the devil exerted himself in such a way that because of disobedience man could not reach that blissful state from which he himself had fallen. And so God, wanting to test his creature, man, about the extent of his obedience to him—not for himself, for whom all things are patent and open, but for the edification of posterity—said: "Of every tree of paradise you shall eat: but of the tree of knowledge of good and evil that is in the middle of the garden, you shall not eat."[8]

5. And as God created man with this capacity, so that out of his own free will man could stand if obedient, or, if disobedient, fall, the apostate angel spoke to the woman through the snake, saying: "'Why has the Lord God commanded you, that you should not eat of every tree in paradise?' And the woman answered him, saying, 'Of the fruit of the trees that are in paradise we do eat; but of the fruit of the tree which is in the midst of paradise God has commanded us that we should not eat and that we should not touch it,

6. Is 14.12.

7. Augustine, *City of God* 22.1.

8. Gn 2.16–17. Liudprand added the detail of the tree's location from Gn 3.3.

lest perhaps we die.' And the serpent said to the woman, 'No, you shall not die the death; for God does know that on whatsoever day you shall eat thereof, your eyes shall be opened, and you shall be as gods, knowing good and evil.' And the woman saw that the tree was good to eat, and fair to the eyes and delightful to behold, and she took of the fruit thereof, and did eat, and gave to her husband, who did eat. And the eyes of them both were opened."[9] They had not been created with closed eyes, but had wandered blind and fumbling through the garden of delights. Why, then, had their eyes been opened, except to desire each other, and to undergo bodily death, the punishment devised for the sins, so that now there was not a mere material body, which could, had they remained obedient, change into the better spiritual form without death, but now there was corporeal death, a law for their limbs that conflicted with the law of the mind?[10]

6. And in order to anticipate your unspoken question, O Jew: God did well to allow the temptation of man, who he foreknew would give in to it. For the real reason is that no great praise was in store for man if, despite everything, he could live righteously, so that no one could induce him to live unrighteously. Such would be the case if man had it in his very nature to be able, and in his free will to desire, to deny consent to the tempter, with the help of him who resists the haughty and gives grace to the humble. For every day we see the human species ceaselessly tempted, with God's permission, in order to test and exercise its virtue; for it is a more glorious victory not to give in when tempted than not to be able to be tempted.

7. Therefore God, grieving that man, his creature, was deceived by the devilish trick, wanted to free him from the jaws of a well-earned death not by an act of sheer omnipotence, but also with an admixture of holy reason. But if you say, "Why did he want to free only his creature man, and not his creature the angel?" this is the answer. The creature called angel, because unburdened by

9. Gn 3.1–7.
10. Augustine, *Commentary on Genesis* 11.31.

the weight of any flesh, uninduced by anyone's blandishments, but only puffed up with his own malice, was not worthy to be freed by any redemption. Man, instead, oppressed by the mass of his flesh, instigated by the serpent's hint, *was* worthy to be liberated by the Lord's grace. In the book of Genesis the most holy prophet Moses, full of the foresight of God's spirit, was silent about the crime of the unredeemable apostate angel, but described the sin of redeemable man. Since the merit of no angel would be enough for redeeming the whole world, God did not want to free man through a creature—that is, through an angel—but through the Source— that is, through the uncreated Creator. Truly I call God's Son the uncreated but begotten Source, who became man with the help of the Holy Spirit from a virgin mother at the end of the ages. That, O Jew, is what scandalizes you; that is what you, unhappy one, refuse to hear.

8. You say that it is written: "Hear, O Israel, the Lord your God is one. You shall love the Lord your God"[11] and "him only shall you serve."[12] You say, "If God is one, how can you confess that God the Father is in heaven, and God the Son (with the help of that third God, the Holy Spirit) is in the womb of a virgin? But let it be thus: let there be three Gods, O Christian, as you confess. I want you to explain by what arrangement it could happen that the pure, holy, uncorrupted, immaculate Divinity could adhere to corruptible flesh without contamination and corruption." O Jew, I grant you asked a most useful question, and one very necessary for all the faithful, and unwittingly you fired arrows with which you will wound yourself. I am forbidden by the very words of the Lord to reveal his mysteries to you who do not believe, or rather will not believe. (He spoke thus to the prophet Ezekiel, saying: "I will make your tongue stick fast to the roof of your mouth, and you shall be dumb, and not as a man that reproves, because they are a provoking house. The sons of Israel do not want to hear you, since they do not want to hear me.")[13] Nevertheless, I will try to explain your

11. Dt 6.4–5. 12. Mt 4.10.
13. Ezek 3.26.

question as best I can, on account of the simple-mindedness of some believers, relying on the help of him who "made the tongues of infants eloquent."[14]

9. I say, O foolish one, that there is nothing which human frailty can say worthily of God. For when we call him Godhead, or Divine Lord, we use two or three syllables, and we present something worthy of him insofar as pertains to the pettiness of man, since we cannot find another more excellent name. Indeed, insofar as pertains to the immensity and dignity of God's majesty, given that we confess that there is nothing outside him, nothing beyond him, nothing above him, and we confess everything to be in him and under him, it is absurd to think that we can enclose such ineffable, in fact imponderable, Divinity in two or three syllables.[15] Moreover, I declare it not just incongruous, but downright mad to compare anything to him from whom living things take the source of their existence. Yet the minds of simple people are less able to understand the subtleties of such a great Divinity, unless we draw them to an understanding of the invisible by comparing it with visible things. So let your silliness listen to this, along with the simple folk, and not to contribute to your improvement but to compound your perdition: in the midst of visible and corporeal things was a creature created by a Creator. The creature chose three words as if for three distinct things. In truth, the three words demonstrate a single substance, and, when you say one of them, you mean the two others at the same time, not in a unity of words or in a mixture of functions, but in their communion of substance. Something can work without something else, even though it cannot exist without that something else.

10. When you name the sun, or a fire, you understand heat and light to be in them, but, in terms of words, the sun or a fire is one thing, and light and heat are quite different. For light plainly illuminates and heat dries. Even a blind man can feel heat without the illumination of light, and we, too, talk about the brightness of

14. Wis 10.21.
15. Augustine, *On Christian Doctrine* 1.6.

the sun or of a fire while not feeling their heat. And while there are three words—that is, "sun," "light," "heat"—they have the same substance, not different ones. And as they have the same nature, substance, and function, and there is at the same time almost the same property of function for each of the words, we do not speak of three suns or three lights or three heats, but of a single sun. Thus it is that, when you name it, you do not mention the words "heat" and "light," but you intend the substance of those words to be one.

11. Therefore, if it is possible to treat created things in this way, why do you call God the Father, God the Son, and God the Holy Spirit three Gods and not one, namely, God the Father, from whom are all things; God the Son, through whom are all things; and God the Holy Spirit, in whom are all things? That holy old man, the patriarch Abraham, knew this inseparable holy Trinity and indivisible Unity perfectly well. When he saw three angels, "he ran to meet them from the door of his tent in the heat of the day and bowed down to the ground in adoration, and he said"—and not, mind you, as if they were three, but as if he addressed a single person—"Lord, if I have found favor in your eyes, pass not away from your servant, but I will fetch a little water"; and, as if he understood three persons in a single substance, he spoke again as if addressing three, not one, saying, "and wash your feet, and rest yourselves under the tree."[16]

12. What do you think your, and indeed *our*, most holy prophet Moses realized regarding the unity of the Trinity and the tripleness of the Unity when, describing this vision, he said: "The Lord appeared to Abraham in the vale of Mamre as he was sitting at the door of his tent. And when he had lifted up his eyes, there were three men standing near him; as soon as he saw them, he ran to meet them"?[17] Tell me, I say, *please* tell me: if Abraham did not

16. Gn 18.2–4. In the first quotation, Abraham uses the singular possessive adjective *tuus*, and in the second, the plural *vester*. See also Augustine, *Questions on the Heptateuch* 1.33 and *On the Trinity* 2.10.

17. Gn 18.1–2.

believe in the one trinitarian God, why did he describe first the Lord and then three angels appearing? If holy Abraham did not believe in the trinity of the one God, why did he speak of the three angels not as three, but as if they were one, when he said, "I worship the Lord"? For although we use colloquial language, according to whose barbarous custom, even when we greet a single person, we say, "Hello to everyone," you can see the holy patriarch did not speak in that sense.[18] Indeed, he first said, "Lord, if I have found favor in your eyes"—and did not mean "in the eyes of all of you"—"pass not away from your servant." He did not say, "Pass not away from the servant of all of you." Hence, now that we have removed any ambiguity on the matter, we can assert that he understood the angels whom he saw as three persons to be one divine essence.

13. Therefore, O Jew, according to my modest intelligence you have God the unbegotten Father, God the Son, begotten and not made by the Father, and God the Holy Spirit, neither made nor begotten by, but proceeding from, the Father and Son.[19] And these three Persons are not three Gods, but one uncircumscribed, ineffable, immortal God. When we preach of the crucifixion, death, and burial of God's Son, the Lord Jesus, we do not say that he is made out of the invisible and immortal majesty, since he is co-eternal and consubstantial with the Father; instead we aver that he is from that matter which he took on from his virgin mother. For neither the Father nor the Holy Spirit, but the Son alone was incarnated, and incarnated so that he could free us by this mystery from the devil's power, and not simply by an act of his power, but by just and true reason.

18. The Latin plural greeting used here (*avete*) was hardly an everyday colloquialism, nor really a "barbarism" since classical authors knew it.

19. Without actually using the "Filioque clause" Liudprand espoused the idea that the Holy Spirit proceeded from the Father and from the Son, as papal liturgies began to do in the early eleventh century. In northern Europe the clause had been added to the Nicene Creed under the Carolingians. From the ninth century this clause generated liturgical controversy between Latin and Orthodox Christians, though easterners recognized its theological value.

14. The Word of the Lord, "by whom the heavens were created," did not become man so that Divinity or the power of the Divinity might lessen. Rather, it happened so that, remaining as it was, the Divinity took on something it was not, in order that it might liberate what it had made. This Divinity's humanity had, just like a real man, a real soul in which resided the fullness of all the Divinity. But let me say it to you more plainly, even if it is more uncomfortable for you; the same One who allowed your ancestors to cross the Red Sea with dry feet became, in more recent times, a man and was born to a virgin mother, Mary. Now, in order for it to be easier for you to believe this than to argue back, listen to what your own Scripture says: "And man is, and who knows him?"[20] And again: "Detach yourself from man, whose breath is in his nostrils, for he is reputed high."[21]

15. Moreover, assuming that Christ was not God and at the same time man, but only a man, having trusted in the experience of victory over the first man, the devil tried to win over with the weapons of temptation him whom he considered to be only a man, not knowing that he was God. Truly, the devil's temptations were conquered by our Savior, though the devil gloried in his victory over our first ancestor. Imagine, therefore, by what musings the devil became agitated when he acknowledged that he had found a man in whom there was nothing bad. For he must have said, "This fellow surpasses Moses and Elijah by far, if he is scarcely hungry on the fortieth day of his fast; and though I see him to be unusually free of sin, still by his hunger I recognize not God but a man." And, so that guile might trick guile, he must also have mused, "If I can knock off this one, who is without sin, I will make the whole world subject to me, since aside from him I see no one without sin." Encouraged, but also deceived, by this thought, the devil not only turned your ancestors, O Jew, from his salvific teachings, but even instigated them to kill him. In the end he was crucified, as he consented; he died, since he wanted to; he descended into the

20. Jer 17.9.
21. Is 2.22.

underworld, as he did not fear it; from there, since none could resist him, he snatched those whom he had elected, for whom he had descended from heaven, and he led them with him, back to the heavens whence he had come.

16. If the devil dragged our first forefather to his death, the price of disobedience, why did he want to give death to the God-man Jesus, the holy priest unsullied by sin? Had Adam not sinned, he would never have tasted death; but why did he want to nail Christ, who did not sin, to the cross? Yet it was very well done! As the devil sought to snatch what was forbidden, he rightly lost the acquisitions that he was clutching. Keep in mind that the power of God is mixed with just, holy, and true reason. It was just, indeed most just, for the devil to lose that which he was confident he rightly controlled, through the power of the immortal and righteous God. For he tried to extinguish by execution on the cross the God-man who was holy, pious, and free from any taint of sin, and wanted to lead him to the darkness of death (where the devil justifiably rejoiced in keeping humanity).

17. Nor should it be thought that our Lord Jesus Christ somehow condemned the devil unjustly. Life was without beginning, without end, eternal, by whose partaking all those who are seen to live are alive. Truly, when death saw life coming its way, it was unable to resist this vitality, and, having abandoned everything, death fled, lest it be discovered by life. And since this is why I rejoice and exult, I want to pose a philosophical dilemma to you, O Jew. The dialecticians assert that two opposites cannot be simultaneously true, whether in a matter of essence, or of absence, or in particular qualities.[22] We all, however, recognize that death and life are opposites of each other, so they cannot both prevail in the same case. With one prevailing, the other is necessarily absent. But you do not deny that God is life and the devil is death: "That's right," you say. If, therefore, it is so, indeed *because* it is so, death condemned *itself*

22. According to the Aristotelian *Categories* 18, PL 32.1432–37, which was considered an Augustinian translation in the early Middle Ages.

unjustly, when it wanted life to come to it, but could not withstand
life's presence.

18. That is why we Christians celebrate Easter: in this victory we
cheer, and we exult in this freedom. If you glory in temporal freedom, achieved by God's servant Moses, we rejoice in the eternal va-
riety, given us by Christ Jesus, Son of God. Yet I have heard certain
people from your community say that, on account of the crime of
disobedience, Adam and his descendants incurred not death of the
soul, but only bodily death.[23] That is utterly wrong. For Scripture
does not say, "On the very day you eat, you will become mortal"
but rather "you shall die."[24] And without a doubt both soul and
body, not just the body, were threatened with death.[25] To think
anything else is both childish and demented.

19. It did not slip my memory, ω ἄπιστε,[26] that you suggested I
discuss how the uncorrupted, immortal Son of God could cling to
a corruptible and mortal humanity without himself becoming corrupted.[27] That Solomon whose multifarious wisdom you cannot
deny he received from the Lord, foresaw the Incarnation by God's
inspiration when he wrote, "Wisdom has built herself a house."[28]
By that he means the Son of God prepared himself an appropriate
dwelling in the Virgin, which was holy, uncorrupted, and worthy of
him, and whence he took on that enfleshed form which his Father
had placed a little lower than the angels, and under whose feet the
Father had subjected everything. Can you deny what holy David
said to God, namely, "What is a man that you are mindful of him,
or the son of man, that you are concerned about him? And you
have made him a little lower than the angels; you have crowned him
with glory and honor; you have given him power over the works of
your hands; you have placed all things under his feet"?[29]

20. If you want to learn truly about holy Scripture, while dili-

23. An insight into the kinds of encounters between Christian clerics and Jews
that lay behind Liudprand's "dialectical" sermon.

24. Gn 2.17.   25. Augustine, *City of God* 13.12.
26. "O faithless one."   27. See section 8, above.
28. Prv 9.1.   29. Ps 8.5–8; Heb 2.6–8.

gently examining your prophets, do not neglect the letter which the most blessed Paul, first a follower of Gamaliel but then of Christ, wrote to your people. In it, researching the arcana of your law, you will find the very same exposition of the short verse I cited above. "For he has not subjected to angels the world to come, whereof we speak."[30] To whom, then, did he subject it if not to his Son? For in subjecting all things to Jesus, "he left nothing that is not subjected to him. But we do not yet see all things subject to him. For we see Jesus made a little lower than the angels, and crowned with glory and honor because of his having suffered death, so that by the grace of God he should taste death for all. For it became him, for whom are all things and through whom are all things, who brought many sons into glory, to perfect through sufferings the pathbreaker of their salvation. For both he that sanctifies and they who are sanctified are all from one: for which cause he is not ashamed to call them brethren, saying, "I will declare your name to my brethren, in the midst of the congregation I will praise you."[31]

21. If these tangible and literal examples do not please you who are alive, consider this visible sun, when its rays pierce murky things or are divided by the branches of a tree. Sunshine neither is soiled by the murk nor is divided or diminished by being struck. It is no wonder, then, that the uncorrupted, immortal God can take on the mortal form of man, whom he came to liberate, without any detriment to himself. Truly, since I can see that your heart is shrouded and unknowingly you carry sealed instructions for your own death, as unwitting Uriah did (I mean the Law, which you do not understand), I have no desire to argue further with you. Instead I will describe to the faithful, and not to argumentative folk, the pearl, that is, the doctrine worthy of God.[32] For our God wants "to bring

30. Heb 2.5.

31. Heb 2.8–12.

32. Here Liudprand changed imagined audience, and style of address, for his homily. The preceding section resembles a schoolroom exercise, while the latter section is much closer to normal tenth-century sermons (also in length: by contemporary standards Liudprand's homily is very long, and is thus less likely to have been delivered as recorded. Atto of Vercelli, a near contemporary of Liudprand, considered more than eight paragraphs of text an excessive strain on listeners. He wrote an abbreviated ver-

forth praise out of the mouths of infants and sucklings, to silence the enemy and the foe."[33]

22. Therefore, dearest brothers, as we are celebrating Holy Easter, let us imitate within ourselves what we see being celebrated outside.[34] "For the king's daughter is all glorious within."[35] Nothing is properly good for us, but is actually detrimental, if we do not fulfill with deeds that which we say with words. Easter is called a passage,[36] and we celebrate it reverently when we pass to virtue, having abandoned vice. I do not want to think that any one of you believes he will fail either to be punished for his vices or crowned for his virtues in the world to come. Clearly, "if with this life only in view we have hope, we are of all men the most to be pitied."[37] I say this, too, my brothers, because while I see some who perform evil deeds without fear of God, I declare them dreamers who do not believe in the coming judgment. Even if they truly believe this, by not following justice they earn themselves a greater punishment.

23. I see several evil people who turn away from evil purely out of fear of some mortal king and on account of corporeal death, but who do not give up anything on account of the immortal God, the King of Kings, who can without end torment body and soul. My brothers, what on earth will these fellows say when they see the powers of heaven moving, and every earthly tribe mourning over them, and each, according to his deeds, receiving judgment? It is possible to reduce considerably the present torment by either good works or saintly intercessions, or even by the hope of future corrections in

sion of his Pentecost sermon, which is already itself much shorter than Liudprand's homily, "lest profane people grow restless": see PL 134.849).

33. Ps 8.3.

34. Easter, the most important feast on the Christian calendar, was often the occasion for Christians' expression of anti-Jewish sentiment (see section 15 above, for instance). This may explain the logic behind the awkward juncture between the first twenty-one sections of the homily (a dialogue between Christian and Jew) and the last seven (an exhortation to the Christian clergy to improve their behavior in light of the season).

35. Ps 44.14.

36. This was a homilists' trope, based on the etymology of the word *Pascha*, the Greek translation of the Hebrew word *Pesach* (Passover): see Hrabanus Maurus's Easter sermon, PL 110.34; or Maximus of Turin, PL 57.364.

37. 1 Cor 15.19.

one's deeds; but, my brothers, these fellows will not reduce their own toil except by whatever good deeds they perform in this life. Anyone who does not have oil in the church lamps, that is, a good deed in conscience, when he desires it from wise maidens, will not be able to obtain any, and, when he goes off to buy more oil, returning to the wedding after the doors are already shut, he will not be able to get in.[38] Thus says the blessed apostle Paul: "Behold, now is the acceptable time; behold, now is the day of salvation!"[39] On exactly such days as this, let us show ourselves to be ministers of God.

24. If it pleases you that we preach about the pious and forgiving God, let it also frighten you that we profess faith in a true and just Judge. He grants us great kindness and charity when, through his preachers, he announces the future prize and torment. For he who takes care to warn us of how we are able to elude the punishment does not wish to punish us, because of his kindness. Through his own self our Lord Jesus Christ deigned to come down from the heavens and indicate the glory of the world to come as we can earn it, and avoid eternal damnation; this he does not scorn to announce daily through us, his unworthy servants.

25. He recognized that we cannot ascend to heaven by our goodness alone. Therefore he took care to prepare a ladder for us in the neediness of the poor. By this ladder, if we want, we can climb to him. Nor was it out of any want of power that God desired there to be some who are poor and some who are rich, for "the earth is the Lord's, and the fullness thereof; the world, and all who dwell therein."[40] Why, then? God mercifully wished there to be poor people in this life for the salvation of the rich, so that just as the rich might make the poor participate in their wealth by the love of true charity, equally the poor might give the rich a share in their eternal bliss. It is on account of this that the gospel text says, "Make friends for yourselves with the mammon of wickedness so that, when you fail, they may receive you into everlasting dwellings."[41]

26. When one sees a pauper, and not just a pauper but, even

---

38. A paraphrase of Mt 25.1–13, the parable of the ten maidens.
39. 2 Cor 6.2.   40. Ps 24.1.
41. Lk 16.9.

more troubling, a blind man weak in every limb, and one for whom the lack of belongings takes the place of toil, each of us should consider that he himself could be deprived one day of all use of every limb. To us, on the contrary, to whom strength of body was given sparingly, but to whom health was granted, with God's help, on top of this the delightful responsibility of wealth was offered. My brothers, could not the divine goodness have made us needy and weak, and them strong and mighty, if it wanted to? What did we do for God, to deserve such privileges? Nothing, I say! What can we do to compensate him for such gifts? There is nothing more wholesome than what we have learned from his generosity: "You shall love the Lord your God with your whole heart, and with your whole mind, and with your whole strength, and your neighbor as yourself."[42] There is no offering more wholesome, no sacrifice more pleasing to him than this.

27. "I truly love my neighbor," you say. "How is it that you love your neighbor," God answers back, "when you do not visit the sick, and do not listen when people call out to you?" This is the most detestable among our deeds, my brothers. If we catch sight of the kinsfolk of kings and the powerful of this world, we receive them with great honor, and even fawn over them, arguing with them in hopes they will accept our gifts; and, what is more serious still, we offer them not any old gift, but the things we hold dearest. We not only fail to give the kinsfolk of Jesus Christ our Lord any gifts, but often we do not deign to notice them, and, if occasionally we desire to show mercy to their moaning and struggling, we disdain to do it ourselves, and whatever measly thing it is that we offer them, we do not deliver it in our own hands, but through a lowly servant. Therefore, what will the Lord say to us at the reckoning of our good and bad deeds? I shudder lest it be that which we read Abraham said in response to the miserly rich man: "Son, remember that you in your lifetime have received good things, and Lazarus in like manner evil things; but now here he is comforted, whereas you are tormented."[43] My brothers, may God avert this terrible sentence from us!

42. Lk 10.27.
43. Lk 16.25. Liudprand made light of this episode in *Retribution* 6.10, above.

28. Perhaps one of you is saying to himself, in silent thought, "If it is as you teach, why, O bishop, do *you* not hear the poor calling out to you while you keep the warehouses full?"[44] And in the same breath you add, "As I pass over those things which now glisten with freshness, the indigence of the poor could be relieved by those things which we heard, and even saw, were cast into the mud on account of age and the stink of worms." If it is so, my brothers, I do not defend myself or anyone else who is doing such things, but most vehemently declare that I judge such a person to be dead while living. Believe me, nothing will be judged more harshly against this faithless person, whoever he is. For the faithful brothers brought such abundance to the church for the sustenance of the poor, and no bishop should act as the owner of such things, but only as the faithful distributor of them.[45] For the substance belongs to the poor, to whom the bishop was appointed to be a faithful dispenser. For he who denies to the poor that of which he has plenty will be forced in the severe examination of judgment to declare why he illicitly stole.

29. But you, my brothers, if by chance we do any ill, ignore it. Instead, try to do the good deeds about which we preached to you. I ask you, what good will it do you if you are tormented as accomplices of the sinful bishops? Their double "Oh, woe! Woe!" will not help your single "Woe!" nor will some company in your torment be able to relieve the pain of burning. Above all, let this torment be averted by him who for our salvation became man and died on the cross, and who, descending to the underworld, undid the power of the devil, destroyed death, placed his elect in the heavenly seat, and for us believers was resurrected on the third day and appeared alive again, namely, Jesus Christ our Lord, who with God the Father and the Holy Spirit lives, and, as God, is glorified for all time. Amen.

44. See Lk 12.16–20.

45. Failure to spend their wealth and behave generously, also toward the indigent who made up a tenth of the population, earned tenth-century bishops censure: see H. Fichtenau, *Living in the Tenth Century* (Chicago: University of Chicago Press, 1991), 184–85, 197–99, 368.

✺ CONCERNING KING OTTO

1. It was the period when Berengar and Adalbert ruled, or rather ravaged, in Italy and, to be more truthful, exercised their tyranny.[1] The supreme pontiff and universal Pope John XII, whose church was then all-too-familiar with the savagery of the aforementioned Berengar and Adalbert, sent [two] ambassadors of the holy Roman church, that is, John the cardinal deacon and Azzo the archivist, to Otto, the most serene and pious king (now august caesar).[2] With prayerful letters and indicators of the situation, the messengers were to beg that, for the love of God and of the holy apostles Peter and Paul, who the pope hoped would be the ones to absolve his own sins, the king would free the pope himself and his ward, the Roman church, from the tyrants' fangs, and return them to their original health and liberty.[3]

1. Berengar II and his son Adalbert (whose name Liudprand spelled several ways) were crowned on December 15, 950; unsure of his Italian policy, Otto I entrusted them with the kingdom of Italy in 952. They held power until 962 and created trouble for Otto thereafter.

2. After 959 Adalbert raided the Sabina, northeast of Rome, from Spoleto. Beneventan lords menaced Rome's territory from the south, too.

3. Otto had sought emperorship in 951, only to be rebuffed by Alberic, then lord at Rome. Egged on by his son Liudolf and brother Henry of Bavaria, he campaigned in Italy 951–52 in defense of the widow of King Lothar II of Italy (†950), Adelheid (whom Otto married, gaining rights over the kingdom); he also sent his son Liudolf to overthrow Berengar there in 957. Otto was thus known to have an interest in Ital-

While the Roman ambassadors were pleading this case, the venerable man Walpert, archbishop of the holy Milanese church, having been freed half-dead from the rage of the same Berengar and Adalbert, sought out the power of the above-mentioned Otto, then king and now august caesar. He indicated he could not bear and endure the savagery of Berengar and Adalbert, nor that of Willa, who had appointed Manasses, the bishop of Arles, to the Milanese see, contrary to all law and decency.[4] He claimed, quite reasonably, this was a calamity for his church, since it snatched away what ought to belong to him and his people. But after this there followed Waldo, bishop of Como, crying out that he had been stricken with an injury not unlike that which Berengar, Adalbert, and Willa had inflicted on Walpert.[5] There also came from Italy many men of clerical and secular status; among them the illustrious margrave Otbert hastened with the papal ambassadors, seeking aid and advice from the most holy Otto, then king and now august caesar.[6]

2. The most pious king was moved by the tearful requests of these people, and, considering not his own interests, but those of Jesus Christ, he appointed his own son king, equal to himself, while he was still a boy, though this was contrary to custom, and left him in Saxony.[7] As for himself, having gathered his forces, Otto came

---

ian affairs. The powerful foreign lord was the *deus ex machina* of tenth-century Italian politics: see *Retribution*, passim.

4. Liudprand had promised to discuss this issue in *Retribution* 4.7. Manasses's defection from the Berengarian camp in 951 created difficulties for the new king, who promptly deposed him. Berengar's wife Willa was introduced in *Retribution* 4.8.

5. Waldo became bishop during the aristocratic upheavals that brought Berengar to power between 947 and 950. His presence in the Italian delegation to Otto meant that aristocratic support for Berengar had waned after a decade of his rule.

6. Otbert I († before 978), founder of the Obertenghi clan that came to dominate northwestern Italy, especially Liguria, exploited the demise of the march of Ivrea under King Hugh (†948) to build a territorial base at the expense of Berengar, whose power base Ivrea was.

7. The numerous deaths of Ottonian rivals in the 950s gave Otto I enough security to have his son Otto II elected and crowned east Frankish king in summer 961: T. Reuter, *Germany in the Early Middle Ages* (London: Longman, 1991), 158–59. Otto II was only six, but secured dynastic succession.

quickly to Italy.[8] There he expelled both Berengar and Adalbert from the kingdom, so fast that it was clear he had the most holy apostles Peter and Paul as allies. Thus the good king, gathering what had been scattered and shoring up what had been broken, returned to each what had been his. Last, he headed for Rome to do the same.

3. There he was received with wondrous pomp and new ceremonial, and he received the anointment of imperial rule from the same supreme pontiff and universal pope John.[9] But here he did not merely restore properties; he also honored the church with sizeable gifts of gems, gold, and silver.[10] Otto further accepted the oath of Pope John and all the magnates of the city, over the most precious body of St. Peter, to the effect that they would never help Berengar and Adalbert. After this Otto returned promptly to Pavia.

4. Meanwhile this same Pope John, forgetful of the oath and promise which he had made to the holy emperor, sent word to Adalbert that he should come to him, affirming to him by oath that he would help Adalbert against the might of the most holy emperor. For the holy emperor had so terrified Adalbert, persecutor of the churches of God and of Pope John, that, abandoning Italy altogether, he had gone to Fraxinetum to entrust himself to the faith of the Saracens.[11] The just emperor could not fathom why Pope John now loved that same Adalbert whom he had earlier attacked with strenuous hatred. On account of this, having summoned some of his intimates, Otto sent inquiries to Rome about whether this was true.[12] And when his messengers arrived there they got the following response, and not just from any person, but from all (or a few) of the Roman citizens: "There appears to be some

8. In August 961.

9. On February 2, 962, together with Adelheid.

10. On February 13th Otto confirmed the traditional Carolingian privileges of the papacy in the *Privilegium Ottonianum*.

11. He also went to Corsica, a dependency of Tuscany, whence he sailed to Civitavecchia (then Centocelle) in northern Latium: see chapter 7. The faithlessness of Adalbert, who looted churches and abandoned his supporters, made him a fitting ally for the infidel Saracens.

12. In late 962.

parallel between why Pope John hates the most holy emperor, who freed him from the hands of Adalbert, and why the devil hates his Creator. The emperor, as we have experienced the matter, knows, works for, and loves what pertains to God, protects church and secular affairs with arms, improves them by his customs, and cleans them up with his laws; Pope John is against all these things. Nor is what we are revealing hidden from the people. Take as witness the widow of the pope's own soldier Rainerius, to whom, burning with blind lust, John gave control of many cities and even the holy golden crosses and chalices of blessed Peter. Take as witness the case of John's aunt Stephana, who left this life recently, bleeding from the baby she had conceived with him. And even if all are silent about this, the Lateran palace, once shelter of the saints and now a brothel for prostitutes, will certainly resound over his coupling with his aunt, sister of the other concubine Stephania. Another witness is the absence hereabouts of women of all nations except the Roman, since they fear to visit the thresholds of the apostles for the sake of prayer, since they heard that a few days ago several women, married, widowed, and virgins, were forcefully raped there. A further witness is the condition of the churches of the holy apostles, which do not leak in a few drops of rain, but let in deluges onto the very sacrosanct altars. How the sodden roof-beams do terrify us! When we request holy services there, death reigns in the roofing, preventing us from praying as much as we wanted to, and driving us to depart from the house of God. Our last witnesses are both the artificial, reed-like thinness of some women, and also the more normal shapes of other ones: to Pope John it is the same whether they wear down the blackened paving stones with their feet or if they arrive [at his residence] with the aid of big horses. Thus there is as great discord between the pope and the holy emperor as by lot separates wolf and lamb. So that he may carry out his desires with impunity, John is grooming Adalbert to be his father, protector, and defender."[13]

13. In 955, a year after his powerful father's death, John XII was elected pope at age eighteen. He was twenty-five or so at this time, young for a high-ranking cleric.

5. When he had listened to this report from his returning messengers, the emperor said: "He is a child. John will easily shift his opinion under the influence of good men. I will hope for his honest change of heart, brought about by kind persuasion, so that he may easily lift himself out of these vices. We will say with the prophet, 'This is the change of the right hand of the Most High.'"[14] And he added: "Because the order of things requires it, first let us cast the rebellious Berengar from Montefeltro; then let us meet the lord pope for a fatherly rebuke. If not through his own will, at least through his sense of shame he will transform himself into a perfect man. In this way, perhaps, forced to take on good habits, he will feel ashamed to become unaccustomed to them all over again."

6. Having done these things, Otto left Pavia by ship and reached Ravenna by following the course of the river Po. Proceeding from there, he besieged Montefeltro, also called St. Leo, where Berengar and Willa were.[15] There the aforementioned pope directed to the holy emperor two messengers, namely, Leo, then chief secretary of the holy Roman church and now in the same see as vicar of St. Peter, prince of the apostles, and Demetrius, the more illustrious of the Roman nobles. They were to say that it was hardly surprising if up to this point, conquered by the fire of youth, John did some childish things. Now the time had come when he should try to live by a different standard. John, too, relayed certain things, deceitfully: namely, that the holy emperor had violated the promise of his faithfulness when he bound by oath to himself, and not to the pope, the people who were staying in that place; and that Otto had welcomed Bishop Leo and Cardinal Deacon John, who had been unfaithful to the pope.[16] To this the emperor replied: "I give thanks for the rectification and change in customs which John has

14. Ps 76.11.

15. Otto captured Willa in June 962 on the lake of Orta near Varese; in May 963 San Leo, in the Marches, fell, and Berengar II was exiled to Bavaria with his wife.

16. John referred to the terms of the *Privilegium Ottonianum* of early 962. Its first fourteen titles guaranteed papal sovereignty over extensive territories in central Italy, including the Marches.

promised. Consider carefully whether the complete subversion of my promise may be true, which he asserts I made. We promised to return all lands of St. Peter that should fall under our power, and it is for this reason that we strive to cast Berengar with his whole following out of this castle. For by what title can we return this land if beforehand we do not take it from the grasp of the violent and submit it to our power? As to Bishop Leo and Cardinal Deacon John, who were unfaithful to the pope, whom he accuses us of welcoming, in this period we neither saw nor welcomed them. With the lord pope directing them to leave for Constantinople to cause us trouble, they were captured at Capua, according to what we heard.[17] With them, we heard, were captured also Saleccus, a Bulgarian by birth, by education a Hungarian, a very close associate of the lord pope, and Zacheus, an evil man, ignorant of divine and profane letters, who was recently consecrated bishop by the lord pope and sent to the Hungarians to preach that they should attack us. We would never have believed anyone who said the pope did these things, except that there were letters worthy of trust, sealed with lead and bearing his inscribed name on them."

7. Having done these things, Otto sent to Rome the bishops Landward of Minden from Saxony and Liudprand of Cremona from Italy with the aforementioned messengers.[18] They were to satisfy the lord pope that Otto was innocent. The righteous emperor also attached soldiers to their party so that if the lord pope did not believe it, by a judicial duel they could prove the truth. Thereupon, when the aforementioned bishops Landward and Li-

17. Unlike Otto, John had had little luck in his maneuvers to win support from southern Italy's Lombard rulers: see G. Loud, "Southern Italy in the Tenth Century," *New Cambridge Medieval History* 3, ed. T. Reuter (Cambridge: Cambridge University Press, 1999), 624–30; B. Kreutz, *Before the Normans* (Philadelphia: University of Pennsylvania Press, 1991), 102–6. His alleged attempt to form an alliance with the Byzantine emperor stumbled on their enmity. Capua was the first major center on the main (Appian) highway south from Rome, on the obvious route for anyone heading for Byzantine territory in southern Italy.

18. In the late summer of 963. Landward of Minden (†969) was a close ally of the Ottonians whose see was rewarded with privileges and immunities.

udprand arrived at Rome and in the pope's presence, they were received with such honors that it was quite obvious to them with what deep loathing the pope disliked the holy emperor. While they spoke, however, in an orderly fashion about the things they were instructed to relay, the pope would not receive an oath nor the proof of the duel, but remained in the same hard-headed positions as before. Craftily, after eight days he sent Bishop John of Narni and Cardinal Deacon Benedict back with them to the lord emperor, reckoning that by means of his subtleties he could deceive Otto, whom it is very difficult to take in with words. Before their return, Adalbert, with the pope beckoning, returned from Fraxinetum and reached Civitavecchia. Then he set out for Rome, where he was not repudiated by the pope, as he should have been, but welcomed with pomp.

8. While these things were happening, the hot season, boiling over with the rays of Phoebus, pushed the emperor far from the Roman walls;[19] but when the returning virgin star brought pleasant mildness, having gathered his troops, he came to Rome because the Romans were secretly beckoning him.[20] Why did I say "secretly," since the larger part of the nobles among the Romans occupied the castle of St. Paul, and invited the holy emperor in, having handed over hostages?[21] And why do I delay the conclusion so long? Once the emperor was encamped next to the city, the pope and Adalbert fled Rome at the same time. The citizens received the holy emperor with all his men into the city, promised fidelity again, and added to this a firm oath that they would not elect or ordain a pope without the consent and election of the lord emperor caesar augustus and of his son King Otto.

9. After three days, with both the Roman people and bishops

19. Boethius, *Consolation of Philosophy* 1.6.1–2. The danger of malaria in the Roman Campagna, and Italy in general, for the unacclimatized, were tropes that medieval historians used often.

20. In November 963. There is little evidence that Otto enjoyed much support in Rome.

21. St. Paul Outside-the-Walls lay south of Rome, along the Tiber, and was hence fortified.

requesting it, there was a great gathering in the church of St. Peter. And there sat with the emperor:

Archbishops from Italy: Deacon Rodalf took the place of the patriarch of Aquileia Ingelfred, who suddenly sickened in that same city, the city of his birth; Walpert of Milan; Peter of Ravenna.

From Saxony: Adeltac the archbishop and Landward bishop of Minden.

From Francia: Otker, bishop of Speyer.

From Italy: Humbert of Parma; Liudprand of Cremona; Herenald of Reggio.[22]

From Tuscany: Cuonrad of Lucca; Everarius of Arezzo; the Pisan; the Sienese; the Florentine; the Pistoian; Peter of Camerino; the Spoletan.

From the Romans: Gregory of Albano; Sico of Ostia; Benedict of Porto; Lucidus of Gabi; Theophylact of Palestrina; Wido of Silva Candida; Leo of Velletri; Sico of Blera; Stephen of Ceri; John of Nepi; John of Tivoli; John of Oriolo; Romanus of Ferentino; John of Norba; John of Veroli; Marinus of Sutri; John of Narni; John of the Sabina; John of Gallese; the Falerian; the Alatrian; the Ortan; John of Anagni; the Trevian; Sabbatinus of Terracina; Cardinal Stephen, archpriest of the *titulus* of Nereus and Achilleus;[23] Leo priest of the *titulus* of Balbina; Dominic of the *titulus* of Anastasia; Peter of the *titulus* of Damasus; Theophylact of the *titulus* of Chrysogonus; John of the *titulus* of Equitius; John of the *titulus* of Susanna; Peter of the *titulus* of Pamachius; Hadrian of the *titulus* of Callixtus; John of the *titulus* of Cecilia; Hadrian of the *titulus* of Lucina; Benedict of the *titulus* of Sixtus; of the *titulus* of Santi Quattro Coronati;[24] Stephen of the *titulus* of Sabina; Cardinal Benedict the archdeacon; John the deacon; Bonofilus the car-

22. Humbert replaced Wido of Modena as royal arch-chancellor after 961, and the powerful Modenese bishop, Berengar's mainstay after 947, is conspicuously absent from this list. He was reintegrated afterwards, when Otto realized the difficulty of ruling Italy without local magnates' cooperation.

23. A *titulus* was one of the most ancient and prestigious churches in the city of Rome. Clergy attached to titular churches held high posts in the papal administration.

24. Liudprand omitted the name.

dinal deacon; the papal palace supervisor; George the supervisor's aide; Stephen the advocate for the poor; Andrew the treasurer; Sergius the master of the *defensors*; John the bursar; Stephen; Theophylact; Hadrian; Stephen; Benedict; Azzo; Hadrian; Romanus; Leo; Benedict; Leo; and also Leo and Leo the archivists; Leo master of the papal choir; Benedict the subdeacon and almsgiver; Azzo; Benedict; Demetrius; John; Amicus; Sergius; Benedict; Ursus; John; Benedict the subdeacon; the under-food-distributor; and Stephen the arch-acolyte with all the acolytes and parish clergy.

From the nobles of the Roman city: Stephen the officer, son of John;[25] Demetrius Meliosi; Crescentius "of the marble horse";[26] John surnamed Mizina; Stephen son of Imiza; Theodore son of Rufina; John of Primicerio; Leo of Cazunuli; Rihkard; Peter of Canaparia;[27] Benedict with his son Bulgamino.

From the people, Peter who is also called Imperiola was there with all the Roman militia.[28]

10. Thereupon, with all these people seated and keeping very quiet, the holy emperor spoke thus: "How proper it would be for the famous and holy lord Pope John to be present at this council! Truly I ask you, O holy fathers who shared the same life and the same occupations with him, why he declined to join such a splendid gathering."[29] Then the Roman bishops and cardinals, priests

25. Stephen was *superista*, a Carolingian-period title for the chief military officer of the Lateran. See T. Noble, *The Republic of St. Peter* (Philadelphia: University of Pennsylvania Press, 1984), 248–49.

26. The Crescentii became a leading Roman aristocratic clan in the wake of the Ottonian rise: see *Medieval Italy. An Encyclopedia*, ed. C. Kleinhenz (New York: Routledge, 2004), s.v.

27. This surname was also attached to powerful Roman clerics of the period. (In the earliest years of the eleventh century John Canaparius, abbot of St. Bartholomew's on the Tiber island, wrote the first *Life of St. Adalbert*.)

28. This impressive list helps to show that Otto's unprecedented deposition of a reigning pope had the support of Rome's and the empire's secular and ecclesiastical community: it reassures readers that the action enjoyed consensus and was not an overbearing individual's whim. But its presence in the narrative is a sign of unease over the proceedings: see Sutherland, *Liutprand*, 91–93.

29. Traditionally, no one had the right to sit in judgment over popes, and John was upholding canon law by refusing to attend this synod.

and deacons, along with all the people said: "We marvel that your most holy prudence wants us to recount this, which is hidden from the inhabitants of neither Spain nor Babylon nor India. John is not one of those 'who come in the clothing of sheep, but inwardly are ravening wolves.'[30] He rages so openly, he carries on the devil's business so publicly, that he uses no roundabout methods." The emperor answered: "It seems just to us that the accusations against John be specified; then we shall determine by common counsel what we should do."

Then there stood up the cardinal priest Peter, who testified that he saw John celebrate the mass and not take communion. John, bishop of Narni, and Cardinal Deacon John claimed to have seen him ordain a deacon in the horses' stable and not at the right times. Cardinal Deacon Benedict along with other deacons and priests said that they knew he made a profit from ordinations of bishops and that at Todi he had ordained a temporary, ten-year bishop. They said it was not necessary to relate anything about sacrileges, since we could learn more by looking around than by listening to them. Concerning John's adultery, they said they had not seen it with their own eyes, but they knew for certain that he had debauched the widow of Rainerius and Stephana, his father's concubine, and the widow Anna with her niece, and had turned the holy [Lateran] palace into a house of ill repute and brothel. They said that he went hunting publicly; he blinded his spiritual advisor Benedict, who promptly died of it; he killed John the cardinal subdeacon by amputating his genitals; he set fires; they testified that he girded himself with a sword and wore a helmet and breastplate. Everyone, clergy and laity alike, called out that he drank wine for the love of the devil. They said that he invoked the help of Jupiter, Venus, and other demons while playing dice. They professed that John did not celebrate matins and the canonical hours, nor did he protect himself with the sign of the cross.

11. Having heard all this, since the Romans did not understand

30. Mt 7.15.

176

didn't begin

his own language, that is, the Saxon tongue, the emperor instructed the Cremonese bishop Liudprand to express what follows to all the Romans in the Latin language.[31] Rising up, he began thus: "It often happens, and we think ourselves experienced in this regard, that those in high positions are smeared by the false accusations of the envious; the good is just as distasteful to bad people as the bad is to good people. Therefore, the accusation against the pope that just now Cardinal Deacon Benedict read out and made along with you, we regard as uncertain, and we are unsure whether the zeal of justice or a jealous impiety may be driving it forward. Because of this, though I am unworthy, according to the authority of the dignity granted to me, in the name of God, whom no one can deceive, even if he wants to, and of his holy uncorrupted Virgin Mother Mary, and in the name of the most precious body of the prince of the apostles, in whose church these things are being recited, I request that no accusation be cast against the lord pope for wrongdoing that has not been perpetrated by him and seen by the most trustworthy men."

Then the bishops, priests, deacons, and the rest of the clergy, and the whole Roman people, as if a single body, said: "If Pope John did not commit shameful crimes, both the ones that Deacon Benedict read out, and more ghastly and greater ones, too, let not the prince of the apostles, the most blessed Peter, absolve us from the shackles of our crimes, he who by his mere word closes paradise to the unworthy and opens it to the just. Rather, let us be bound by the chains of anathema, and on the last day let us be placed on the left side, with those 'who have said to the Lord God: depart from us, we desire not the knowledge of your ways.'[32] For if you do not accept our faithfulness, at least you ought to believe the troops of the lord emperor, against whom John charged five days ago, girt with a sword, bearing a shield, helmet, and breast-

31. This was the high point of Liudprand's career. He never explains why in later councils he was not given the honor of representing Otto again. His tactful way of pointing out that Otto knew little Latin cannot have been the reason.

32. Jb 21.14.

plate. Only the Tiber, which flowed between them, prevented John, decked out like that, from being captured by the imperial troops." Immediately the holy emperor said: "There are as many witnesses to that as there are fighters in our army." The holy council said: "If it pleases the holy emperor, let a letter be sent to the lord pope so that he may come here and clear himself of all these accusations." Then a letter to this effect was sent to John.

12. "To the supreme pontiff and universal pope lord John, Otto, the august emperor by divine clemency, along with the archbishops and bishops of Liguria, Tuscany, Saxony, and Francia, sends greetings in the Lord. Arriving in Rome in God's service, while we asked of your sons, that is, the Roman bishops, cardinals, priests, and deacons, and also all the people, about your absence, and about the reason why you did not want to see us, though we are the defenders of your church and person, they held forth with such stories about you, and so obscene, that if they were told about actors they would still occasion us embarrassment.[33] And lest all these stories should be hidden from your excellency, we will describe briefly to you a few of them, since, even if we tried, a whole day would not suffice to spell them all out individually. You should know that you are accused of homicide, perjury, sacrilege, and of the crime of incest within your own family and with two sisters, and the accusations come from all sorts of people, both of your own and of the other order, and not just from a few people. They say something else horrible to hear, namely, that you drank wine for love of the devil; that you invoked the help of Jupiter, Venus, and other demons in the game of dice. Therefore, with all our strength we pray your paternity, do not elude coming to Rome and clearing yourself of all these charges. If by chance you fear the violence of the unruly mob, we affirm to you by oath that nothing will be done that goes

33. Liudprand expressed the opinion, common in Latin literature, that actors are immoral people. Given that his accomplished contemporary Hrotswita of Gandersheim wrote plays intended (it seems) to be performed by the nuns of her aristocratic Ottonian nunnery, more than one opinion about actors' behavior co-existed in tenth-century Ottonian Europe.

beyond the sanctions of the holy canons. Given on the eighth day before the ides of November."

13. When he read this letter, he wrote a defense like this: "Bishop John, servant of the servants of God, to all bishops. We heard it said that you want to make another pope. If you do this I excommunicate you through God almighty, so that you may not have the faculty of ordaining no one and celebrating the mass."[34]

14. While this letter was being read at the holy council, there arrived clergymen who had been absent earlier: from Lotharingia, Heinrich, bishop of Trier; from Emilia and Liguria, Wido of Modena, Gero of Tortona, Sigulf of Piacenza. With their counsel, the council replied thus to the lord pope: "To the supreme pontiff and universal pope lord John: Otto, the august emperor by divine clemency, and also the holy council congregated at Rome to serve God, send greetings in the name of the Lord. This aforementioned council, which met on the eighth day before the ides of November, sent you a letter outlining the words of your accusers and the causes of the accusations. In this same letter we asked your excellency, as is just, to come to Rome and to clear yourself of the accusations. We got back from you, however, a letter not of the kind the occasion called for, but of the kind the vanity of imprudent men inspires. The excuse for not coming to the council must be reasonable; but messengers from your excellency must be on hand who demonstrate that you declined the holy council's invitation either because of illness or because of certified difficulties. There is material written in your own letter that no bishop, but only childish ignorance, could deign to write. For you excommunicated all so that they would have the right to sing masses and ordain ecclesiastical officers if we were to constitute another bishop for the Roman see. Indeed, it was written as follows: 'you may not have the faculty of ordaining no one.' Until now we thought and truly believed that two negatives make an affirmative, unless of course your authority undoes the maxims of the earliest Latin authors.

---

34. Pope John's double negative is supposed to belittle him and reduce his authority. See chapter 14, below.

But we answer your intent, not your actual words. If you do not put off coming to the council and clearing yourself of the accusations, we will obey your authority without any hesitation. But if—and may it not be so!—you elude coming and clearing yourself of the capital crimes ascribed to you, especially since there is nothing preventing you from coming, neither the need to sail the seas, nor bodily infirmity, nor the length of the journey, then we shall ignore your excommunication. Instead we shall turn it back upon you, since we can rightly do that. For Judas, the betrayer and seller of our Lord Jesus Christ, received, along with the others, the power to bind and loose from the Master, who used these words: 'Amen, I say to you, whatsoever you shall bind upon earth, shall be bound also in heaven; and whatsoever you shall loose on earth, shall be loosed also in heaven.'[35] As long as he was good among the disciples, he could bind and loose. But after that he became a murderer on account of greed and sought to extinguish the life of all: whom then could he loose among the bound, or bind among the loose, unless it was himself, whom he choked to death with a most miserable rope? Given on the tenth day before the calends of December and sent through Hadrian, cardinal priest, and Benedict, cardinal deacon."

15. When these messengers reached Tivoli, they did not find him; for now he had left and was carrying his bow amidst the fields, nor was there anyone who could indicate to them where he was. Since they could not find him, they returned to the holy council, now gathered for a third time, with the original letters. Soon the emperor spoke: "We awaited his arrival so that, with him present, we could complain of what he did to us. But since we know for sure that he will not be present here, we beg that you diligently listen to how perfidiously he acted toward us. We inform you archbishops, bishops, priests, deacons, and other clergy, and also counts, judges, and all the people, that this same Pope John, oppressed by Berengar and Adalbert, who rebelled against us, sent messengers to us in

35. Mt 18.18.

Saxony, asking that we come to Italy for the love of God and free him and the church of St. Peter from their jaws. It is not necessary to say how much we achieved with the help of God, since you see it around here. Once snatched from their clutches by my intervention and returned to his due honor, he forgot the oath and fidelity he promised me over the body of St. Peter, then had Adalbert come to Rome, and held the city against me, sparked revolts, and, with our own soldiers looking on, he became a war leader, wearing breastplate and helmet. Let this holy council now say what it decrees about all this."

To this the Roman pontiffs and the rest of the clergy and the whole people answered: "An unheard-of wound must be healed with an unprecedented cauterization! If, by his corrupt morals, he were harmful just to himself and not to everyone, it should be somehow tolerated. But how many people who had been chaste beforehand became unchaste through imitation of him! How many upstanding men have now become criminals through the example of his ways! We plead therefore that the greatness of your imperial authority cast this monster, redeemed from his vices by no virtue whatsoever,[36] out of the holy Roman church, and appoint another man in his place, one who is worthy to lead us by the example of his good ways, who himself lives righteously and offers us an example by living well." Then the emperor said: "What you say pleases us, and nothing would delight us more than that such a man, worthy to be placed at the head of this holy and universal see, could be found."

16. Once these things had been said, all spoke with a single voice: "Having rejected John the apostate for his reprobate morals, we elect as our shepherd and supreme universal pope of the holy Roman church Leo, the venerable first secretary of the holy Roman church, an esteemed man and one worthy of the highest priestly rank."[37] When all had said this aloud for a third time, with the

---

36. Juvenal, *Satires* 4.2–3.

37. The narrative does not follow the protocols of papal election as imagined by the Ottonians and spelled out in the *Privilegium Ottonianum* of early 962. Otto is not

emperor assenting, they led the aforementioned Leo to the Lateran palace according to custom, singing the lauds, and at the specified time they administered holy consecration to the highest priesthood in the church of St. Peter, and promised by swearing oaths that they would be faithful to him in the future.[38]

17. Once these things had been done thus, as the most holy emperor was hoping to stay in Rome with few retainers, lest he exhaust the Roman people through the multitude of his army, he gave many license to return north. When John, who was called pope, learned this, not unaware of how easily money can corrupt the minds of the Romans, he secretly sent messengers to Rome, promising the money of St. Peter and all the churches if they were to attack the pious emperor and lord pope Leo and butcher them most impiously.[39] Why do I delay the conclusion so long? With their trumpets blaring the Romans hastened against the emperor so as to kill him, trusting in, or being deceived by, the smallness of the imperial army, and encouraged by the promise of money. The emperor himself rushed against them, towards the Tiber bridge that the Romans had blocked with carts. His strong soldiers, with breasts hardened by war, intrepid with weapons, leapt at them, and, like hunters of birds, terrified the multitude, with none able to resist. Neither the dens, nor the baskets, nor the curved wooden beams, nor the sewer tunnels could offer any protection for those in flight.[40] They were killed, therefore, and, as happens with men that strong, most were struck in the back. Who then of the Romans would have survived the massacre if the holy emperor had not been inclined to that mercy which he did not owe them at all, and had not called back his men, still thirsting to kill?

18. Thus, once all the rebels were overpowered, and hostages

---

represented selecting the candidate for the tiara. Instead, Liudprand stresses decision-making by consensus, which was how German aristocratic politics were supposed to work.

38. Unlike other tenth-century popes, this Lateran high official kept his name, becoming Leo VIII.

39. In January 964.

40. See *Retribution* 1.35 for similar imagery.

had been taken from the survivors, the venerable Pope Leo threw himself at the feet of the emperor and begged him to return the hostages to the Romans and commend the pope to their trust. At last, through the plea of the venerable Pope Leo, the holy emperor returned the hostages to the Romans, though he was certain they would start up what I am about to relate; therefore, he entrusted the same pope to the trust of the Romans just as a lamb might be entrusted to wolves. Lastly, leaving Rome, he set out toward Camerino and Spoleto,[41] where he had heard Adalbert was.

19. Meanwhile some women, with whom John, who was called pope, had exercised the offense of his lust (and they were neither plebeian nor few), incited the Romans to drop the supreme and universal Pope Leo, elected by God and themselves, and accept John back into the city. When they did this, through God's mercy the venerable Pope Leo was freed from their grasp, and, along with a few followers, he set out for the clemency of the most pious Emperor Otto.

20. Then the holy emperor mobilized his army and prepared to return to Rome, bearing bitterly so great an insult—since the abdicated John had shown faithlessness through the expulsion of the lord Pope Leo *and* through John the cardinal deacon and Azzo the secretary, of whom the former's right hand and the latter's tongue, two fingers, and nose were cut off. Yet before the troops of the holy emperor had gathered, since the Lord wished to show to all centuries how justly Pope John had been repudiated by his bishops and all the people, and how unjustly afterwards he was received back in Rome, while John was taking his pleasure with the wife of some man on a certain night outside of Rome, he was struck in the temple by the devil so that within the space of eight days he had died of the wound.[42] But by the inspiration of the same one who

41. These cities anchored central Italy's most important territorial units; they had been strongholds of Berengarian sentiment since the 940s.

42. On February 26, 964. In Liudprand's account, this is the sole direct supernatural intervention. For the rest Otto is God's effective agent on earth. See P. Garbini, "Scrittura autobiografica e filosofia della politica nei *Gesta Ottonis* di Liutprando," *La cultura* 32 (1994): 482.

had struck him, John did not take the Eucharist of the last rites, according to what we heard often and under oath from his relatives and other hangers-on who were present.

21. Once he was dead, all the Romans, forgetful of the oath they swore to the holy emperor, made Cardinal Deacon Benedict pope; beyond that, they promised with an oath that they would never abandon him, but would defend him against the power of the emperor.[43] Having heard this, the emperor surrounded the city and permitted no one to leave who did not have his limbs severed, and he afflicted the city with catapults and hunger until he could seize it, though the Romans were unwilling, and could return the venerable man Leo to his proper see, and could have the invader of the supreme see, Benedict, brought into his presence.[44]

22. With lord Leo, supreme and universal pope, sitting in the Lateran church, and the most holy emperor Otto, as well as the Roman bishops, the Italian, Lotharingian, and Saxon archbishops, bishops, priests, deacons, and the whole Roman people, whose names are written below, there entered the invader of the apostolic see, Benedict, led in by the hands of those who had elected him, clad in the papal vestments.[45] The cardinal deacon Benedict addressed him: "By what authority, what law, O invader, did you usurp these pontifical robes, and in the presence of our lord the venerable Pope Leo, whom you elected to the pinnacle of apostolicity, along with us, having accused and recused John? Can you deny that in the presence of the lord emperor you swore an oath never to elect or ordain a pope along with the other Romans, except with his consent and that of his son King Otto?" Benedict replied: "If I have sinned, have mercy on me." Then the emperor, having spilled some tears, demonstrating how merciful he was, asked the council not to show prejudice against Benedict. If he wanted to and was

43. Benedict V was elected in May 964.

44. This siege took place in June 964.

45. The public ritual signaled the submission of the Roman aristocracy (and the success of Ottonian consensus politics) and sanctioned the legitimacy of John XII's deposition: Sutherland, *Liutprand*, 92.

able, he should answer the interrogation and defend his case; and if he could not or did not want to, and declared himself guilty, he should find some clemency, for fear of God. Having heard that, Benedict quickly cast himself at the feet of lord Pope Leo and the emperor, and shouted out that he had sinned and that he was an invader of the holy Roman see. After that he took off the pallium,[46] which he returned to the lord Pope Leo, along with the pontifical staff, which he was holding in his hand. The pope broke the staff and showed the broken pieces to the people. Then he instructed Benedict to sit on the floor, and he removed the tunic, which they call *planeta*, and also the stole. After that he said to all the bishops: "We deprive Benedict, invader of the apostolic see, of every episcopal and priestly honor. On account of the generosity of the lord emperor Otto, thanks to whose efforts we are returned to our proper see, we allow him to keep the rank of deacon; and not now in Rome, but in the exile to which we send him . . ."[47]

46. This white woolen band, embroidered with crosses, was worn around the shoulders. It was a symbolically important part of high-ranking clerics' vestments, particularly of bishops and archbishops.

47. The text is incomplete. Benedict V died in exile in Hamburg in 965/6. Otto III had his body reburied in Rome some decades later, and there is evidence that even some German clerics, like Thietmar of Merseburg (*Chronicon* 4.62), disapproved of his deposition: Reuter, *Germany*, 171; M. Lintzel, *Studien über Liutprand von Cremona* (Berlin: Verlag Dr Emil Ebering, 1933), 19–34.

THE EMBASSY OF LIUDPRAND
THE CREMONESE BISHOP
TO THE CONSTANTINOPOLITAN
EMPEROR NICEPHOROS PHOCAS
ON BEHALF OF THE AUGUST
OTTOS & ADELHEID

Liudprand, bishop of the holy Cremonese church, wishes, desires, and hopes that the Ottonians, the utterly unconquered, august emperors of the Romans, and the most glorious august empress Adelheid[1] may always be well, prosper, and triumph.

1. What the reasons were why you did not receive a letter or a messenger from me sooner, the following explanation will make plain. We arrived in Constantinople on the day before the nones of June (968) and, as an insult to you, we were received in a shameful way, rudely and shamefully handled. We were closed into a certain mansion, quite big and open, which neither protected from the cold nor kept out the heat; armed soldiers were stationed there as guards, who forbade all my people from leaving and others from

---

1. Widow of the Italian king Lothar who married Otto I in 951, bore him Otto II and Mathilda, was crowned empress in 962, and wielded great power until her death in 999. Liudprand mentioned her in *Retribution* 4.13. He was hostile to her father Rudolf (*Retribution* 2.60–67).

entering. This house, open just to us who were shut within, was so remote from the imperial palace that one became short of breath not by riding there, but even by walking. It added to our disastrous position that the wine of the Greeks was undrinkable for us because of their commingling pitch, pine sap, and plaster in it; for that house was waterless, and we could not even extinguish our thirst with water that we would buy with the money that had been given us. On top of this great woe was placed another woe; a man, that is, the guardian of the house,[2] who oversaw the daily expenses, one whose equal, if you seek him, will be found, perhaps, in hell, but not on earth. For like a flooding torrent he poured onto us whatever calamity,[3] whatever robbery, whatever cost, whatever sorrow, whatever misery he could dream up. Never in 120 days did a single one pass that did not provide us with a moan or sorrow.[4]

2. On the day before the nones of June, as we wrote above, we arrived at Constantinople, before the Carean gate,[5] and we waited with our horses until the eleventh hour,[6] under rain that was not light. At the eleventh hour, since Nicephoros did not consider us worthy to ride horses that your clemency had outfitted with such elegance,[7] he ordered us to come in, and we were led to the aforementioned ugly, waterless, wide-open marble house. On the eighth day before the ides, the Saturday before Pentecost,[8] I was led into the presence of the emperor's brother Leo, the chief of staff at the court and minister, where we were exhausted by a great altercation over your imperial title. For he called you not "emperor,"

2. The text here is corrupt.

3. Is 30.28.

4. From June 4th to October 2nd, according to Liudprand's own account.

5. Close to the Great Palace, the main imperial residence.

6. Following classical tradition, the Byzantines divided daytime into twelve hours that expanded and contracted in length according to the season and latitude. Thus Liudprand waited until almost dusk. See also *Retribution* 5.21, n. 37.

7. Horses, especially the magnificent ones that Otto seems to have furnished his messengers, conferred status to their riders, and Nicephoros deprived the visitors of a chance to flaunt their mounts.

8. An important Christian holiday observed fifty days after Easter to celebrate the apostles' mission. In 968 Pentecost fell on June 7th.

that is, βασιλέα in his tongue, but rather, out of disdain, ῥῆγα, that is, "king" in our tongue. When I answered this by saying that the meaning was the same even if the signifier is different, he told me I had come not for the sake of peace, but to squabble; and thus, rising up in rage, he accepted your letter in a truly insulting way, through an interpreter and not into his own hands. And what a man was Leo, fairly imposing, falsely humble, one who would pierce the hand of a man who leaned against him.[9]

3. On the seventh day before the ides, the holy day of Pentecost itself, I was led before Nicephoros[10] in the residence called Στεφάνα, in Latin the "Crown Palace";[11] he is a quite monstrous man, dwarfish, with a fat head, and mole-like by virtue of the smallness of his eyes, deformed by a short beard that is wide and thick and graying, disgraced by a finger-like neck, quite like Hyopas because of the abundance and thickness of his hair, in color quite like the Ethiopian whom you would not like to run into in the middle of the night,[12] with an extended belly and scrawny buttocks, very long hips measured against his short height, small legs, flat feet, dressed in an ornamental robe, but one old and, by reason of its age and daily use, stinking and faded, with Sicyonian footgear on his feet,[13] provocative in his speech, a fox in his slyness, a Ulysses in his perjury and mendacity. My lords the august emperors always seemed handsome to me, but how much more handsome you seem after him! Always you seemed elegant, but how much more elegant after him! Always you seemed mighty, but how much mightier after him! You always seemed nice, but how much nicer after him! You always seemed full of virtue, but how much more virtuous after him! There sat on the left, not aligned with him but far behind,

9. A reference to Is 36.6, where the Assyrian general advancing on Jerusalem likened Egypt, unreliable ally of Judah, to a flimsy walking stick.

10. After a brilliant military career Nicephoros II Phocas, acclaimed by the troops in Cappadocia, entered Constantinople and ruled Byzantium, 963–69. To sustain a connection with the legitimate Macedonian dynasty, he kept Basil II and Constantine VIII, sons of Theophano and his predecessor Romanos II, in the palace.

11. There was a Coronation Hall in the Great Palace.

12. Juvenal, *Satires* 5.53–54.

13. Considered unmanly by Cicero, *De oratore* 1.54.231.

two small emperors, once his rulers, now subject to him. This was the beginning of their narrative:

4. "We should have, indeed we wished to welcome you kindly and magnificently; but the impiety of your lord does not permit it, a man who arrogated Rome to himself with a hostile occupation, who took it by force from Berengar and Adalbert,[14] against all law and custom, who killed some of the Romans by the sword, others by hanging, deprived others of their eyes, consigned still others to exile, and on top of that attempted to subdue to his power the cities of our empire by murder and arson.[15] And since his wicked scheme could not have the desired outcome, having faked peace, now he sent us you, as a κατάσκοπον, or spy, an instigator and agent of his malice."

5. To which I replied: "My lord did not invade the Roman city by force or in a tyrannical way, but rather he freed it from the yoke of the tyrant, or tyrants.[16] Were not effeminates lording it over Rome,[17] and, what is more serious and sordid, were not whores doing the same? Back then, I think, your power was snoozing, along with that of your predecessors, who in name alone, and not in actual fact, are considered emperors of the Romans.

"If they were powerful, if they were emperors of the Romans, why were they leaving Rome to the power of the whores? Were not some of the most holy popes expelled, others so cast down they did not have enough to pay their daily expenses or for charity? Did not Adalbert send a libelous letter to Romanos and Constantine,

14. Adalbert (†c.975) and his father Berengar II (†966) were the kings of Italy whom Otto I subjected in 951 and deposed in 962, but who provided continuous resistance thereafter. Their control of Rome was always nominal (see *Concerning King Otto* 15). Liudprand recorded their deeds in *Retribution* 5.

15. In 965 Otto I had crushed a revolt against "his" pope, Leo VIII (*Concerning King Otto*, 17–18). In 967 and 968 he had campaigned, with modest success, in Byzantine Italy. The failure of the 968 attack on Bari did not alter Byzantine opinions of this hostile deed.

16. Liudprand often portrayed the doings of powerful Roman clans as immoral, and Rome as needing a purifying external intervention, like Otto I's in 962. See G. Arnaldi, "Liutprando di Cremona: un detrattore di Roma o dei romani?" *Studi romani* 53 (2005): 12–50.

17. See Is 3.4.

your imperial predecessors? Did he not strip the churches of the most holy apostles with his robbery? Which of you emperors, led by zeal for God, bothered to avenge such an unworthy crime and return the holy church to its proper condition? You neglected to, but my lord did not neglect it, he who, arising from the ends of the earth and coming to Rome,[18] cast out the impious ones and returned every right and privilege to the vicars of the holy apostles. Afterwards, following the decrees of the Roman emperors Justinian, Valentinian, Theodosius,[19] and others, he felled, throttled, hanged, and relegated to exile those who rebelled against him and the apostolic lord, people who were violators of oaths, sacrilegious, torturers of their apostolic lords, or robbers. If he had not done these things, he would be an impious, unjust, cruel tyrant. It is manifest that Berengar and Adalbert, having become Otto's soldiers, took the golden scepter of the Italian kingdom from his hands and, in the presence of your servants who are alive to this day and live in this city, promised loyalty by swearing an oath.[20] And since, with the devil instigating, they perfidiously violated it, he rightly deprived them of the kingdom as deserters and rebels against him, which you would do, too, to any subjects who afterwards became rebels."

6. "But," he said, "a soldier of Adalbert's does not acknowledge this version." To which I answered: "If he contradicts it, one of my soldiers will demonstrate that it *is* so in a duel tomorrow, if you order it."

"It may be that he did these things, as you say, rightly," he said. "Now explain why the boundaries of our empire are attacked by war and fire. We were friends, and thought of making an indissoluble alliance by marriage."

7. "The land," I said, "which you relate as being part of your

18. See Jer 6.22.

19. Famous late antique emperors who added to the corpus of Roman law.

20. This emphasis on the feudal bonds (sworn at Augsburg in 952) between Otto and Berengar and Adalbert reminded readers of the inappropriateness of the vassals' later behavior, and the righteousness of Otto's actions toward them. *Retribution* 5.12–13 was more ambiguous about the nature of Otto's settlement with Berengar.

empire, the indigenous people and language show to be part of the Italian kingdom. The Lombards held it by might, and Louis, the emperor of the Lombards and Franks, freed it from the hand of the prostrated Saracen hordes.[21] Landulf, prince of the Beneventans and Capuans,[22] subjugated it by force to himself for seven years, nor would it have escaped the yoke of subjection to him and his successors up to the present day, if the emperor Romanos had not bought the friendship of our King Hugh by handing over a vast sum—and this was the reason why he united in marriage his nephew and namesake to the illegitimate daughter of our King Hugh.[23] And as I see it, you ascribe to my lord not kindness, but powerlessness, because after acquiring Italy and Rome he left them to you for so many years. The alliance of friendship that you say you wanted to make by marriage, we consider a fraud and a trick; you demand a truce that no real reason compels you to demand, nor us to grant. Truly, so that lies may be removed, let not the truth be silent. My lord sent me to you so that, if you want to hand over in marriage to his son, my lord Otto the august emperor, the daughter of the emperor Romanos and the empress Theophano, you affirm it to me by oath, and I, by way of recompense for this concession, will affirm by swearing an oath that my lord will do and observe this-and-that. But my lord now proffers an excellent guarantee of friendship to your brotherly highness, since he has subjected all Apulia[24] to your power, thanks to my intervention,

21. The Carolingian ruler of Italy Louis II (850–75) captured Bari from the Arabs in 871. Westerners often called Muslims Saracens, thus assigning them biblical origins (related to Abraham's wife Sarah).

22. Landulf II (†943) succeeded in re-establishing Beneventan rights to rule northern Apulia in the 920s. Benevento and Capua were important cities (and states) in the Lombard area of southern Italy. After 900 they were ruled by members of the same family, in effect fusing together. See *Retribution* 4.9 for some context.

23. Romanos II (†963) married his son to a daughter of King Hugh of Italy in 944: *Retribution* 5.15, 5.20.

24. This Byzantine-ruled province in southeastern Italy was contested between southern Lombard rulers, Arab invaders, and occasionally western emperors. Compared to southwestern Italy, Apulia was less Hellenized, as large segments of it had been subject to the dukes of Benevento in the eighth and ninth centuries.

to whose instigation instead you say a misdeed is due. There are as many witnesses to this as there are inhabitants in all Apulia."[25]

8. "The second hour," Nicephoros said, "is now past.[26] We are now to celebrate the προέλευσις, that is, the procession. We do what is now scheduled; against these assertions of yours, if it proves opportune, we shall answer later."

9. It does not bother me to describe this προέλευσις, and it will not bother my lords to hear of it. A copious multitude of merchants and common people, decked out with quite thin little shields and cheap spears, gathered for this solemnity to welcome and praise Nicephoros, occupied the sides of the roads forming walls, almost, from the palace of Nicephoros to Sancta Sophia. That the larger part of this mob had proceeded to this praise session with bare feet increased the whole event's shamefulness: I believe they thought they could better adorn their holy προέλευσις this way. But even his nobles, who crossed through the same plebeian and barefooted multitude with him, wore oversized tunics much tattered by age. They would have marched much more decorously wearing their everyday clothes: there was no one there whose ancestor owned the tunic when it was new.[27] No one was decorated with gold there, no one with jewels, except Nicephoros alone, whom the imperial ornaments, cut and made for the physiques of his predecessors, rendered uglier. By your health, which is dearer to me than my own, a single one of the costumes of your nobles is more costly than one hundred of those, and more! I was led to that προέλευσις and placed in a higher place, next to the *psaltas*, or chanters.

10. While that monster proceeded, almost crawling, the adulating *psaltas* called out: "Here comes the morning star, there arises Eous, he reflects the sun's rays with his glare, the pallid death of the Saracens, Nicephoros the μέδων" (that is, the "prince"). And they sang

25. Liudprand's claims to intercession in southern Italy are not substantiated elsewhere.

26. It was roughly 8:00 A.M. See n. 6 above.

27. The Byzantine aristocrats' antique attire conferred authority. In the west, new clothes did the same.

on, "Μέδοντι" (that is, "to the prince") "Nicephoros, may there
be πολλὰ ἔτη" (that is, "many years"). "O nations, worship him,
adore him, and to him alone bow your necks!"[28] How much more
accurately they might have sung: "Come, burnt cinder, μέλας,[29] old
hag in your walk, elfin in your expression, boor, jungle-wanderer,
goat-footed, horned, double-limbed, bristly, wild, bumpkin, barbarian, hard and hairy one, rebel and Cappadocian!"[30] Thereupon,
puffed up by those lying songs, he entered Sancta Sophia with his
lords the emperors following him from far off and prostrating
themselves on the ground in a kiss of peace. In the church his ar-
mor-bearer with an arrow for a pen set down the era that was under
way, doubtless in which time he had begun to rule, and in this way
any who did not see it understand what era it is.[31]

11. That same day he ordered me to be his dinner guest. He did
not, however, consider me worthy to be placed before any of his
nobles, so I sat fifteenth from him, and where there was no table-
cloth.[32] Of my party, not only did no one sit at table but none even
saw the house in which I was dinner guest. At this dinner, quite
foul and repulsive in the manner of all drunkards' gatherings, im-
pregnated with oil and sprinkled with a really awful fish sauce,[33] he

28. A fairly accurate representation of the formal acclamations offered to Byzantine
emperors on ceremonial occasions. On such events, see A. Berger, "Imperial and Ecclesiastical Processions in Constantinople," in *Byzantine Constantinople*, ed. N. Necipoğlu
(Leiden: Brill, 2001), 73–87.

29. "Dark one."

30. For the implications to postclassical audiences of being from Cappadocia, see
R. Van Dam, *Kingdom of Snow: Roman Rule and Greek Culture in Cappadocia* (Philadelphia:
University of Pennsylvania Press, 2002), chapter 1.

31. Perhaps an echo of ancient Roman timekeeping practices whereby nails were
affixed in the wall of the Capitoline temple of Jupiter. Elsewhere (*Retribution* 3.37)
Liudprand called Constantinople's grandest church by its traditional Greek name,
Haghia Sophia.

32. Rank and ceremonial order mattered to tenth-century aristocrats, and his seating was an issue that Liudprand knew would strike a chord with his western audience:
see H. Fichtenau, *Living in the Tenth Century* (Chicago: University of Chicago Press,
1991), 8, 32–33.

33. *Garum* was the ketchup of the ancient world, made of fermented fish parts. It
was industrially produced in postclassical Italy, though Liudprand affects the disgust

asked me a lot of questions about your power, and a lot about your realms and soldiers. When I would answer appropriately and truthfully, "You lie!" he said; "the soldiers of your lord are ignorant of horse-riding and do not know about infantry combat! The size of shields, the weight of breastplates, the length of swords, and the heft of helmets does not allow them to fight in either way!" Then, chuckling, he said, "Also their gullets' voracity prevents them, that is, the gluttony of their stomachs; their gut is their god,[34] their courage is debauchery, their steadfastness is drunkenness, going without rations is their undoing, and fear is their sobriety. Nor is there a large number of fleets afloat on the sea serving your lord; to me alone belongs the steadfastness of sailors, to me who will attack him with fleets and demolish his maritime cities in war and reduce to ashes those that are close to rivers. Who, I ask, can resist me even on land, with scanty forces? Otto's son was not absent, his wife was not missing, the Saxons, Swabians, Bavarians, and Italians were all with him; yet when they both did not know how and were not able to take one tiny city that resisted them, how will they resist me when I arrive, followed by armies numerous

'as are the crops of Gargarus, as are the grape bunches on Methymna, as are the stars in the sky, as are the waves in the sea'?"[35]

12. He did not permit it when I wanted to respond to this and throw out a counter-argument worthy of his inflation; instead he added, as if to insult us: "You are not Romans, but Lombards!" Though he wanted to say something beyond this and waved his hand so that I would be quiet, I spoke out, upset: "The annals recognize that fratricidal Romulus, from whose name they are called

---

of a northern European landlubber. But the sauce was known to the monks of St. Gall: see J. Koder and T. Weber, *Liudprand von Cremona in Konstantinopel* (Vienna: Verlag der Österreichischen Akademie der Wissenschaften, 1980), 87.

34. Phil 3.19.

35. Liudprand quotes Ovid, *Ars Amatoria* 1.57–59. In the reported speech Nicephoros refers to Byzantine amphibious operations in Sicily and southern Italy between 964 and 967. In spring 968 Otto abandoned his siege of Bari, crucial administrative center and port in Byzantine Italy, but a second attack on Calabria followed the same year.

Romans, was born to a whore, that is, he was generated in defilement; and he made a refuge for himself where he welcomed defaulted debtors from foreign climes, runaway slaves, murderers, and people who deserved death for their crimes, and he attracted such a throng of such people that he called them Romans; from this aristocracy there arose those whom you call *cosmocrators*, or emperors.[36] We, that means the Lombards, Saxons, Franks, Lotharingians, Bavarians, Swabians, Burgundians, so disdain them that we utter no other insult than 'You Roman!' to our enemies when aroused, and we understand that single term, the name of the Romans, to include every baseness, every cowardice, every kind of greed, every promiscuity, every mendacity, indeed every vice.

"Since you say we are unwarlike and ignorant of riding skills, if the sins of the Christians merit that you persist in this harshness, the coming wars will demonstrate what type of men you are and how pugnacious we are."

13. Nicephoros, angered by such words, called for silence with his hand and ordered the long, narrow table removed and myself returned to the hated house or, if I were to speak more truthfully, prison. There, after two days I was afflicted by such a deep prostration, first through my indignation and then the heat and thirst, that there was no one among my retainers who did not fear his last day approached after having drunk from my same cup. Why, I ask, did they, too, not fall ill, whose drink was brine in lieu of fine wine, whose bedding, in lieu of hay, straw, or even earth, was hard marble, who had stone in lieu of a pillow, whose wide-open house did not protect from heat, rain, or cold? Even health itself, poured over them, could not save them if it wanted to![37] Therefore, debilitated by my own suffering as well as that of my men, having summoned the guardian, or rather my persecutor, I arranged, not just by pleas but by paying a price, that he would deliver to the brother of Nicephoros my letter, saying things like this:

36. Liudprand drew on Paul the Deacon, *Historia Romana* 1.1–2. But even in antiquity Rome's founding myths were sometimes denigrated (e.g., Livy, 1.4.7).

37. Terence, *Adelphoe* 761–62.

14. "Bishop Liudprand to Leo, chief of staff and minister τοῦ δρόμου:[38] The sufferings which I am undergoing here will not wear me out if the most serene emperor is thinking of granting the request on account of which I came; only that through a letter from me and a messenger my lord Otto should be told that I am not delaying the matter here. But if the emperor considers the matter differently, there is here a freight ship of the Venetians, which hastens to depart; let him permit me, sick as I am, to board it so that, if the time of my collapse were to arrive, at least my corpse may be welcomed by the land of my birth."

15. When he read this, he ordered me to come to him after four days. There sat with him to debate your matter men very learned according to their tradition, strong in their Greek language, Basil the head of the imperial bedchamber, the first secretary, the chief of the imperial wardrobe, and two teachers. This was the beginning of their narration:

"Explain, brother, what the cause might be that you wore yourself out to announce." When I spelled out to them the recompense of kinship which would be the opportunity for endless peace, they said: "It is unheard-of for the *porphyrogenita* of a *porphyrogenitus*, that is, the daughter born in the purple to one who was himself born in the purple, to be mixed up with the peoples.[39] Truly, since you seek such a rarefied thing, you will receive what pleases you only if you give what is appropriate, that is, Ravenna and Rome with all the lands, uninterrupted, which extend from there to us here. If you in fact desire friendship without kinship, let your lord allow Rome to be free, and also let him hand over into their original slavery the Capuan and the Beneventan princes, formerly slaves of our holy empire and now rebels against it."[40]

38. The "logothete of the drome" was a title that referred to responsibility for the public postal system and, by extension, foreign affairs and communications. See D. Miller, "The Logothete of the Drome," *Byzantion* 36 (1966): 438–70.

39. In *Retribution* 1.6–7 Liudprand explains the term *porphyrogenitus*. "Peoples" here means foreign, non-Byzantine, or barbarian populations.

40. H. Mayr-Harting, "Liutprand of Cremona's Account of his Legation," *English Historical Review* 116 (2001): 539–56, thinks that the real purpose of this text was to

16. To them I said: "Even you are not unaware that my lord has mightier Slavic peoples under him than the king of the Bulgarians, Peter, who led off in marriage the daughter of the emperor Christopher!" "But Christopher," they said, "was not born in the purple."

17. "In truth," I said, "whom does Rome serve, that you clamor for it to wish to be freed? To whom does she pay tribute? Was she not serving whores before, and, with you snoozing and certainly not showing any valor, did not my master, the august emperor, free her from so base a form of servitude? As he was *cosmocrator*, the august emperor Constantine, who built this city on his own name, contributed many gifts to the holy apostolic Roman church, and not just gifts in Italy, but in almost all the western kingdoms and in the eastern and southern ones, too, namely, in Greece, Judea, Persia, Mesopotamia, Babylonia, Egypt, and Libya, as testify his charters that are in our possession.[41] Rightly my lord handed over to the vicar of the most holy apostles whatever belonged to the church of the most holy apostles in Italy, and Saxony, Bavaria, and all the kingdoms of my lord; and if it happened that my lord kept back anything from all of these, whether cities, manors, soldiers, or a single family, then I have denied God.[42] Why does not your emperor do the same thing, so that he returns to the church of the apostles its properties that are in his realms and thus renders richer and freer that church which, through the toil and generosity of my lord, is already rich and free?"

18. "But he will do that," said Basil, the head of the imperial bedchamber, "when he makes Rome and the Roman church obe-

---

convince these southern Lombard princes to support Otto instead of Byzantium. Pandulf Ironhead (†981) ruled Capua and Benevento alongside his brother, Landulf (†969). They entered Otto's allegiance early in 967; in recompense, Pandulf also received the central Italian states of Camerino and Spoleto.

41. An early reference to the *Donation of Constantine*, an eighth-century forgery designed to increase papal jurisdiction, which became an instrument of papal propaganda in the high Middle Ages.

42. After the hints in chapter 5, here Liudprand refers explicitly to the *Privilegium Ottonianum* of February 962, whereby the freshly crowned emperor reaffirmed Carolingian grants of land and rights to the papacy.

dient to his nod." Then I said, "A certain fellow, having suffered much harm from another, approaches God with these words: 'Lord, avenge me of my enemy!' God answered him: 'I will do it,' he said, 'on the day when I will give to each according to his deeds.' But the fellow replied, 'How late!'"[43]

19. Then all except the emperor's brother left the disputation shaking with laughter, and ordered me to be led back to the hated house and to be guarded with great care until the feast day of the holy apostles, celebrated by all clerics.[44] On that feast day I was quite sick, but nevertheless he ordered me and the messengers of the Bulgarians, who had arrived the day before, to meet him at the Church of the Holy Apostles. When, after the wordiness of the chants and of the celebration of the masses, we were invited to table, he placed the messenger of the Bulgarians, shorn in the Hungarian style, girt with a bronze chain, and—as my mind suggested to me—not yet baptized, at the furthest end of the table (which was long and narrow) but closer than me to himself, obviously as an insult to you, my august lords. For you I underwent contempt, for you I was disdained, for you I was scorned; but I give thanks to the Lord Jesus Christ, whom you serve with your whole spirit, that I was considered worthy to suffer insults in your name. Truly, my lords, I left that table considering the insult not to me, but to you. As I sought to leave, indignant, Leo, the chief of staff and brother of the emperor, and the first secretary, Simon, followed behind me, howling: "When Peter the emperor of the Bulgarians led off Christopher's daughter as spouse, symphonies, that is, accords, were written and sealed with oaths, so that we would give precedence to, give honor and favor to the Bulgarians' apostles, that

43. The joke weaves together citations of Lk 18.3 and Ps 61.13.

44. The feast of the apostles Peter and Paul (June 29th) should not have required much explanation, but its date fits most tidily into the narrative (the next firm date, thirteen days before the calends of August, comes in chapter 29). The feast of the Transfiguration would make more sense, as it was less well established and was not universally accepted in the west until the 1400s. Leo VI introduced it to Constantinople, though it was not unknown there beforehand. Traditionally it was celebrated on August 6th, too late for the logic of the narrative.

is, the messengers, above the apostles of all the other nations. That apostle of the Bulgarians, though he is, as you say (and it is true), shorn, unwashed, and girt with a bronze chain, nevertheless is a noble, and we judge it unpropitious to give precedence over him to a bishop, especially one of the Franks. And since we perceive you bear this without dignity, we will not allow you to return to your hostel now as you think, but will force you to savor the food with the slaves of the emperor in a certain cheap inn."

20. To them I answered nothing because of a boundless pain within my heart; but I did what they had ordered, considering dishonorable a table where precedence is given to a Bulgarian messenger over not me, that is, Bishop Liudprand, but over one of your messengers. But the holy emperor alleviated my pain with a great gift, sending me from his most refined foods a fat goat, one of which he himself had eaten, totally overloaded with garlic, onion, leeks, drowned in fish sauce, which I wish could appear on your own table, my lords, so that, whatever delectables you did not believe fitting for a holy emperor, at least, after having seen these ones, you might believe it.

21. When eight days had passed, once the Bulgarians had gone, thinking I would esteem his table highly, he invited me, still quite sick, to eat with him in the same place. The patriarch was there, along with many bishops, in whose presence he proposed to me many issues concerning the Holy Scriptures, which I elegantly explained with the Holy Spirit inspiring me.[45] And suddenly, so as to make a joke of you, he asked what councils we accept. When I answered the Nicean, Chalcedonian, Ephesian, Antiochene, Carthaginian, Ankaran, and Constantinopolitan, he said, "Ha! Ha! He! You forgot to say the Saxon one! If you ask why that one is not in our books, I answer because it is primitive and it could not yet make it through to us."[46]

---

45. Patriarch Polyeuktos (†970), whose long tenure was characterized by testy relations with the emperor Nicephoros.

46. The humor depends on historical knowledge of the antiquity of eastern Mediterranean Christianity compared with the more recent christianization of Sax-

22. To that I answered: "In whatever limb illness prevails, there it must be driven out by cauterization. All the heresies originated from you, and they flourished among you; they were stifled, they were killed by us, that is, the westerners. Roman and Pavian councils, although held often, we shall not count here. But it was a Roman cleric, later the universal pope Gregory, who is called Dialogus by you, who freed Eutychius, heretical patriarch of Constantinople, of his heresy.[47] That same Eutychius not only said, but even taught, proclaimed, and wrote, that at our resurrection we would assume flesh that is not real, as we have here on earth, but somehow imaginary; his book of error was incinerated by Gregory in an orthodox way. But Ennodius, the Pavian bishop,[48] was sent here, to Constantinople, by the Roman patriarch, on account of a certain other heresy, which, once he had suppressed it, he reshaped into an orthodox and catholic form. After it accepted news of holy baptism and of God, the Saxon nation was never stained with heresy so that a council was held there to correct error, since there was none. As you call the faith of the Saxons primitive, I confirm the very same thing. For among them the faith of Christ is always primitive and not old, where good works follow upon belief; here the faith is certainly not primitive, but old, where belief does not unite with good works but instead is disdained on account of its age, like some old garment. But I know for sure that a council was held in Saxony wherein it was discussed and established that it is more honorable to fight with spears than with pens, and to accept death before turning one's back on the enemy; and your army is now learning all about it." In my heart I said, "And how pugnacious the Saxons are, may the outcome itself show!"

23. He ordered me to rush to him in the palace in the afternoon

---

ony. The seven late antique "Ecumenical Councils" to which Liudprand referred had established the framework of Christian belief and practice. Under Otto numerous councils in Saxony focused on the Slavic missions.

47. Before becoming pope (†604), Gregory the Great had been papal legate to Byzantium and had opposed Patriarch Eutychius's (†582) teachings on the resurrection.

48. A competent aristocratic administrator and writer, who died in 521, and had been papal legate to Constantinople.

of that same day, though I was weak and beside myself to the point that women I met in the street who earlier with wondering minds called out, "Mana! Mana!" now, pitying my pitiful condition, beating their breasts with their fists, would say, "Tαπεινὲ καὶ ταλαίπωρε!"[49] May what I prayed for, with my hands outstretched to the heavens, both for Nicephoros as he approached, and for you, who were absent, come true! Still I want you to believe me that he induced me to no small laughter, sitting as he was, quite tiny on a quite big, impatient, and unbridled horse. My mind pictured to itself that kind of doll your Slavs tie onto the young horse they send out unbridled to follow the lead of its mother.

24. Once these things had been done, I was led to the aforementioned hated house, to my fellow citizens and roommates, by now five lions, where I was granted conversation with no one except my people for over three weeks. Because of this, the notion that Nicephoros wanted never to send me home formed in my mind, and measureless sadness piled illness on illness in me, so that I would have died if the Mother of God had not obtained reprieve through her prayers from her Creator and Son, which was revealed to me by a vision, not an imaginary one but a real one.

25. During these three weeks Nicephoros held a *metastasis*, or prolonged stay, outside Constantinople at a place called Εἰς πήγας, or "At the Springs,"[50] and he ordered me to come there. And though I was so sick that not just standing but even mere sitting seemed a heavy burden to me, he required me to stand before him with my head uncovered, which was entirely wrong for my bad health. And he said: "The messengers of your King Otto, who preceded you last year, promised me with an oath—and the documents of the oath-taking are available here—that he would never scandalize our empire in any regard. Do you want a greater scandal than that he calls himself emperor, and usurps for himself the *themes* of our em-

49. "Miserable and unhappy man!" The earlier utterance is obscure; it may mean, "O my mother," but clearly was intended to convey admiration for the bishop's physical appearance.

50. Across the Golden Horn from the Great Palace.

pire?[51] Both cannot be tolerated, and, if both are unsupportable, this is not tolerable, indeed impossible even to hear about: that is, that he names himself emperor. But if you confirm the same oaths that your predecessors did, the majesty of our empire will quickly send you home prosperous and rich." He did not say this because he hoped that you would observe the terms, if my stupidity had accepted them, but he wanted to have in his hands something he could show in future times to his own credit and our dishonor.

26. To which I replied: "Recently my most holy lord, because he is very wise and full of the Spirit of God, foreseeing what you assert, lest I should cross the boundaries which he established for me, wrote out an ἐντόλινα, or document of instruction, which he even marked with his own seal, lest I should do differently.[52] You know, my august lord, in what a spirit of trust I say this—let the ἐντόλινα be brought into our midst, and whatever it instructs I will confirm to you by an oath. If these aforementioned messengers promised, swore, undersigned things exceeding the orders of my lord, it is as Plato said, 'checking the facts rests on the chooser, God is beyond blame.'"[53]

27. Once these things were finished, he came to the subject of the most noble princes, the Capuan and Beneventan, whom he named slaves and on account of whom a deep-seated pain wracks him. "Your lord," he said, "accepted under his tutelage my slaves; if he does not send them back and restore them to their original slavery, our friendship will fall away. They themselves petition to be received into our empire; but our empire rejects them so that

51. Byzantine military/administrative districts were called *themes* after the seventh century. The *themes* in question, Langobardia (now Apulia) and Sicilia (now Calabria), were creations of the late 800s (see Loud, "Southern Italy," 624). In 967 Otto's Venetian intermediaries and Nicephoros's envoys had met in the southern Balkans; see below, chapter 31.

52. Evidently Otto's prior Venetian messenger had promised more than Otto intended to deliver. The use of letters of instruction like Liudprand's here had begun under the Carolingians: see D. Queller, *The Office of Ambassador in the Middle Ages* (Princeton: Princeton University Press, 1967), 123–25.

53. *Republic* 10.617e.

they may learn and experience how dangerous it is for slaves to elude masters, to flee slavery. And it is more proper for your lord to hand them over as a friend than for him to send them to me against his will. They will plainly learn, if life lasts, what it means to trick a master, what it is to desert slavery; and, as I believe, they are even now feeling what I am talking about, with our troops who are beyond the sea executing the order."

28. He did not permit me to reply to these words, but, though I was desirous of leaving, he ordered me to return to his table. There his father sat down, a man, it seemed to me, born a hundred and fifty years before. In their praises, or rather venting, the Greeks sang out, asking God to multiply his years, just as his son's. From this we can discern how ignorant the Greeks are, how enamored of their glory, what adulators, how greedy. They wish upon an old man, indeed a walking corpse, what they certainly know nature itself will not allow; and the walking corpse rejoices that these things are wished upon him which, he knows, God would not do, and which would not be good for him, but bad, even if God did do them. Why, I ask, did they call out at Nicephoros to rejoice in the titles "peaceful" and "morning star"? Believe me, it is not praise, but insult, to call an impotent man virile, an ignorant man wise, a short man great, a black man white, a sinner saintly. And whoever enjoys being acclaimed more for others' deeds than for his own is most like those birds whose vision the night illuminates and the day blinds.

29. But let us return to the matter at hand. At this dinner he ordered to be read aloud the homily of the blessed John Chrysostom on the Acts of the Apostles, something he had not done before.[54] After the end of this reading, when I asked for license to return to you, nodding with his head that it would be done, he ordered me to be taken back by my persecutor to my fellow citizens and roommates, the lions. When this was done, I was not again received by

54. St. John Chrysostom (†407), "the golden-mouthed," was one of the most prolific late antique theologians, one of the Greek Church Fathers.

him until the thirteenth day before the calends of August, but I was carefully guarded lest I might benefit from the speech of anyone who could tell me of his deeds. Meanwhile he ordered Grimizo, Adalbert's messenger, to come to him, whom he ordered to return with his naval expedition.[55] There were twenty-four warships,[56] two ships of Russians,[57] two Gallic ships; I do not know if he sent more that I did not see. The strength of your soldiers, my lords, august emperors, does not need to be encouraged by the impotence of enemies, which it has often proved against those peoples, even the least of which, and the ones weakest by comparison with the others, cast the Greek power down and made it tributary: for just as I would not frighten you if I spoke of the Greeks as very strong people, similar to Alexander of Macedon, so I will not egg you on if I tell of their impotence, which is very real. I want you to believe me—and I know you will believe me—that forty of your men could kill off all that army of theirs, if a moat and walls did not prevent it. As I see it, he placed at the head of his army a sort of man—I called him "sort of man" since he ceased to be male and did not become a woman—to insult you.[58] Adalbert informed Nicephoros that he had eight thousand armored men with whom, and with the Greek army helping, he said he would put you to flight or overwhelm you; and he asked your imitator to send him money with which he would induce them to fight more eagerly.

30. But now, my lords, "see the snares of the Greeks and learn all of them from this one crime."[59] Nicephoros gave to that slave, to whom he entrusted the mustering and leadership of the army, a

55. To create difficulties for Otto, Nicephoros kept diplomatic ties with Berengar's son Adalbert, a focus of anti-Saxon sentiment in Italy.

56. Medieval seacraft were flexible, and these *chelandia* could serve multiple purposes (e.g., as transport vessels). They were oar-powered.

57. Probably the Varangian guard, elite mercenaries recruited in the Scandinavian settlements on Russia's rivers.

58. Eunuchs were much used in Byzantine administration because of their inability to form biological families, and thus because of their presumed greater loyalty to the emperors.

59. Virgil, *Aeneid* 2.65–66.

quite large sum of money for this reason: so that, if Adalbert came
to him with seven thousand armored men and more, as he had announced, then he should distribute that gift to them, and Cona,
his brother, should attack you with his own and the Greek army,
while Adalbert should be carefully guarded at Bari until his brother
returned, having obtained victory; but Nicephoros also ordered that
if, when Adalbert arrived, he did not lead that many thousand men,
then he should be seized, subdued, and handed over to you when
you arrived there, and, on top of that, the money which was supposed to go to Adalbert should be given into your hands.[60] O great
warrior! O loyal man! He seeks to harm the one for whom he prepares a defender, and he prepares a defender for the one he desires
to destroy! To neither is he loyal, to both disloyal; he does what he
did not need to do, he needs to do what he did not do. But let that
be: he did what suits the Greeks! Let us return to our subject.

31. On the fourteenth day before the calends of August, with me
looking on from that hated house, he sent off that hodge-podge
naval force. On the thirteenth, a day when the lighthearted Greeks
celebrate the ascension of the prophet Elijah to the heavens with
stage performances, he ordered me to come to him.[61] And he said
to me: "Our empire plans to lead its troops against the Assyrians,
not against those who worship Christ, as your lord does.[62] Last
year I wanted to do this very thing, but having heard that your lord
wanted to invade territories of our empire, having let off the Assyrians, we turned the reins back toward him. Dominic the Venetian, his messenger, met us in Macedonia and, through much hard
work and sweat, tricked us by swearing an oath stating that your
lord never would plan such a thing, let alone do it, so that we returned home. Go back, therefore" (and when I heard that I quietly

60. Adalbert did not in fact show up with an army at Bari; Otto's troops chased
him north through the Apennines in summer 969.

61. This feast occurred on July 20th.

62. The Byzantine army was on the offensive against its Islamic neighbors in eastern Anatolia in the 960s, and Antioch, the major city on the southern edge of the
Tauros range, fell to Byzantium in 969. To call Byzantium's eastern neighbors Assyrians gave the war biblical overtones.

said, "Thank God"), "and tell your lord this-and-that; if he makes me his drinking companion, then come back."

32. "Let your most holy imperial authority order me," I said to him, "to fly back quickly to Italy, and be sure that my lord would carry out what your imperial authority wants, and I shall return to you, happy." With what thoughts I said this did not, alas, escape him. For, chuckling, at the same time he nodded his head and, with me bowing to the ground and proceeding outside, he ordered me to stay outside and to come to another dinner reeking of garlic and onion, smeared with oil and fish sauce. That day, by great pleas I managed things so that my gift, which he had often disdained, he finally condescended to accept.

33. Thus with us sitting at a table that was long without width, covered over its width with a drape, but almost bare on its extremities, he made fun of the Franks—under which name he understood both the Latins and the Germanic peoples; and he asked me to explain in what place my city and bishopric lay and what name it enjoyed. To that I answered: "Cremona, a place quite close to the Po, king of Italian rivers.[63] And since your imperial authority prepares to send war ships there—let it be advantageous to me that I saw you, let it be useful to have met you—give that place peace, so that, through you, it may live on a bit longer, as it cannot resist you!" But that sly fellow recognized I said that εἰρωνικῶς;[64] with lowered eyes he promised he would do it and he swore to me on the power of his imperial rule that I would undergo nothing bad, but would, as I wished, quickly arrive at the port of Ancona with his war ships; and he swore it to me, having struck his breast with his fingers.

34. Notice how impiously he perjured himself. These things were done and said on the thirteenth day before the calends of August, on the second day of the week; from that day until the ninth I received no stipend from him, when there was such a shortage in Constantinople that with three gold coins I could not refresh my twenty-five followers and the four Greek guards at one dinner. On

63. Virgil, *Georgics* 1.482.
64. "In an ironic way."

the fourth day of that same week Nicephoros left Constantinople, heading for the Assyrians.

35. On the fifth day of the week his brother summoned me and began thus: "With the holy emperor having departed, I remained at home today to carry out his dispositions; now, if the desire of seeing the holy emperor grips you, and if you have anything that you have not yet said, state it plainly." To whom I said: "I have no reason either to see the holy emperor or to tell new things; I ask this one thing, according to the promise of the holy emperor: namely, that I may be conducted to the port of Ancona by war ships." Once he heard this, as the Greeks are always ready to swear on other people's heads,[65] he began to swear he would carry it out, swearing by the head of the emperor, by his own life, by that of his children—and may God protect them according to what truth he spoke! When I said, "When?" to him, "As soon as the emperor has left," he answered, "for the commander,[66] under whose hand is all power over ships when the holy emperor has left, will take care of you." I left him, happy, toyed-with by that hope.

36. After the next day, that is, Saturday, Nicephoros ordered me to hasten to Umbrias, a place eighteen miles from Constantinople;[67] and he said: "I thought a somehow great and honest man had come here so that, having carried out my will in every regard, you would institute a perpetual alliance between your lord and me. And since you do not want to do this because of the hardness of your heart, just one thing I would obtain, which you can do with just cause, namely, arrange that your lord will bring no aid to the Capuan and Beneventan princes, my slaves, against whom I am preparing to fight. Let him who does not give his own property at least surrender ours. It is well known that their forefathers and ancestors bore tribute to our empire; but the army of our empire will work those two into doing the same thing in a short time."[68]

65. Juvenal, *Satires* 6.16–17.
66. *Droungarios* was the normal title of the main Byzantine naval commander.
67. The palace of Bruas lay on the Asian side of the Sea of Marmara.
68. The coastal duchies of south Italy, dependent on overseas commerce, exposed to Byzantine naval incursions, had deeper traditions of friendship with Byzantium

To which I replied: "In the first place, those princes are nobles and soldiers of my lord, who, if he detects your army rushing on them, will send them troops with whom to crush yours, and they will succeed in taking from you the two *themes* which you hold across the [Adriatic] sea."

Then, all agitated and puffed up like a toad: "Leave!" he said. "On myself, on my parents who made me such as I am,[69] I will arrange things so that your lord worries about something other than defending runaway slaves!"

37. And as I was going out, he ordered the interpreter to make me his table guest; and, having summoned the brother of those same princes and Bysantius of Bari, he ordered great insults to be vomited forth against you and the Latin and German peoples.[70] Truly, when I left that vile dinner, they secretly sent messengers after me and swore that they, who had been howling, had said all that not spontaneously but at the emperor's bidding and because of his threats.

But at that same dinner the same Nicephoros asked me whether you had preserves, that is, hunting grounds, or if, instead of preserves, you had wild donkeys or other animals.[71] When I affirmed to him that you had preserves, and animals in the hunting grounds, with the exception of wild donkeys, he said: "I will lead you to our preserve, whose enormity, as well as the wild, that is woodland, donkeys, you will marvel to see." Thus I was led to a rather big

---

and had indeed paid tribute in the ninth and tenth centuries, although Gisulf I of Salerno (†977) never acknowledged Otto's sovereignty. But for the inland polities (like Capua and Benevento) tribute payment was untraditional.

69. Virgil, *Aeneid* 10.597.

70. Southern Italian rulers periodically visited Constantinople (Guaiamar I of Salerno in 887, Landulf I of Benevento in 910), and Byzantium supported a group of expatriate aristocrats. Here Liudprand referred to Romuald, brother of Pandulf I of Capua-Benevento. Given the cooperative nature of rule in that principality, a brother had a credible claim to power, and might become a useful diplomatic lever for the Byzantines.

71. Since Roman times, well stocked hunting grounds and dominion over exotic animals contributed to the stature of the powerful. See P. Dutton, *Charlemagne's Mustache* (New York: Palgrave Macmillan, 2004), 43–68, for some early medieval context.

preserve, hilly, overgrown, unpleasant, and as I was riding with a hat on, when the chief of staff saw me from far off, he quickly sent me a directive through his son that it was unlucky for anyone wearing a hat instead of a hood to enter wherever the emperor was. To him I said: "Our women ride wearing tiaras and hoods; we men ride wearing hats. Nor is it proper for you to compel me to change my ancestral custom here, since we allow your ambassadors to keep your ancestral customs when they visit us. For with us they ride, walk, and sit at table long-sleeved, wrapped up, with brooches, long-haired, wearing a long tunic, and, something that seems especially unseemly to all of us, they alone kiss our emperor with uncovered heads," and I quietly added, "May God not permit them to do it any more!"[72]

"Go back then!" he said.

38. When I was doing just this, there rushed toward me some of those creatures they call wild donkeys, mingled with some wild goats. But, I ask, what kind of wild donkeys? The very same kind as are tame at Cremona. The same color, the same shape, the same ears, equally vocal when they begin to bray, not uneven in size, the same speed, equally tasty for wolves. When I saw them I said to my Greek riding companion: "I never saw such creatures in Saxony." "If," he said, "your lord shall be kind to the holy emperor, he will give him many of these animals, and it will be no small glory for Otto, when he shall possess what none of his predecessors in lordship even saw." But believe me, my august lords, my brother and fellow lord bishop Anthony can give you some that are not inferior, as prove the markets that are held in Cremona, but those go about that are called domesticated, not wild donkeys, and are not bare-backed, but bearing loads.[73] But when the words written

72. As Liudprand had some familiarity with imperial etiquette, his *faux pas* cannot have been innocent (see *Retribution* 6.5). He knew that western elites considered their attire an indispensable part of their persona, a message about their identity, and expected this account to scandalize his readers.

73. Liudprand disapprovingly referred to Bishop Anthony of Brescia (†969) in *Retribution* 5.29.

above were announced to Nicephoros, he gave me license to go, having sent me two wild goats. The following day he, too, left for Syria.

39. But I ask you to note why he led the army against the Assyrians just now. The Greeks and the Saracens have books that they call ὁράσεις, or visions, of Daniel, and I call Sibylline books, in which it is found written how many years a certain emperor may live, what the nature of future times under his rule may be, whether peace or hostility shall prevail, whether things shall favor or hamper the Saracens.[74] In them you read that in Nicephoros's times the Assyrians shall not be able to resist the Greeks and he will live for seven years only; after his death an even worse emperor—though I doubt one could be found—and more of a weakling is supposed to arise, in whose reign the Assyrians are supposed to prevail, so that they are supposed to acquire everything by force, right up to Chalcedon,[75] which is not at all far from Constantinople. They both pay close attention to the schedules; for one and the same reason the Greeks, encouraged, now hound their enemies, and the Saracens, dispirited, do not resist, awaiting the time when they in turn shall hound their enemies and the Greeks again will not resist.

40. But a certain Hippolytus, a Sicilian bishop,[76] wrote the very same thing about both our bishop and our people—I now call "our" any people that is subject to your empire—and I wish it may turn true, what this man wrote about the present times! According

74. Apocalyptic literature based on the more future-looking sections of the book of Daniel was always popular in Byzantium, and in the 960s would have had special resonance for Macedonian loyalists seeking to undermine Nicephoros Phocas's reign: see P. J. Alexander, *Byzantine Apocalyptic Literature* (Berkeley: University of California Press, 1985), 96–104, 120–21. Such prophetic literature was equally popular in the west. One such text was called "Prophecies of Daniel." The *Sibylline Books* were a collection, much varied over time, of ancient, late antique, and later prophecies, with political and eschatological overtones, that enjoyed great popularity throughout the Middle Ages.

75. Across the Sea of Marmara from Constantinople and famous in Christian history for a council held there in 451.

76. Alexander, *Byzantine Apocalyptic Literature*, 100–101, argues that "Hyppolitus" was an inference by Liudprand on the authorship of anonymous eschatological tracts.

to what I heard from men who have knowledge of these books, the rest of what he wrote has been fulfilled up to now. And we shall offer here one of his many sayings in the midst of this account. For he says that scripture shall now be fulfilled which says, λέων καὶ σκίμνος ὁμοδιώξουσιν ὄναγρον in Greek, and in Latin, "The lion and the cub together shall exterminate the wild donkey."[77] Its interpretation according to the Greeks: the lion, that is, the emperor of the Romans or Greeks, and the cub, that is, the king of the Franks, together in these current times shall exterminate the wild donkey, that is, the African king of the Saracens. This interpretation does not seem to me true since the lion and the cub, though unequal in size, still are one in nature, species, and habits; and, as my knowledge suggests to me, if the lion should be the emperor of the Greeks, it would not be likely that the cub would be the king of the Franks. Although both may be men, just as both the lion and the cub are animals, nevertheless they are as distant in customs, I do not say as one species is from another, but as tangible things are from intangible ones. The cub is removed from the lion in nothing but age; the same shape, the same ferocity, the same roar. The king of the Greeks is long-haired, tunic-wearing, long-sleeved, hooded, lying, fraudulent, merciless, fox-like, haughty, falsely humble, cheap, greedy, eating garlic, onions, and leeks, drinking bath-water; by contrast the king of the Franks is nicely shorn, in attire that differs from women's clothing, hat-wearing, truthful, guileless, quite merciful when appropriate, strict when necessary, always truly humble, never cheap, not a consumer of garlic, onions, and leeks so that he might thereby spare animals and accumulate money, having sold them instead of eating them. You heard the difference; do not accept this interpretation, for either it is about the future or it is not true. For it is impossible that Nicephoros, as their lies assert, might be the lion, and Otto the cub, who together exterminate everything.

77. In Byzantine apocalyptic writings, the wild donkey was associated with Arabia and Islam: see W. Brandes, "Liudprand von Cremona und ein bisher unbeachteter West-Östliche Korrespondenz über die Bedeutung des Jahres 1000," *Byzantinische Zeitschrift* 93 (2000): 447.

For the Parthian shall drink from the Arar River in exile, or Germany of the Tigris,[78] and both shall wander across the other's borders before Nicephoros and Otto come together in an alliance and unite by treaty.

41. You heard the interpretation of the Greeks; now listen to that of Liudprand the Cremonese bishop. I say—and I do not only say, but I assert—if that scripture is to be fulfilled in the current times, the lion and the cub, father and son, Otto and Otto, unequal in nothing, distant from each other in age alone, together in this present time shall exterminate the wild donkey, that is, the woodland donkey Nicephoros, who may fittingly be compared to a woodland donkey on account of his empty and mindless vainglory and the incestuous marriage with his mistress and co-godparent.[79] If this wild donkey is not now exterminated by our lion and cub, Otto and Otto, the father, that is, and the son, the august emperors of the Romans, what Hippolytus wrote will not prove true. The interpretation of the Greeks, outlined above, is to be discarded. But, O good Jesus, eternal God, Word of the Father, who spoke to us unworthy ones not by a voice, but by inspiration, may you will no other interpretation than mine to be accurate for this prophecy. Order that this lion and this cub exterminate and humiliate this wild donkey in his body, so that, returning to his place and subjected to his lords, the emperors Basil and Constantine, his soul may be saved on the day of the Lord.

42. Yet the astronomers pronounce this same outcome about you and Nicephoros. It is a thing I call astounding. When I talked it over with a certain astronomer, who accurately described your

78. Virgil, *Bucolics* 1.61–62. Such thirsty migrations are deemed most unlikely.

79. Theophano (†c.976) was the widow of Romanos II whom Nicephoros married in 963, shortly after attaining power. She fostered his fall, perhaps imagining that the putschist John Tsimiskes would marry her. But her second marriage had incurred ecclesiastical disfavor, and she was banished. Nicephoros, whose career flourished under Romanos II, was godfather to Theophano's children and as such a member of her family, debarred by canon law from marrying her. This is why Liudprand called the liaison adulterous (see 52, below) and incestuous (here), and made fun of the relationship, especially Theophano's position of authority over her second husband, by calling her "mistress" (*domina*) of her husband.

appearance and customs, my august lords, and those of your august peer, he also outlined all my past as if it were present.[80] Nor did he omit anything regarding my friends or enemies, about whom my mind suggested to me that I ask, whose condition, appearance, and habits he did not describe. He predicted for my future every calamity that later struck me during this trip. But let everything he said be a lie; I ask that only one thing be true, namely, what he predicted you would do to Nicephoros! If only it would be, if only it could be! Then I would consider the harm that has happened to me as nothing.

43. The same Hippolytus also writes that not the Greeks, but the Franks shall crush the Saracens. Three years ago the Saracens, encouraged by this reading, prepared war against Manuel the patrician, nephew of Nicephoros, in the Sicilian sea near Scylla and Charybdis.[81] When they had squelched his numberless troops, they captured him and hanged him with his head severed. When they captured his companion of equal rank, who was of the neutered gender, they did not deign to kill him, but they sold him, broken and worn by his long captivity, for such a price that no one of sound mind would possibly ever pay it for that type of person.

Nor was it with dampened spirits that a little later they rushed, emboldened by this same reading, against the commander Exaconta; when they turned him to flight, they mangled his troops in every way.

44. But there is something else that propels Nicephoros to lead troops against the Assyrians now. For at the present time, with God ordaining it, famine consumes every region of the Argives[82] so that a gold coin could not buy two Pavian measures of grain, and this in places where abundance usually reigns. An infestation of mice augmented this scourge, but Nicephoros further exacer-

80. Liudprand's seer knew not just about Otto I and Adelheid, but also about their heir Otto II, who had been crowned co-emperor on Christmas Day 967, aged 12.

81. The Straits of Messina. The debacle Liudprand describes took place in 964. A Byzantine expedition to bolster the last Sicilian strongholds against the Arabs was routed on land and at sea.

82. An old-fashioned, classicizing way of naming the Greeks, or Byzantines.

bated it because at harvest time, with the landowners complaining, he amassed crops from every land, having paid a tiny price. When he did the same thing near Mesopotamia, where an abundance of crops grew in the absence of mice, he could have equaled the multitude of sand grains in the sea with the abundance of the harvest he stockpiled.[83] Therefore, when famine raged horribly everywhere, through his mean deal, with the pretext of war he gathered to himself a militia of eighty thousand mortal men, to whom throughout a whole month he sold for two gold coins what he had bought for one. These, my lord, are the things that drove Nicephoros to lead troops against the Assyrians now. But what kind, I ask, of troops? Truly, I answer, not men but hominids, whose mouth is as foul as "their right hand is cold in war."[84] Nicephoros did not mind their quality, but only their quantity; and too late will he regret just how dangerous that miscalculation shall prove for him, when they, unwarlike but encouraged by their numbers, shall be crushed by a few of our troops, knowledgeable in war, indeed, thirsting for it.

45. While you besieged Bari, a mere three hundred Hungarians surrounded five hundred Greeks near Thessalonica and led them off captive to Hungary.[85] That exploit, since it worked so successfully, drove two hundred Hungarians to do the same in Macedonia, not far from Constantinople; since they imprudently returned on a narrow path, forty of them were captured whom now Nicephoros, having removed them from captivity and dressed them in most precious clothes, trained as protectors and defenders of his person, leading them with him against the Assyrians. You can truly discern what sort of army is his from this, since those who outclass the others are Venetians and Amalfitans.[86]

83. The Mesopotamian *theme* defined the easternmost Byzantine-held territory in Anatolia, whence very successful campaigns against the Caliphate's Syrian provinces were launched in 968–69.

84. Virgil, *Aeneid* 11.338–39.

85. Otto's ability to stem Hungarian raids into his realm is contrasted here with Hungarian successes in the southern Balkans, subject to Byzantium.

86. Venice and Amalfi were ports in Italy whose warm relations with Byzantium afforded them commercial advantages; but merchants were not expected to make good soldiers.

46. Now, forgetting all these things, consider what happened to me. On the sixth day before the calends of August, outside of Constantinople at Umbrias I received permission from Nicephoros to return to you. And when I reached Constantinople, the eunuch Christopher the patrician, who managed affairs in Nicephoros's place, informed me that I could not leave then as the Saracens had taken over the sea and the Hungarians the land: it remained for me to wait until they retreated. But both, alas, were lies! Then guards were posted who forbade me and my party to exit from the house. Seizing the paupers of Latin tongue who came to me for the favor of alms, they beat them and took them into custody; they did not allow my grecologue, that is, a man versed in the Greek tongue, to go out, not even to buy supplies, but only the cook, ignorant of the Greek tongue, who conversed as a buyer with the seller not by signs of signs, but with movements of the fingers or the head, and who bought as much food with four coins as the grecologue with one.

And when one of my friends would send spices, breads, wine, and apples, the guards sent the messengers away overwhelmed by slaps, having spilled everything onto the ground. And unless divine mercy had set a table for me against those who torment me, that form of death they had prepared for me would have been accepted; but the One who permitted my temptation mercifully gave me endurance. This kind of danger vexed me in Constantinople from the second day before the nones of June to the sixth before the nones of October, that is, for one hundred and twenty days.

47. Truly, so as to increase my calamities, on the feast of the Assumption of the holy Mother of God and Virgin Mary[87] there arrived, bearing no good omens for me, the messengers of the apostolic and universal lord Pope John, with letters through which they prayed Nicephoros, the emperor of the Greeks, to form kinship and a firm alliance with his beloved spiritual son Otto the august emperor of the Romans. I, who so often seem wordy and

---

87. August 15th. Throughout the *Embassy* Liudprand employed the Christian high feasts to anchor the chronology. Pentecost, the Apostles' feast, the Assumption, and St. John's feast day gave the reader a sense of the length of time elapsing between events.

long-winded on other topics, seem as dumb as a fish on the subject of how this phrasing, these titles, sinful and rash according to the Greeks, did not cause the death of their bearer, why they did not choke him before he read them out. The Greeks scolded the sea; even more they cursed its calm surface, wondering why it could bear this sin, why the waves had not opened up and swallowed the ship. "It did not trouble him to refer in writing to the emperor," they said, "to the only universal, august, great emperor of the Romans, Nicephoros, by the title 'of the Greeks,' and to some poor barbarian fellow by the title 'of the Romans'! O heavens! O earth! O sea![88] But what," they said, "shall we do to these wicked criminal men? They are poor, and, if we kill them, we shall pollute our hands with plebeian blood; they are ragged, they are slaves, they are peasants, and, if we whip them, we will dishonor not them but ourselves, since they are unworthy of the golden Roman whip and of any such torments. O, if only one were a bishop, the other a margrave! After the sting of flexible branches, after the plucking of their hair or beards, sown up into leather sacks they could be sunk in the sea. But let them be spared," they said, "and until the most holy emperor of the Romans, Nicephoros, learns of these evils, let them waste away under heavy guard."

48. When I learned all this, I considered them happy because they were poor men, and myself unhappy because rich. When I was at home, my own will excused me for my poverty, but once I was in Constantinople, fear itself said I had the wealth of Croesus.[89] Always poverty had seemed burdensome to me; now it seemed light, now accepted, now something to be embraced—to be embraced because it did not allow its adepts to be destroyed, its subjects to be whipped; and since this poverty defends its own only at Constantinople, may it be beloved there alone.[90]

49. Therefore, with the apostolic messengers hauled off to pris-

---

88. Terence, *Adelphoe* 790.

89. A proverbially rich king of ancient Lydia.

90. Tenth-century Byzantine politics included disagreements on the "poor church," or whether clerics should have access to economic privileges and wealth.

on, that official letter was sent to Nicephoros in Mesopotamia, whence the one who bore the message of reply did not return until two days before the ides of September. On the day when he returned he avoided me; after two days, that is, on the eighteenth day before the calends of October, by pleas and gifts I arranged to worship the life- and health-giving wood;[91] there, in such a great tumult of worshipers, hidden from my guardians, certain people approached me who turned my sad mind to glee with furtive conversations.[92]

50. On the fifteenth day before the calends of October, I was called, halfway between life and death, to the palace. And when I came into the presence of the eunuch Christopher the patrician, he rose to greet me with three others, welcoming me kindly. The beginning of their report went like this:

"The pallor around your mouth, the thinness in all your body,[93] the shaggy hair, the beard, unkempt by your standards, make clear that immense distress is in your heart, because the time for your return to your lord has been postponed. Truly, we pray you not to grow angry with the holy emperor or with us: we will now relate the cause of your delay. The Roman pope—if indeed he should be called pope, who gave communion and celebrated services with the apostate, adulterous, sacrilegious son of Alberic[94]—sent a letter to our most holy emperor, which was worthy of himself but unworthy of the recipient, calling the emperor 'of the Greeks' and

91. A relic of the holy cross, perhaps one in the Great Palace of the emperors or in Haghia Sophia. The Exaltation of the Cross was celebrated on September 14th.

92. Perhaps these were Macedonian loyalists, displeased with Nicephoros's usurpation, with whom Liudprand had formed contacts during his earlier Constantinopolitan visits. Local friendships are also mentioned in chapters 29 and 46. See M. Lintzel, *Studien über Liudprand von Cremona* (Berlin: Verlag Dr Emil Ebering, 1933), 48.

93. Ovid, *Metamorphoses* 2.775.

94. Alberic (†954) was a member of the most powerful Roman clan and was one of the "tyrants" whom Liudprand chastised in chapter 5. Alberic's son Octavian (†964) became Pope John XII in 955. John XIII (†972) sent the letters in question; he was a close ally of Otto I, and had crowned Otto II emperor nine months earlier. His ecclesiastical career before his pontificate required acknowledgement of the sometimes scandalous John XII.

not 'of the Romans'; it is not ἀμφίσβητον[95] that it was done with your lord's advice."

51. "What words," I said to myself, "do I hear? Let me die: it is beyond doubt I will now take the short road to the guardhouse!" "But listen," they said, "we know you want to say the pope is the most stupid of all men; say it, and we, too, profess it." But I said, "I will not utter it." "Then listen: the empty-headed and bungling pope is ignorant of the fact that holy Constantine translated the imperial symbols here, and brought the entire senate and the whole Roman knighthood, and left at Rome only lowly dependents, that is, fishers, food-peddlers, bird-hunters, bastards, plebeians, and slaves. Never would the pope write such things unless with the instigation of your king; and how dangerous it was for both of them, unless they take it all back, the coming times will prove."

"But the pope," I said, "noble in his simplicity, thought that to write such a thing was praise for the emperor, not insult! We certainly know Constantine the Roman emperor came here with the Roman knighthood and founded this city in his own name; but since you have changed the language, customs, and dress, the most holy pope thought the name of the Romans would similarly displease you, as does their costume. If life abides with him, he will make this clear in future letters, whose opening address will be this: 'John the Roman pope to Nicephoros, Constantine, and Basil, the great and august emperors of the Romans.'" Why I said this, I ask that you note well.

52. Nicephoros rose to the pinnacle of power by perjury and adultery. And since the well-being of all Christians falls under the responsibility of the Roman pope, let the lord pope send a letter much like a tomb to Nicephoros, for tombs are all white outside[96] but inside are filled with the bones of the dead. Within, the letter should scold him about the perjury and adultery through which he attained lordship over his lords; it should invite him to a council

95. "Uncertain."
96. Mt 23.27.

and threaten anathema if he were not to come. If the opening address is not as I suggested, it would never be delivered to him.

53. Now let us return to our subject. When the aforementioned princes heard my promise about the opening address, thinking it contained no trickery, they said: "We give you thanks, O bishop; it is proper for your mediating wisdom to intercede in these important matters. You alone among the Franks do we like, but when they have rectified their depravities, with you exhorting them, we shall like the rest of them, too, and when you come to us again you shall not leave without gifts." Quietly I said, "Nicephoros will give me a golden crown and scepter if I ever come here again!"

"But tell us," they said, "does your lord wish to establish an alliance by marriage with the most holy emperor?" "When I came here, he wanted to," I said; "but as he has not received any letters, though I have been tarrying here a long time, he thinks me imprisoned and fettered by you σφάλμα, that is, wrongly; now his whole spirit seethes, as she-lions do when their cubs are stolen,[97] and until he shall have taken revenge with righteous harshness, he both abhors the marriage and boils over with rage against you."

"If he shall try anything," they said, "neither Italy, we declare, nor even impoverished, furry, that is to say, leather-clad Saxony, where he was born, shall afford him refuge;[98] through our money, which gives us power, we shall induce all the nations to attack him and we shall shatter him like some ceramic, that is, a pottery vase that cannot be fixed once broken. And since we think you have bought certain cloaks for his splendor, we decree that they be brought forth here; the ones that are suited to you shall be marked with a lead seal and left to you; and those which instead are κολυόμενα, that is, articles forbidden to all nations except us Romans, shall be seized, once their price has been reimbursed."

54. When this was done, they took from me five very precious purple robes, judging that you and all the Italians, Saxons, Franks,

97. Hos 13.7.8.

98. Liudprand stressed the "barbaric" attire of northern Europeans to contrast with the silks over which argument was about to erupt.

Bavarians, Swabians, indeed all the nations, are unworthy to go about decked out in cloth of that quality. But how unsuitable and how insulting it is that soft, effeminate, long-sleeved, tiara-wearing, hooded, lying, unsexed, idle people strut around in purple, while heroes, that is, strong men, who know war, full of faith and charity, in submission to God, full of virtues, do not! What is an insult, if that is not?[99]

"But where," I said, "is the emperor's word of honor? Where the emperor's promise? For when I bade him farewell, I asked that he allow me to buy cloths at whatever price for the honor of the church;[100] and he said, 'Whichever ones and however many you want,' saying, ποιότητα καὶ ποσότητα, that is, 'quantity and quality.' He plainly did not make a distinction by saying, 'with these and those excepted.' His brother Leo, the chief of staff, is a witness; the interpreter Euodisius, John, and Romanos, are witnesses; and I myself am witness, who would have understood what the emperor said even if the interpreter had been absent."

"But those things are κολυόμενα, that is, forbidden," they said, "and if the emperor said what you claim he said, he could scarcely intend such cloths as you dream of; for we ought to outclass other nations in dress just as in wealth and wisdom, so that those who have a unique grace in their virtues may have also a unique beauty in their clothes."

55. "In what way can this attire," I said, "be considered unique, when in our countries cheap women and parasitic dependents use them?" "Whence," they said, "do they come to you?" "Through the Venetian and Amalfitan traders," I said, "who support their lives with our foodstuffs by bearing such cloth to us." "Well, they will not do it any longer," they said; "they will be closely scrutinized, and, if any one is found with this type of thing, he will pay the penalty, beaten with sticks, his hair shaved off."

99. Terence, *Andria* 237.

100. Though Liudprand uses the term "pallium" (see *Concerning King Otto*, chapter 22), he seems to mean a silk tapestry, a popular decoration in western churches, rather than clerical attire.

"In the time," I said, "of the emperor Constantine of blessed memory I came here, still a deacon, not a bishop, and not sent by an emperor or a king but by the margrave Berengar, and I bought many more, and more precious, cloths than these, which were neither scrutinized nor seen by the Greeks, nor marked with lead.[101] Now that, with God granting it, I am a bishop and sent by the magnificent emperors Otto and Otto, father and son, I am so greatly disgraced that my cloaks are marked in the way of the Venetians' and those that seem of a certain price are confiscated even though they are being carried back for use in churches entrusted to me. Will you not tire of insulting me, indeed of insulting my lords, for whose sake I am insulted to the extent that I am kept under guard, that I am tormented with hunger and thirst, that I do not return to them but am detained here, until finally, on top of the affronts against them, you despoil me of my own goods? Confiscate only the ones that were bought; at least release those that were given as gifts by friends!"

"The emperor Constantine," they said, "a mild man, one who always stayed in the palace, made the nations friends of his by that kind of thing. Nicephoros instead is a *basileus*, a ταχύχειρ man, that is, one eager for combat;[102] he avoids the palace like the plague, and he is called by us almost a lover of rivalry and an argumentative fellow; he is one who does not make the nations friendly to himself by paying them, but by terror and the sword he makes them subject to himself. And, so that you may recognize how highly we esteem your lords the kings, those cloths of this color that were given, and those that were bought, shall return to us in the same way."

56. Once these things had been said and done, they gave me a χρυσοβούλιον, that is, a letter written and sealed in gold, to be brought to you; but to my mind it was not worthy of you. For they produced another letter sealed in silver and said: "We judge your pope unworthy to receive an imperial letter; the chief of staff,

101. He had come in 949, sent by Berengar just before King Lothar's death: see *Retribution* 6.
102. Literally, "quick-handed."

the emperor's brother, sends him a quite appropriate letter, not through his poor messengers, but through you, to the effect that he should recognize he is thoroughly ruined unless he recants."[103]

57. When I received this letter, they dismissed me, saying farewell to me, giving me quite cheerful, quite loving kisses. But while I was withdrawing, they sent a message after me quite worthy of them, if not of me, to the effect that they would only furnish horses to me and my followers, but none for the baggage; so that, greatly troubled, as the situation required, I gave to my διασώστη, that is, my guide, property priced at fifty gold pieces.[104] And as I did not have anything with which I could repay Nicephoros for his evil deeds then and there, I wrote these verses on the wall of my hated house and on the wooden table:

> Do not trust the word of the Argive; let it remain far from you,
>   O Latin,
> To believe it, and remember not to meditate on their words!
> If he can win thereby, in what a holy way does the Argive perjure
>   himself!
> With veined marble this lofty house lies open with high windows,
> This waterless house, accessible only to its prisoner,
> Welcoming the cold, nor repelling the rage of summer's heat;
> From Italy Liudprand the prelate in the city of Cremona,
> Having reached Constantinople for the love of peace,
> Was shut in here for four summer months.
> The emperor Otto descended on Bari,
> Seeking by blood and fire together to subject those places to himself,
> But the victor returned the Byzantine cities through my pleas.
> Lying Greece promised him a daughter-in-law;
> If only she had never been born! Neither would it pain me to have
>   come,
> Nor, O Nicephoros, would I have measured your spite,

---

103. Rather than John XIII's association with his predecessor (above, chapter 50), it was his creation of an archbishopric at Benevento, and the attendant subordination of Apulia's bishoprics to an archbishop whom Byzantium did not control, that disturbed the Byzantines. See chapter 62 below.

104. Perhaps to hire additional beasts of burden. Or perhaps property that Liudprand lost "on duty" and that he hoped to have reimbursed.

You who prohibit a stepdaughter to unite with the son of the master.
Now the day is imminent when, incited by harsh furies,
Let God not prevent it, Mars will rage through the whole globe,
And through your crime the peace everyone longed for shall fall
   silent.[105]

58. Having written these verses, six days before the nones of October, at the tenth hour, I departed with my guide by boat from that city once most opulent and flourishing, now starving, perjured, lying, fraudulent, rapacious, greedy, stingy, dinner-driven; and in forty-nine days by donkeyback-riding, by horseback-riding, by walking, fasting, thirsting, sighing, crying, moaning I came to Naupactis, which is a Nicopolean city.[106] There, when my guide abandoned me, he commended me to two messengers who would lead me to Otranto[107] across the sea, having embarked me on two small ships. And since by the terms of the *entolina*, or written instructions, they did not have the right to requisition supplies from the Greek princes, everywhere they were spurned, and we were not nourished by them, but they by us. How often did I mull over that Terentian verse within my head: "Those you send as defenders need a protector themselves."

59. Thus, having departed from Naupactis nine days before the calends of December, in two days I reached as far as the river Euenos, since my companions did not stay in the ships, which could not hold them, but followed along the shore.[108] Having been deposited at the Euenos river, we saw that Patras[109] lay on the other shore of the sea, eighteen miles distant. The site of an apostle's

105. Liudprand cites his contemporary Rather, bishop of Verona, Virgil, and Juvenal, in this lyric.

106. Naupactis lies on the northwestern rim of the Gulf of Corinth, in mainland Greece. Details on Liudprand's travels are in M. McCormick, *The Origins of the European Economy* (Cambridge: Cambridge University Press, 2001), 447, 462–64, 490–91, with maps on pp. 487, 532.

107. On Italy's Apulian coast, under Byzantine control.

108. The short Euenos River rises from the southern Pindus and discharges into the Gulf of Patras between Naupactis and Missolonghi.

109. An Ionian port in Peloponnesian Greece, traditionally regarded as the site of the martyrdom of the apostle Andrew; see chapters 51–65, "The Acts of Andrew," in

passion that we had visited and worshiped on the way to Constantinople, we now neglected to visit and worship—I confess my sin! The inexpressible desire to return to you and see you, my august lords, caused this; and if it had not been for this one thing, I think I would have suffered eternal death.

60. For a south wind strove against me, fool that I am, and churned up the sea with waves from their deepest abodes. And since it did this for consecutive days and nights, on the day before the calends of December (the very day of the passion, that is)[110] I understood that this was happening to me on account of my crime. "Vexation alone will make you understand what you hear."[111] Hunger oppressed us powerfully; the inhabitants of the land were thinking of killing us so as to take away our things from us; lest we escape, the sea churned with waves. Then, turning toward the church, which I could see, weeping and moaning, I said: "Saint Andrew the apostle, I am a servant of your fellow fisherman, fellow brother, and fellow apostle Simon Peter. I did not disdain the site of your passion nor turn from it out of haughtiness; a burning longing for a glimpse of the august ones, my love of the august ones, drove me to return home. If my sin moved you to indignation, let the worthiness of my august lords elicit your mercy. You do not have anything to grant your brother; instead, grant something to the august Ottos who love your brother by clinging to him who knows all. You know with how much labor and sweat, by how many vigils and expenses, they enriched, honored, exalted, and returned to its proper state the Roman church of your brother the apostle Peter, having torn it from the hands of the impious. If my deeds cause my downfall, let their merits free us; and do not cause sorrow in this circumstance, that is, in regard to me, whom they sent, to those Ottos whom your brother in faith and blood,

---

The Apocryphal New Testament: A Collection of Apocryphal Christian Literature in an English Translation, trans. J. K. Elliott (Oxford: Oxford University Press, 1993).

110. St. Andrew's martyrdom was celebrated on November 30th.

111. Is 28.19. At the end of his text Liudprand turns to Jewish prophetic literature to enhance the dramatic impact of his woeful tale.

the apostle Peter, prince of the apostles, desires in other regards to rejoice and prosper."

61. This, my lords august emperors, in all truth is not adulation, nor do I now sew a pillow under my elbow;[112] it is true, I say. After two days, the sea was calmed by such tranquility, through your merits, that, when the sailors fled from us, we sailed ourselves to Leucada, that is, a hundred and forty miles, suffering no harm or difficulty except a little bit at the mouth of the river Acheloös where the wave of the sea beats back its swift current.[113]

62. Therefore, most potent august ones, how will you recompense the Lord for all these things by which he rewarded you through me? I will tell you how. This God wants, this he seeks; and, although he can do this without you, nevertheless in this case he wants there to be *hypurgos*, that is, assistants. For actually he gives that which is offered to him, and protects what he demands from us, so that he may crown what he achieves with it. I ask you to pay attention.

Since Nicephoros is a man impious toward all churches, out of that hatred which he feels abundantly towards you he ordered the Constantinopolitan patriarch to expand the Otrantine church into an archbishopric, and to forbid the divine mysteries to be celebrated any longer after the Latin manner in all Apulia and Calabria,[114] but only after the Greek. He says past popes were merchants who sold the Holy Spirit, by whom all things are given life and ruled, "who fills the earth and has knowledge of the voice,"[115] who is coeternal and consubstantial with God the Father and his Son Jesus Christ, without a beginning, without end, eternally true, whose price cannot be evaluated but who is acquired by the pure of heart

112. See Ezek 13.18.

113. The Acheloös flows from the Pindus into the Gulf of Patras near Missolonghi. Leucada (or Santa Maura) lies between Corfu and Cephalonia, close to Paxos, where Liudprand spent some time: see *Retribution* 3.1.

114. Byzantine-ruled province in southwestern Italy where Greek was the prevalent spoken language, unlike Apulia. There is no Byzantine evidence for this unlikely provision.

115. Wis 1.7.

for as great a price as they can afford. Therefore Polyeuktos, the Constantinopolitan patriarch, wrote a privilege for the Otrantine bishop, according to which, by his authority, that bishop should have the right to consecrate the bishops of Acerenza, Tursi, Gravina, Matera, Tricarico, all sees where it is manifest that consecration pertains to the apostolic lord.[116]

But why do I rehearse this, since the very Constantinopolitan church is rightly subject to our holy catholic and apostolic Roman church? We know, indeed we observe, that the Constantinopolitan bishop does not use the pallium unless with our holy father's permission.[117] In fact, when that most impious Alberic, whom greed had filled, not drop-by-drop, but as a rushing torrent, usurped the Roman city to himself, and held the apostolic lord under lock and key as if he were his personal slave, the emperor Romanos established his son the eunuch Theophylact as patriarch;[118] since the greed of Alberic was not concealed from him, having sent him quite large gifts, he caused a letter to be sent in the pope's name to the patriarch Theophylact; by the authority of this letter first he, then his successors, used the pallium without the permission of the popes. Out of this disgraceful transaction the execrable custom arose that not only patriarchs, but even the bishops of all Greece use pallia. How wrong this is it is not the task of the critic to say.

My advice is that a holy council be held, and that Polyeuktos be called to it. If he does not wish to come and correct his *sphalmata*, that is, his vices, as described above, according to the canons, let what the most holy canons decree be done to him.

116. The Adriatic port city of Otranto was more securely Byzantine than the inland towns mentioned here, and its bishop was more likely to advance Byzantine interests. In 968 Otto's creature John XIII had elevated Benevento to archiepiscopal status, giving it authority over Byzantine-controlled bishoprics in Apulia, and this was the Byzantine retaliation, inspired by Patriarch Polyeuktos: see Loud, "Southern Italy," 630–33.

117. Eastern archbishops never had received their pallia (here the liturgical vestment) from Rome. See n. 100 above on the pallium.

118. Romanos I's 16-year-old son, long groomed for the post, became patriarch in 933. After his death in 956, and the end of his father's regime, he was denigrated as frivolous and irreverent.

In the meantime you, most potent august lords, should work at what you began. Execute things so that, if Nicephoros, whom we resolved to censure according to the canons, does not wish to obey us, let him hear from you, whose troops that mummy does not dare to face. That, I say, is what the apostles, our lords and fellow soldiers, want us to do. Rome ought not to be treated basely by the Greeks because the emperor Constantine left the place; rather, it should be all the more greatly worshiped, venerated, and adored because the apostles, the holy doctors Peter and Paul, went there. But let it suffice to me to have written about these things until, with God granting it through the prayers of the most holy apostles, I, who have been snatched from the hands of the Greeks, come to you; and then let it not be tiresome to say out loud what it is now annoying to write here. Now let us return to our subject.

63. Eight days before the ides of December we came to Leucada, where we were most inhumanely received and treated by the eunuch-bishop of that place, just as we were everywhere else by the others. In all of Greece I did not discover any hospitable bishops—and I speak the truth, I do not lie. They are rich, but they are poor: rich in gold coins filling a bulging chest with which one gambles; poor in servants or tools. They sit at bare, small tables, serving themselves ash-baked bread, and then not drinking, but sipping bath water in a tiny glass.[119] They themselves do the selling and buying for the household; they open and close their own doors; they themselves are the table servants, the stable hands, the capons—ha! I had meant to write *caupons*, but truly the thing itself, which is true, compelled me to write the truth, even involuntarily. For we say that they are capons, that is, eunuchs, which is not canonical; and they are also *caupons*, that is, innkeepers, which is also against the canons—whose tough dinner is introduced by and concluded with lettuce, "lettuce of the sort that used to end the

---

119. Such parsimonious behavior would be particularly praiseworthy during the Advent fasting season, the very time of Liudprand's visit to Corfu. Liudprand objected to the temperature of the water, to him suitable for bathing but not drinking (see also chapter 40 above). On the temperature of drinking water, see P. Squatriti, *Water and Society in Early Medieval Italy* (Cambridge: Cambridge University Press, 1998), 38–41.

dinners of our ancestors."[120] I would judge such paupers happy if they imitate the poverty of Christ in this; but a "holy hunger for gold"[121] and a cold coin motivate them. Even so, may God spare them! I think they do this because their churches pay tribute. The Leucadan bishop swore to me that every year his church must pay Nicephoros a hundred gold coins, and the other churches more or less the same, according to their wealth. And how unjust *that* is the deeds of our most holy father Joseph demonstrate, he who permitted the land of the priests to be free from tribute although he subjected all Egypt to tribute to the pharaoh during a time of famine.[122]

64. Thus, nineteen days before the calends of January, leaving Leucada and sailing ourselves—since, as we wrote above, the sailors had fled—fifteen days before the kalends we reached Corfu. There, before our disembarkation from the ship a certain officer ran toward us named Michael Chersonitis, that is, from the place called Cherson,[123] a man with a white head, a cheery face, good with words, always jolly with laughter but, as became clear later, a devil in disposition.[124] God actually showed me this by clues that would have been obvious if my mind had been able to understand them. For, as soon as he gave me the kiss of peace, a sentiment he did not bear in his heart, the whole island of Corfu, which is large, shook; nor just this once, but it quaked through and through three times that same day.[125] After four days, that is, on the eleventh before the calends of January, while, seated at table, the man who was lifting his heel against me was eating bread,[126] the sun, ashamed of

120. Martial, *Epigrams* 13.14.   121. See Virgil, *Aeneid* 3.57.
122. Gn 47.22.   123. In the Crimea.

124. For attempts at a "who's who" for this section see R. Morris, "'O Michaeles Michaeles': A Problem of Identification in Liudprand's *Legatio*," *Byzantion* 51 (1981): 248–54. This Michael seems to have been the governor of the Byzantine *theme* of Cephallenia.

125. No one else seems to have recorded this earthquake; see E. Guidoboni, *Catalogue of Ancient Earthquakes in the Mediterranean Area Up To the 10th Century* (Rome: Istituto Nazionale di Geofisica, 1994), 398–401.

126. Ps 41.7; Augustine, *City of God* 17.18.

a crime so unworthy of its light, hid its rays, underwent an eclipse, and terrified that Michael, but still did not change him.[127]

65. So I will say what I did for him for the sake of friendship and what I received from him by way of recompense. When I was going to Constantinople, I gave his son that most precious shield of yours, gilt and embossed with marvelous craft, which you, my august lords, gave me with other gifts so that I could give it to my Greek friends; now, returning from Constantinople, I gave a most precious cloak to the father. For all of these things he gave thanks as follows: Nicephoros had written that, at whatever hour I should reach him, he should transport me without delay on a war ship to Leo the imperial wardrobe-keeper; this he did not do, but instead he kept me for twenty days, and not at his but at my own expense, until a messenger came from the aforesaid chamberlain Leo, who chastised him because he detained me. And so, when he could no longer bear my pleas, my laments, and sighs, he gave up and he entrusted me to a man so unjust and wicked that he would not even allow me to buy supplies until he had received from me a fine cauldron worth a pound of silver; and when after twenty days, I departed from there, that same custodian to whom I had given the cauldron ordered the ship's captain to allow me to die of hunger, after having cast me off behind the *acroteria*, that is, a certain promontory. He did this because he turned over my cloaks in case I had hidden any purple ones, and though he wanted to receive one of them, he did not get it.

O Michaels, Michaels! Where did I ever meet such men as you, all at the same time? My Constantinopolitan guard Michael commended me to his rival Michael, from bad to worst, from worst man to unjust one. My guide was called Michael, too, a straightforward man whose holy simplicity harmed me almost as much as these ones' perversity. But from these puny Michaels I ran into you,

127. An eclipse was visible throughout Europe on December 22, 968; see D. Schove, *Chronology of Eclipses and Comets, AD 1–1000* (Woodbridge, England: Boydell Press, 1984), 234–36. It was supposed to have terrified an Ottonian army in Calabria: Liudprand may have been gently teasing Otto by evoking it.

great Michael, half-hermit, half-monk.[128] I say, and I say it truly: the bath you assiduously drink for the love of John the Forerunner will not aid you.[129] Those who falsely seek God never deserve to find . . .

128. Perhaps St. Michael Maleinos, uncle of Nicephoros Phocas and idiorhythmic monk.

129. Drinking tepid water, rather than wine, might win the approval of John the Baptist, considered the ideal ascetic in monastic literature.

BIBLIOGRAPHY

INDEX

BIBLIOGRAPHY

Primary Sources

Acta Sanctorum. Aprilis 3. Paris: V. Palmé, 1866.

Ahimaaz. *The Chronicle of Ahimaaz.* Translated by M. Salzmann. New York: Columbia University Press, 1924.

Atto of Vercelli. *Homilies.* In *Patrologia Cursus Completus. Series Latina* 134. Edited by J.-P. Migne. Paris, 1884.

Codex Diplomaticus Cremonae. Edited by L. Astegiano. Bologna: A. Forni, 1983.

Hrabanus Maurus. *Homilies.* In *Patrologia Cursus Completus. Series Latina* 110. Edited by J.-P. Migne. Paris, 1864.

Hrotsvit. *Hrotsvit of Gandersheim: A Florilegium of Her Works.* Translated by K. Wilson. Woodbridge, England: D. S. Brewer, 1998.

Leo of Synada. *The Correspondence of Leo Metropolitan of Synada.* Edited by M. Pollard Vinson. Washington: Dumbarton Oaks Research Library, 1985.

Liudprand. *Liudprandi Cremonensis Opera.* Edited by P. Chiesa. Corpus Christianorum, Continuatio Mediaevalis 156. Turnholt: Brepols, 1998.

———. *Liudprand of Cremona. Relatio de Legatione Constantinopolitana.* Translated by B. Scott. London: Bristol Classical Press, 1993.

———. *The Works of Liudprand of Cremona.* Translated by F. Wright. London: Dutton, 1930.

Maximus of Turin. *Homilies.* In *Patrologia Cursus Completus. Series Latina* 57. Edited by J.-P. Migne. Paris, 1862.

MGH Diplomatum 1. Edited by T. Sickel. Hannover: Hahnsche Buchhandlung, 1879.

Odilo of Cluny. *The Epitaph of Adelheid.* Translated with introduction and notes by Sean Gilsdorf. In *Queenship and Sanctity: The* Lives *of Mathilda and the* Epitaph *of Adelheid.* Medieval Texts in Translation. Washington, DC: The Catholic University of America Press, 2004.

Rather. *The Complete Works of Rather of Verona.* Edited by P. Reid. Binghamton, NY: Medieval and Renaissance Texts and Studies, 1991.

Salzburger Urkundenbuch 2. Edited by W. Hauthaler. Salzburg: Gesellschaft für Salzburger Landeskunde, 1910.

Thietmar. *Ottonian Germany. The* Chronicon *of Thietmar of Merseburg.* Translated by D. Warner. Manchester, England: Manchester University Press, 2001.

Secondary Sources

Alexander, P. J. *Byzantine Apocalyptic Literature.* Berkeley: University of California Press, 1985.

Althoff, G. *Family, Friends and Followers.* Cambridge: Cambridge University Press, 2004.

Angold, M. "Knowledge of Byzantine History in the West." In *Anglo-Norman Studies 25: Proceedings of the Battle Conference 2002.* Edited by J. Gillingham. Woodbridge, England: Boydell & Brewer, 2003. Pp. 19–33.

Arnaldi, G. "Liutprando e la storiografia contemporanea." *Settimane di Studio del Centro Italiano di Studi sull'Alto Medioevo.* Vol. 17. Spoleto: CISAM, 1969. Pp. 497–519.

―――. "Mito e realtà del secolo X romano e papale." *Settimane di Studio del Centro Italiano di Studi sull'Alto Medioevo.* Vol. 38. Spoleto: CISAM, 1991. Pp. 25–53.

―――. "Liutprando di Cremona: un detrattore di Roma o dei romani?" *Studi romani* 53 (2005): 12–50.

Auerbach, E. *Mimesis.* Garden City, NY: Doubleday, 1957.

Bachrach, B. *Early Medieval Jewish Policy in Western Europe.* Minneapolis: University of Minnesota Press, 1977.

Balzaretti, R. "Liudprand of Cremona's Sense of Humor." In *Humour, History and Politics in Late Antiquity and the Early Middle Ages.* Edited by G. Halsall. Cambridge: Cambridge University Press, 2002. Pp. 114–28.

―――. "Men and Sex in Tenth-Century Italy." In *Masculinity in Medieval Europe.* Edited by D. Hadley. London: Longman, 1999. Pp. 119–27.

Bange, P. "The Image of Women of the Nobility in the German Chronicles of the Tenth and Eleventh Centuries." In *The Empress Theophano.* Edited by A. Davids. Cambridge: Cambridge University Press, 1995. Pp. 150–68.

Baronius, C. *Annales Ecclesiastici.* Vol. 10. Rome, 1601.

Berger, D. *The Jewish-Christian Debate in the High Middle Ages.* Philadelphia: Jewish Publication Society of America, 1979.

Berschin, W. *Medioevo greco-latino.* Naples: Liguori, 1989.

Berto, L. "I mussulmani nelle cronache altomedievali dell'Italia meridionale." In *Mediterraneo meridionale.* Edited by M. Meschini. Milan: Vita e Pensiero, 2001. Pp. 3–27.

―――. "La storia degli altri." *Archivio veneto* 155 (2000): 5–20.

Bischoff, B. "Ein Osterpredigt Liudprands von Cremona (um 960)." In his *Anecdota novissima.* Stuttgart: A. Hiersemann, 1984.

Blumenkranz, B. *Les auteurs chrétiens latins du moyen âge sur les juifs et le judaïsme.* Paris: Mouton, 1963.

―――. *Juifs et Chrétiens dans le monde occidental 430–1096.* Paris: Mouton, 1960.

Blumenthal, U.-R. *The Investiture Controversy.* Philadelphia: University of Pennsylvania Press, 1988.

Bougard, F. "Public Power and Authority." In *Italy in the Early Middle Ages.* Edited by C. La Rocca. Oxford: Oxford University Press, 2002. Pp. 34–57.

Brandes, W. "Liudprand von Cremona (*Legatio* 39–41) und ein bisher unbeachteter west-östlicher Korrespondenz über die Bedeutung des Jahres 1000 AD." *Byzantinische Zeitschrift* 93 (2000): 435–60.

Brunhölzl, F. *Geschichte der lateinischen Literatur des Mittelalters*. Munich: W. Fink, 1975.

Buc, P. *The Dangers of Ritual*. Princeton: Princeton University Press, 2001.

―――. "Italian Hussies and German Matrons." *Frühmittelalterliche Studien* 29 (1995): 207–25.

Chiesa, P. *Liudprando di Cremona e il codice di Frisinga*. Turnholt: Brepols, 1994.

Christie, N. "The Alps as a Frontier (AD 168–774)." *Journal of Roman Archaeology* 4 (1991): 410–30.

Colafemmina, C. "Hebrew Inscriptions of the Early Medieval Period in Southern Italy." In *The Jews of Italy*. Edited by B. Cooperman and B. Garvin. Bethesda: University Press of Maryland, 2000.

Colonna, E. "Figure femminili in Liutprando da Cremona." *Quaderni medievali* 14 (1982): 29–59.

―――. *Le poesie di Liutprando di Cremona*. Bari: Edipuglia, 1996.

Colorni, V. "Gli ebrei nei territori italiani a nord di Roma dal 568 all'inizio del secolo XII." *Settimane di Studio del Centro Italiano di Studi sull'Alto Medioevo*. Vol. 26. Spoleto: CISAM, 1980. Pp. 241–307.

Curtius, E. *European Literature and the Latin Middle Ages*. Princeton: Princeton University Press, 1973.

Deliyannis, D. Mauskopf, ed. *Historiography in the Middle Ages*. Leiden: Brill, 2003.

Dolbeau, F. "Le rôle des interprètes dans les traductions hagiographiques d'Italie du Sud." In *Traduction et traducteurs au moyen âge*. Edited by G. Contamine. Paris: Editions du CNRS, 1989.

Dronke, P. *Verse with Prose from Petronius to Dante*. Cambridge, MA: Harvard University Press, 1994.

Dutton, P. *Charlemagne's Mustache: And Other Cultural Clusters of a Dark Age*. New York: Palgrave MacMillan, 2004.

Erdmann, C. *Forschungen zur politischen Ideenwelt des Frühmittelalters*. Berlin: Akademie Verlag, 1951.

―――. *Ottonische Studien*. Darmstadt: Wissenschaftliche Buchgesellschaft, 1961.

Fichtenau, H. "Vom Ansehen des Papsttums im zehnten Jahrhundert." In *Aus Kirche und Reich*. Edited by H. Mordek. Sigmaringen: Jan Thorbecke Verlag, 1983. Pp. 117–24.

―――. *Living in the Tenth Century*. Chicago: University of Chicago Press, 1991.

Fletcher, R., ed. *Moorish Spain*. London: Weidenfeld and Nicolson, 1992.

Gandino, G. *Il vocabolario politico e sociale di Liutprando di Cremona*. Rome: Istituto Storico Italiano per il Medioevo, 1995.

Garbini, P. "Scrittura autobiografica e filosofia della politica nei *Gesta Ottonis* di Liutprando." *La cultura* 32 (1994): 479–86.

Gasparri, S. "The Aristocracy." In *Italy in the Early Middle Ages*. Edited by C. La Rocca. Oxford: Oxford University Press, 2002. Pp. 59–82.

Gay, J. *L'Italie méridionale et l'empire byzantin*. Paris: A. Fontemoing, 1904.

Gibson, M. "Boethius in the Tenth Century." *Mittellateinisches Jahrbuch* 24–25 (1989–1990): 117–24.

Golb, N. *Jewish Proselytism—A Phenomenon in the Religious History of the Early Middle Ages*. Cincinnati: University of Cincinnati Press, 1988.

Guidoboni, E. *Catalogue of Ancient Earthquakes in the Mediterranean Area Up To the 10th Century*. Rome: Istituto Nazionale di Geofisica, 1994.

Hall, T. "The Early Medieval Sermon." In *The Sermon*. Edited by B. Keinzle. Turnholt: Brepols, 2000. Pp. 203–69.

Hofmann, H. "Profil der lateinischen Historiographie im zehnten Jahrhundert." *Settimane di Studio del Centro Italiano di Studi sull'Alto Medioevo*. Vol 38. Spoleto: CISAM, 1991. Pp. 837–905.

Horowitz, E. "'And It Was Reversed': Jews and Their Enemies in the Festivities of Purim." *Zion* 59 (1994): x.

Jussen, B. *Spiritual Kinship as Social Practice. Godparenthood and Adoption in the Early Middle Ages*. Newark, DE: University of Delaware Press, 2000.

Keller, H. *Adelherrschaft und städtische Gesellschaft in Oberitalien, 9. bis 11. Jahrhundert*. Tübingen: M. Niemeyer, 1979.

Koder, J., and Weber, T. *Liudprand von Cremona in Konstantinopel*. Vienna: Verlag der Österreichischen Akademie der Wissenschaften, 1980.

Kolditz, S. "Leon von Synada und Liudprand von Cremona." *Byzantinische Zeitschrift* 95 (2002): 509–84.

Kreutz, B. *Before the Normans*. Philadelphia: University of Pennsylvania Press, 1991.

Leonardi, C. *Letteratura latina medievale*. Florence: SISMEL-Edizioni del Galluzzo, 2002.

––––––. "Intellectual Life." In *The New Cambridge Medieval History*. Vol. 3. Edited by T. Reuter. Cambridge: Cambridge University Press, 1999. Pp. 186–210.

Levine, R. "Liudprand of Cremona: History and Debasement in the Tenth Century." *Mittellateinisches Jahrbuch* 26 (1991): 70–84.

Leyser, K. "Ends and Means in Liudprand of Cremona." In his *Communications and Power in Medieval Europe. The Carolingian and Ottonian Centuries*. London: The Hambledon Press, 1994. Pp. 125–42.

––––––. "Liudprand of Cremona, Preacher and Homilist." In his *Communications and Power in Medieval Europe. The Carolingian and Ottonian Centuries*. London: The Hambledon Press, 1994. Pp. 111–24.

––––––. *Medieval Germany and its Neighbours*. London: The Hambledon Press, 1982.

––––––. *Rule and Conflict in an Early Medieval Society*. Oxford: B. Blackwell, 1979.

––––––. "Theophanu Divina Gratia Imperatrix Augusta." In *The Empress Theophano*. Edited by A. Davids. Cambridge: Cambridge University Press, 1995. Pp. 1–26.

Lintzel, M. *Studien über Liudprand von Cremona*. Berlin: Verlag Dr Emil Ebering, 1933.

Llewellyn, P. *Rome in the Dark Ages*. London: Constable, 1993.

Loud, G. "Southern Italy in the Tenth Century." *New Cambridge Medieval History*. Vol. 3. Edited by T. Reuter. Cambridge: Cambridge University Press, 1999. Pp. 624–44.

Lukyn Williams, A. *Adversus Judaeos. A Bird's Eye View of Christian Apologiae Until the Renaissance*. London: Cambridge University Press, 1935.

Malkiel, D. "Jewish-Christian Relations in Europe, 840–1096." *Journal of Medieval History* 29 (2003): 55–83.

Mango, C. *The Brazen House*. Copenhagen: I Kommision hos Munksgaard, 1959.

Mayr-Harting, H. "Liudprand of Cremona's Account of his Legation to Constantinople and Ottonian Imperial Strategy." *English Historical Review* 116 (2001): 539–56.

Mazo Karras, R. *Sexuality in Medieval Europe*. London: Routledge, 2005.

McCormick, M. *The Origins of the European Economy*. Cambridge: Cambridge University Press, 2001.

Mor, G. *L'Italia feudale*. Vol. 1. Milan: F. Vallardi, 1952.

Morris, R. "'O Michaeles Michaeles': A Problem of Identification in Liudprand's *Legatio*." *Byzantion* 51 (1981): 248–54.

———. "Beyond the *De Cerimoniis*." In *Court Culture in the Early Middle Ages*. Edited by C. Cubitt. Turnholt: Brepols, 2003. Pp. 235–54.

Muessing, C. "Sermon, Preacher, and Society in the Middle Ages." *Journal of Medieval History* 28 (2002): 73–91.

Muller-Martens, E. "The Ottonian Kings and Emperors." In *New Cambridge Medieval History*. Vol. 3. Edited by T. Reuter. Cambridge: Cambridge University Press, 1999. Pp. 233–65.

Nelson, J. "Rulers and Government." *New Cambridge Medieval History*. Vol. 3. Edited by T. Reuter. Cambridge: Cambridge University Press, 1999. Pp. 95–128.

Oldoni, M. "Liutprando oltre il magazzino delle maschere." In M. Oldoni and P. Ariatta. *Liutprando di Cremona. Italia e Oriente alle soglie dell'anno mille*. Novara: Europia, 1987.

———. "'Phrenesis' di una letteratura solitaria." *Settimane del Centro Italiano di Studi sull'Alto Medioevo*. Vol. 38. Spoleto: CISAM, 1991. Pp. 1007–43.

Ostrogorsky, G. *History of the Byzantine State*. Oxford: Blackwell, 1956.

Partner, P. *The Lands of St Peter*. London: Methuen, 1973.

Provero, L. *L'Italia dei poteri locali*. Rome: Carocci, 1998.

Queller, D. *The Office of the Ambassador in the Middle Ages*. Princeton: Princeton University Press, 1967.

Rentschler, M. *Liudprand von Cremona*. Frankfurt: Klostermann, 1981.

Reuter, T. *Germany in the Early Middle Ages*. London: Longman, 1991.

Ricci, L. *Problemi sintattici nelle opere di Liutprando di Cremona*. Spoleto: CISAM, 1996.

Roth, C. *History of the Jews of Italy*. Philadelphia: Jewish Publication Society of America, 1946.

Schimmelpfennig, B. *The Papacy*. New York: Columbia University Press, 1992.

Schove, D. *Chronology of Eclipses and Comets, AD 1–1000*. Woodbridge, England: Boydell Press, 1984.

Schramm, P. E. *Herrschaftszeichen und Staatssymbolik*. Vol. 2. Stuttgart: Hiersemann, 1955.

Schulz-Dorlamm, M. "Die Ungarneinfälle des 10. Jahrhundert im Spiegel archäologischer Funde." In *Europa im 10. Jahrhundert*. Edited by J. Henning. Mainz: P. von Zabern, 2002.

Schummer, C. "Liutprand of Cremona—A Diplomat?" In *Byzantine Diplomacy*. Edited by J. Shepard and S. Franklin. Aldershot, England: Variorum, 1992. Pp. 197–201.

Sergi, G. "The Kingdom of Italy." In *New Cambridge Medieval History*. Vol. 3. Edited by T. Reuter. Cambridge: Cambridge University Press, 1999. Pp. 346–70.

Sivo, V. "Studi recenti su Liutprando di Cremona." *Quaderni medievali* 44 (1997): 214–25.

Skinner, P. *Women in Medieval Italian Society 500–1200*. London: Pearson Education, 2001.

Squatriti, P. *Water and Society in Early Medieval Italy*. Cambridge: Cambridge University Press, 1998.

Staubach, N. "Historia oder Satira?" *Mittellateinisches Jahrbuch* 24–25 (1989–90): 461–87.

Sutherland, J. *Liudprand of Cremona*. Spoleto: CISAM, 1988.

Tabacco, G. "Regno, impero e aristocrazie nell'Italia postcarolingia." *Settimane di Studio del Centro Italiano di Studi sull'Alto Medioevo*. Vol. 38. Spoleto: CISAM, 1991. Pp. 243–70.

———. *The Struggle for Power in Medieval Italy*. Cambridge: Cambridge University Press, 1989.

Tellenbach, G. *The Church in Western Europe from the Tenth to the Early Twelfth Century*. Cambridge: Cambridge University Press, 1993.

Toch, M. "The Formation of a Diaspora." *Ashkenas* 7 (1997): 11–34.

———. *Die Juden im mittelalterlichen Reich*. Munich: R. Oldenbourg Verlag, 2003.

Van Dam, R. *Kingdom of Snow: Roman Rule and Greek Culture in Cappadocia*. Philadelphia: University of Pennsylvania Press, 2002.

Vasiliev, A. "Harun ibn-Yahya and his Description of Constantinople." *Seminarium Kondakavianum* 5 (Prague, 1932): 149–63.

Villa, C. "Lay and Ecclesiastical Culture." In *Italy in the Early Middle Ages*. Edited by C. La Rocca. Oxford: Oxford University Press, 2002. Pp. 189–203.

Vinay, G. *Alto medioevo latino*. Naples: Liguori, 2003.

Vinckier, H. "Liudprandi Passio." *Medieval Perspectives* 1.1. (1986): 54–64.

Wemple, S. *Atto of Vercelli*. Rome: Edizioni di Storia e Letteratura, 1979.

Whittow, M. *The Making of Byzantium*. Berkeley: University of California Press, 1996.

Wickham, C. *Early Medieval Italy*. London: Macmillan, 1981.

Wolf, K. Baxter. "Christian Views of Islam in Early Medieval Spain." In *Medieval Perceptions of Islam*. Edited by J. Tolan. New York: Garland, 1996. Pp. 85–107.

INDEX

The Complete Works of Liudprand of Cremona was designed and typeset in Monotype Centaur by Kachergis Book Design of Pittsboro, North Carolina. It was printed on 60-pound House Natural Smooth and bound by Sheridan Books of Ann Arbor, Michigan.